Making the Most of It

Making the Most of It

Theodora FitzGibbon

A cookery book which examines the past,
as a guide to good food on a budget

DECORATIONS BY VAL BIRO

Hutchinson of London

Hutchinson & Co (Publishers) Ltd
3 Fitzroy Square, London W1

London Melbourne Sydney Auckland
Wellington Johannesburg and agencies
throughout the world

First published 1978
Text © Theodora FitzGibbon 1978
Decorations © Hutchinson Publishing Group Ltd

Set in Monotype Times/Univers

Printed in Great Britain by
The Anchor Press Ltd and bound by
Wm Brendon & Son Ltd, both of
Tiptree, Essex

ISBN 0 09 132620 6

For George, who first thought of the idea

Cosmopolitan Cookery
Weekend Cookery
The High Protein Diet and Cookery Book
(*with Dr Michael Hemans*)
Country House Cooking
The Young Cook's Book
Game Cooking
The Art of British Cooking
Eat Well and Live Longer
(*with Dr Robert Wilson*)
A Taste of Ireland
A Taste of Scotland
A Taste of Wales
A Taste of England: the West Country
A Taste of London
A Taste of Paris
A Taste of Rome
Theodora FitzGibbon's Cookery Book
The Food of the Western World
A Taste of the Sea

FICTION
Flight of the Kingfisher

Contents

Introduction

The conception of this book sprang from strong desire: the desire to economize and yet still eat well. In an art as ancient as cookery economic conditions have governed what foods people ate just as much as climate and soil. Fashions change in food as well as in clothes and many things tend to get forgotten. Even varieties of fruit and vegetables have changed and many of the staples of cookery in the sixteenth and seventeenth centuries, such as globe artichokes which grew freely in many cottage gardens, have now become almost a foreign luxury. In 1557 Thomas Tusser, the English poet and farmer, listed some forty-three herbs and vegetables which he considered essential for the kitchen garden. Many of these are now considered wild and are seldom used, although recently there has been an effort to return to some of the ways of our ancestors, especially so far as food is concerned.

People are getting tired of packaged and processed foods, hence the large number of health food shops which abound all over Europe and America. And does it really take so much longer to cook true oatmeal than the quick-cooking kind, or to cook unprocessed rice? I would make a possible exception of potato powder for that has been used for many centuries, and still is in France where it is called *fécule de pomme de terre*, to thicken soups, sauces and for light cakes. It goes without saying that processed foods are more expensive, for the labour involved puts up the cost, and in some cases much of the nutriment has been removed. When one tastes country butter, chickens, and the bread made from stone-ground flour one realizes how much one is missing.

Country people with smallholdings or farms have always known the value of home-produced food. However, the image many people have of the farmhouse kitchen is very romanticized, and the picture of huge joints, lashings of cream and butter, a sort of 'Sunday every day', is far from true. The farmer's wife had, and still has, a long and arduous day, and it was even more so in former times before electric light, washing machines and other modern conveniences. The best meat went to market, as did the butter, cream and cheese, and often the farmer's wife had to feed large families and farm workers on dishes made from vegetables with very little meat, flavoured with herbs and supplemented by filling things such as dumplings, pastry or bread.

The day would start before dawn with a first breakfast of porridge, and then the household would return later in the morning for something more substantial. Meals went on almost all day, so hearty soups, stews and boiled puddings were popular for they could simmer away for hours at the back of the kitchen range. The farmer's wife had to be inventive and creative, and many of those creations have become part of our country's traditional cuisine. The wives of fishermen likewise have sometimes had a hard struggle to feed their children and their menfolk adequately for the arduous life they were subjected to. These conditions have been prevalent not only in Britain and Ireland, but all over the world, so in some cases I have taken dishes from other countries to show how other people coped with similar situations.

I am perhaps fortunate in that I started housekeeping during the last war. Rationing was very severe for some years and sometimes I wonder just how we did all eat, and even entertain on occasion. But it has given me an innate hatred of waste, and it also made me inventive so far as food was concerned. It was a challenge and one that I took up wholeheartedly. I was, however, greatly helped by my Cornish grandmother who seemed to have spent her long and useful life finding out the best ways to do everything. She could literally make a good meal from the sparsest of ingredients, and to a certain extent I have inherited her talent.

One of the factors which has increased the cost of living enormously is the rise in price of gas, electricity and fuel. It is true to say that the majority of people today are better off in many ways but there are still a lot of people on fixed incomes, living either with husband or wife, or alone, to whom the fuel bills are prohibitive. There are many utensils today which are extremely cheap to run and excellent for small or large families. One is the crock-pot slow cooker. This is really on the old hay-box principle and cooks for eight to ten people (or smaller numbers) for the price of an electric light bulb. It has only two heats, high and low, and the cooking times vary between four hours and ten. It is virtually the only form of cooking I know which requires absolutely no attention. For families coming in at odd hours, or for those out at work or even out for the day, it is perfect, as it keeps everything without spoiling on the low setting. For elderly people it has the advantage that there is no bending down and no heavy pots to lift out of an oven, for the cooking can be done on the table. It is the opposite of the pressure cooker which cooks quickly but needs watching, and which I have written about more fully on page 122.

Other electric cookers which use the minimum of fuel are the Nova or Rima infra-red grills and the electric frying-pan or multi-cooker. The former makes excellent toast or toasted sandwiches and cooks steaks, chops and many other foods efficiently. The multi-cooker both fries and braises well: it is also said to roast but the end product does not have the crisp finish of an oven. However, it is a practical, easy and cheap method of cooking.

Families who spend quite a lot of time in the open air, either fishing or picnicking, should acquire a Brooks home smoker. It smokes (using wood shavings and meta fuel or methylated spirits) almost everything from eggs to small joints in about twenty minutes, and once set up it requires only the barest attention. The results are very pleasing and the cost cheap. It can be used in the home as well on a thick baking sheet, but naturally there is a smell of smoke. Those with gardens, however, would find it good for making smoked sausages, cheeses, eggs (which are delicious), fresh fish, kebabs, liver and so on. It is small and portable and (at present) under ten pounds in cost.

Don't forget the steamer for cooking several things at once and use the oven to full advantage by planning what you will cook in it. For instance, a casserole dish, pastry and a milk pudding can all be done together at different levels, putting the pastry at the top.

The Chinese method of cooking chicken (page 107) is a great fuel saver, and don't fill the kettle for a cup of tea, just over the elements is often enough. Likewise, turn down the heat once a pot has come to the boil for the greater heat won't make it cook any more quickly. If you line your grilling pan with foil it not only keeps it clean but the shiny silver surface reflects the heat and cooks everything much more quickly

The liquidizer is good for making quick soups from leftover vegetables, as well as quick pâté: simply cook the liver in a frying-pan then put it into the liquidizer with a pinch of marjoram, salt, pepper and either a little red wine or consommé and liquidize for about 1 minute or until it is all smooth. About 4 tablespoons liquid is enough for 1 lb (450 g) liver.

The freezer can save money too, for you can buy in bulk or when certain foods are cheap: freezing your own fruit and vegetables will cut food bills, and you can save fuel by cooking more than you need of a dish, then freezing half of it.

When one thinks of the primitive conditions of past years and the many comforts we take for granted today, it should not be too difficult to find ways of 'making the most of it'.

All human history attests
That happiness for man – the hungry sinner! –
Since Eve ate apples, must depend on dinner.

LORD BYRON, *Don Juan*, II, xcix

THEODORA FITZGIBBON
Dalkey. Co. Dublin, 1978

1. Soups

Homemade soup is one of the cheapest and easiest methods of serving a hot meal. All countries in the Western world have their own traditional recipes which combine the best of vegetables and good stock, with perhaps an elusive herb giving it a touch of magic. The good peasant and farmhouse soups of France and Italy astonish a palate used to packaged or tinned soups. Unfortunately, with the rise today of the supermarket good marrow or chine bones are not always available for making stock, but on the other hand some stock cubes are quite acceptable although inclined to be salty and fatty. It is always best to make up the stock cubes, leave the liquid to get cold and then remove the fat from the top, as this can often give a greasy flavour to a delicate soup.

Freezer owners are luckier, for if you consign your chicken and other poultry or game carcasses to the deep freeze, then when time permits boil down about two or three carcasses (a pressure cooker is best for this job), strain the liquid, let it cool and de-fat it, then deep-freeze the results in either small or larger amounts, you have excellent stock always to hand. The same applies to meat bones. Do not add too much water to the carcasses or bones lest you make the stock watery; you can always make it weaker if it's too strong, but it's impossible to give strength quickly. Season to taste and add a few herbs and vegetables, so that you have an acceptable clear soup which can either be drunk on its own or be used as a basis for many other soups or casserole dishes. Vegetable water that is not too salty can also be used for stock.

The liquidizer is a mixed blessing. Certainly it makes a soup of freshly cooked or leftover vegetables with milk or stock in seconds, but the homogeneous creamy mixture can be tiring. So for a change sometimes leave the vegetables unblended, or use a vegetable mill which makes the mixture coarser. Don't make a cream soup too thick – it should be the consistency of pouring cream. Flour is a destroyer of taste so only use the minimum. Apart from the cost, I'm also inclined to think cream disguises flavour if used too liberally, but the majority may not agree with me. A little knob of butter, however, added before serving, adds to the taste.

A good soup, followed by cheese and fruit or yoghurt, is a worthy and very nutritious meal for all ages. It also conjures up childhood memories of warm, friendly kitchens, a favourite dog or cat asleep at one's feet, as the delicious steamy soup, its golden trickle of butter making wondrous patterns on the top, slipped so easily down the 'little red lane'.

Artichoke soup was a popular nineteenth-century dish also known as Palestine soup as Jerusalem artichokes are used. The same recipe can also be used for celery, celeriac or salsify. Salsify is known as the 'oyster plant' as it does have a faint taste of oyster about it. When using salsify, add about a teaspoon of anchovy essence which will enhance the flavour.

1 lb (450 g) Jerusalem artichokes	Salt and pepper
2 medium onions	1 pint (600 ml) boiling milk
2 heaped tablespoons butter	1 level tablespoon cornflour
1 pint (600 ml) water	2 tablespoons cold milk

Wash, peel and slice the artichokes and onions. Melt half the butter in a saucepan, and gently sauté the onions, but do not let them colour. Add the artichokes, and shake over a low heat for about 10 minutes. Add the water, season to taste, cover, and simmer for 20 minutes. Put through a vegetable mill, or liquidize until creamy, then put back into a saucepan and add the boiling milk. Mix the cornflour with the cold milk and add to the mixture stirring well all the time. Adjust seasoning, then add the remaining butter in small pieces. Serves 4–6.

Garnishes: Small croûtons of crisply fried bread are good with this soup, but if you're feeling richer than usual try grilling about 2 dozen hazelnuts, then crushing and pounding them. A spoonful added to each helping is quite delicious.

Brotchán roy is a traditional Irish leek and oatmeal soup, which is filling and good. It is also made with young nettle tops (see the chapter on 'Free foods from nature', pages 150–6) and in this form was a favourite with the great Irishman Saint Colmcille. It is said that he saw a poor woman gathering nettles and after inquiring what use she would make of them, tried the dish himself and became fond of it. *Brotchán* is the Irish for broth.

6 large leeks	2 tablespoons flake oatmeal
2 pints (approx. 1 l) milk	Salt and pepper
2 level tablespoons butter	1 tablespoon chopped parsley

Wash the leeks thoroughly to remove grit, trim the tops and make a cross on the green bottom part, then stand the leeks green part down in a deep jug of water for about 1 hour or longer. This ensures that all the gritty particles in the leaves come out easily. Drain them and cut into chunks about 1 inch (25 mm) long. Heat up the liquid with the butter, and when boiling add the oatmeal.

Let it boil, then add the chopped leeks and season to taste. Cover and simmer gently for about 45 minutes. Add the parsley and boil again for 5 minutes. Serves 4–6.

Garnish: The parsley is really the garnish, but if you are serving this soup as a main course, fry or grill some streaky bacon rashers until crisp, remove from the pan and crush them. Sprinkle a little over each helping.

Bortsch is a famous Russian beetroot soup which for centuries has been a staple diet of the Russian peasant, although today it is eaten everywhere, both as a first course and as a main dish.

2 raw peeled medium beetroots	stock, or $\frac{1}{2}$ stock and $\frac{1}{2}$ water
2 large leeks	Salt and pepper
1 carrot	1 cooked medium
$\frac{1}{4}$ small white cabbage	beetroot and its juice
2 tablespoons butter or oil	1 dessertspoon wine vinegar
$\frac{1}{2}$ bayleaf	4 tablespoons sour
Pinch of ground allspice	cream or yoghurt
2 pints (approx. 1 l) rich beef or poultry	

First cook the beetroot in water to cover, either in the oven or on top of the stove for about 40 minutes. Prick lightly to make sure it is done. Prepare and slice all the other vegetables finely, excepting the cooked beetroot. Heat up the butter or oil and turn them, slowly, until softened but not coloured. Then add the bayleaf and allspice and also the stock. Cover and bring to the boil, then simmer for about $1\frac{1}{2}$ hours, seasoning to taste. The beetroots will go a browny colour when cooked, but this does not affect the taste. Just before it is ready add the mashed cooked beetroot and about 4 tablespoons of the juice. Strain through a fine sieve, and add the wine vinegar. Serve hot (but do not reboil for longer than 2 minutes to preserve the colour) or cold, with a spoonful of sour cream or yoghurt in each portion. Serves 4–6.

Caldo verde is a good potato and cabbage soup from the Minho region of Portugal, although it can be found as far south as the Algarve. It is made from large leaves of Portuguese cabbage, known as *couve*, but any dark cabbage or even kale can be used. Stalks should be removed and the cabbage cut as finely as possible. The best way to do this is to crisp up the cabbage in ice-cold water, then to roll up the leaves tightly and cut them as finely as you can with a very sharp knife.

$1\frac{1}{2}$ lb (675 g) potatoes	vegetable oil
Water or stock	(olive oil gives a
Salt and pepper	better flavour)
1 lb (450 g) cabbage	6 slices salami or 3
1 large and 1 medium onion	sliced frankfurters (optional)
$1\frac{1}{2}$ tablespoons olive or	

Peel and boil the potatoes in water or stock to up to 2 inches (50 mm) above the potatoes. When cooked, mash them into the liquid, taste and season, and reheat them. When boiling add the finely shredded cabbage and cook for not more than 15 minutes. When serving add the chopped raw onions and the olive oil to the soup, and if serving as a main course add a slice of sausage to each plate. Serves 4–6. In the North of Portugal this soup is served with maize bread called *broa*, but wholemeal bread is good with it too. This soup can also be made with potato powder or flakes, but add enough water to make it of soupy consistency and do not season without tasting first.

Carrot soup is the *potage Crécy* of France, although that soup is cooked with potatoes as well. Personally, I think that if the carrots are young or of good quality, their own flavour is delicious. Carrot soup, plainly made with water or stock and puréed, is a marvellous cure for diarrhoea in both babies and adults.

1 lb (450 g) carrots	preferably chicken or
1 small onion, leek or	vegetable
shallot	Good pinch of mace
2 level tablespoons	Salt and pepper
butter	1 tablespoon parsley or
1 teaspoon sugar	chervil and a little
2 pints (1 l) stock,	mint

Scrape the carrots and chop them small, and peel and slice the onion. Heat the butter and sweat the carrots and onion in it, but do not let the onion colour. Add all the other ingredients, except the herbs, cover and simmer gently for about ½ hour. Then sieve or liquidize and add the herbs. Serve with croûtons of fried bread. Serves 4–6.

Pumpkin or vegetable marrow can be used instead of carrots, and a pinch of cinnamon is good with them.

Cucumber soup is a pleasant soup to make when cucumbers are cheap, and it is good either hot or cold.

1 large or 2 medium	½ pint (300 ml) creamy
cucumbers	milk
2 level tablespoons	1 small sliced onion
butter	Salt and pepper
2 level tablespoons flour	Parsley or chives
2 pints (approx. 1 l)	Yoghurt
stock, preferably	
chicken	

Peel, seed and chop the cucumbers, heat the butter until foaming but not coloured and lightly cook the cucumber until soft but not brown. Add the flour, let it cook for 1 minute then add the stock, bring to the boil, cover and simmer gently, stirring from time to time. Meanwhile, scald the milk with the onion, then combine both mixtures and season to taste.

Either sieve or liquidize the mixture for 1 minute. If serving cold let it chill, then serve with chopped herbs and a little yoghurt on top. Serves 4–6.

Fish chowder is really a meal in itself and can be made with any of the cheaper white fishes, or even with stock made from fish heads and bones.

2 lb (1 kg) cod, haddock,	3 large peeled tomatoes
whiting, etc., if	1 tablespoon mixed
possible with head	lemon thyme and
and bones	parsley
Salt and pepper	1 heaped teaspoon
2 small rashers streaky	tomato purée
bacon	Juice of 1 lemon
1 medium sliced onion	2 teaspoons
1 lb (450 g) diced	Worcestershire sauce
potatoes	

Try and get the fish skinned and filleted, but keep the bones, skin and heads. Cut the fish into 2 inch (50 mm) pieces and set aside. Put the bones, etc. into a saucepan with 1 pint (600 ml) water, salt and pepper and simmer for about 20 minutes. Then strain it. Chop the bacon into small pieces and fry until the fat is out; in this sauté the sliced onion and potato lightly. Add 2 cups boiling water and the strained fish liquor, the fish, tomatoes, chopped herbs and tomato purée. Cover and simmer for 15 minutes. When done add the juice of the lemon and the Worcestershire sauce and mix well. This soup should be very highly seasoned. Before serving crush up some cream crackers and sprinkle some into each bowl. Or serve with fried bread croûtons rubbed with garlic. Serves 4–6.

Garlic soup is one of the cheapest soups served extensively in Spain, Portugal and also France. It is quick to make, and despite the few ingredients it has a delicate flavour, and is very good for you. George Santayana, the writer and philosopher, gives the version his family used to have in his book *Persons and Places* (Constable, 1944). 'For supper they had each a small bowl of garlic soup – something that my father loved in his old age, and that I also liked, especially if I might break a raw egg into it, as those twelve children were certainly never allowed to do. You fry some garlic in a pan with some olive oil: when crisp you remove the larger pieces of garlic, add hot water according to the size of the family, with thin little slices of bread, no matter how dry, *ad libitum*, and a little salt, and that is your supper.'

It is also delicious with very thin slices of a hard cheese, and vegetable stock with a sliced onion and tomatoes give an excellent taste.

Garlic soup from Salamanca (*sopa de ajo a la Asmesnal*) is a more elaborate version.

3–4 tablespoons oil	Salt and pepper
6 cloves garlic	Small pieces of cubed
6 small crustless slices of	cooked chicken or
bread	salami (*chorizo*),
3 pints (generous 1½ l)	(optional)
boiling water	4 poached eggs
1 teaspoon chopped	
parsley	

Heat the oil in a deep saucepan, then fry the garlic cloves in it and remove them. Fry the bread in the same oil, then add the boiling water, parsley, salt and pepper. Crush the cooked garlic and add it to the soup with the chicken pieces or salami if using. Put 1 poached egg into each plate and pour the hot soup over the top. Serves 4.

Lentil soup is exceptionally nourishing, as are all the dried vegetables such as beans and peas. They contain a lot of protein and make a cheap, filling meal. *See also* the chapter on 'Mainly vegetable and vegetarian dishes' (pages 74–92). The lentils used for this soup are the brown or German lentils, or the green lentils of Le Puy in France. Unlike the orange Egyptian lentils they do not disintegrate while cooking. They can be found in most good delicatessen shops. It is advisable to pick them over before soaking as they sometimes contain little stones. The simplest and cheapest way to cook all the dried vegetable family is in the pressure cooker.

8 oz (225 g) brown	or a few chopped
lentils soaked in cold	bacon rinds
water for at least 3	2½ pints (1¼ l) stock or
hours	water with 1 teaspoon
2 tablespoons oil or	Marmite added
butter	Salt and pepper
1 large onion	Chopped parsley
1 ham-bone if available,	

Drain the soaked lentils, then heat up the oil or butter and lightly sauté the onion with the chopped bacon rinds if you are using them. Add the lentils and the ham-bone if available and mix well. Pour the stock or water and Marmite over (if using a pressure cooker the water should come to about 1½ inches (40 mm) above the lentils), cover and cook gently once it has reached the boil for about 1½ hours, or until the lentils are cooked but not mushy. (Pressure cooking time is 20

B

minutes.) Do not salt until the lentils are cooked, as this is inclined to toughen them. Sprinkle with a little chopped parsley before serving, and if you can afford it a tiny trickle of olive oil on top of each portion gives a true Italian flavour. Serves 4–6.

If about 1½ pints (approx. 1 l) of water are used, and small pieces of either belly of pork, or lamb are added, and it is cooked for about the same time, it makes a very good ragoût. Garlic, bayleaf, and a little thyme can also be added to the ragoût, as well as a little celery if available. If the meat is omitted, or only a little is used it is excellent served with grilled sausages. *See also* Lentil casserole, page 91.

Dried bean soup can be made as lentil soup, with the addition of 2 teaspoons tomato purée.

Lettuce soup is very good for gardeners who sometimes have too many lettuces ready at the same time, or have ones inclined to bolt. It can be served hot or cold.

2 large heads lettuce, or the outer leaves of 4	1 tablespoon flour
1 tablespoon butter or oil	1 pint (600 ml) chicken stock
6 spring onions or equivalent amount of chives	Salt and pepper
	Pinch each of nutmeg and sugar
	½ pint (300 ml) milk

Remove the lettuce leaves from the hard stalks, and trim the leaves, then cut them into fine ribbons. Melt the butter in a saucepan, and very lightly fry the lettuce and chopped spring onions for about 10 minutes, stirring from time to time. Sprinkle the flour over, and then gradually add the stock, stirring all the time. When it is quite smooth, season, add the milk mixing very well, and continue simmering for about 10 minutes. Then either sieve or liquidize for 1 minute. Garnish with a little yoghurt, and serve with fried bread croûtons. Serves 4.

Oatmeal soup is a delicious, inexpensive Scottish soup which has a very creamy and complex flavour.

1 tablespoon butter	½ pint (300 ml) milk
1 large onion	¼ pint (150 ml) light cream or top of milk
2 level tablespoons medium oatmeal	1 tablespoon chopped parsley
Salt and pepper	
1 pint (600 ml) chicken stock	

Melt the butter in a saucepan, then add the finely chopped, peeled onion and cook until soft but not coloured. Then add the oatmeal and seasonings and cook for a few minutes. Add the stock slowly, stirring all the time, bring to the boil, and simmer, covered, for ½ hour. Then either put through a sieve or liquidize for 1 minute. Return to the pan, reheat with the milk, and serve with the cream and chopped parsley as a garnish. Serves 4–6.

See also the chapter on 'Oatmeal' (pages 34–8).

Pea soup (dried) Dried peas are a great and cheap stand-by to keep in the house, for not only do they make excellent soup, but also pease pudding (page 91) which is wonderful on a cold day with salt beef or pork, or even with sausages. It was a staple of the poor in Victorian London, and was sold in the streets from stalls which also sold hot eels. In Mayhew's *London Cries* it says that the charge for half a pint of pea soup was a halfpenny, as were about 5 pieces of eel and some liquor, and they were referred to as 'street luxuries'. It became known in Dickens's time as 'a London particular' from his lines in *Bleak House:* ' "... this is a London particular" ... "A fog, miss," said the young gentleman.' Subsequently a dense London fog became known as a 'peasouper'.

1 lb (450 g) (2 cups) split dried peas, either green or yellow, soaked for at least 4 hours	1 large onion, sliced
	4 pints (2¼ l) water or stock from ham
	1 tablespoon Worcestershire sauce
4 rashers bacon or a ham-bone	Salt and pepper
	Croûtons of fried bread

Soak the dried peas for at least 4 hours if not using a pressure cooker, then drain before using. Cut the bacon into dice (or use a well-covered ham-bone) and let the fat run out in a large saucepan, then lightly fry the onion in it until it is soft but not coloured. Add the peas and the water or stock, cover and simmer for about 2 hours, or until the peas are puréed (pressure cooking time is 15–20 minutes). A few carrots or a stalk of celery can also be added if available. Stir well and taste for seasoning, then add the Worcestershire sauce, stir again and heat up. Serve with fried bread croûtons sprinkled with a little celery salt. If any is left over it can be reheated if more stock or milk is added, as it becomes very thick when cold. Heat it gently, stirring all the time, lest it should burn. Serves about 6–8.

Potato soup is a traditional Irish soup, and was the mainstay of many a family for centuries. It is also a good basic soup from which can be made watercress, chervil or sorrel soup, also *vichyssoise. See also Caldo verde* (page 15). If potatoes are scarce or expensive then it is easily made with dried potato powder. Make it up as directed with boiling water, but thin it down to the right consistency with either milk or milk and water mixed. Reheat and add the finely chopped herbs or use the garnish given below.

2 heaped tablespoons butter	3 pints (approx. 1½ l) of ½ milk and ½ water, or stock and milk
2 medium onions	
2 lb (1 kg) potatoes	Chopped chives or parsley
Pinch of nutmeg	
Salt and pepper	

Heat the butter until foaming, but not brown, then add the sliced onions and cook gently until soft, but do not let them brown. Add the peeled potatoes cut to an even but not too small size (if too small they may break up too quickly and become watery) add the nutmeg and season to taste, then pour over the milk and water or stock. Cover and cook gently for about ½ hour. Then either sieve or liquidize until the soup is puréed. Serve with freshly chopped chives and parsley on top. Serves 6–8.

If making watercress, chervil or sorrel soup, add about 3 tablespoons of chopped leaves and stalk to the potato while cooking, then when liquidizing or sieving add some more leaf, but taste before adding too much. Leeks can be used instead of onions, when it becomes *vichyssoise*. If you have a little drop of cream to add at the last minute it adds to the flavour.

Another delightful variation is to add about 4 large tomatoes (peeled) to the onions or leeks at the beginning of cooking, which gives a fresh taste and makes the soup an enchanting colour. In all cases do not let the soup be too thick – add more milk if the potatoes are the very floury kind.

Garnish: A very good garnish is to fry a few streaky bacon rashers until crisp, then to break them up with a fork and scatter them over the top. Small chunks of cooked fish or, if the budget runs to it, a scattering of shrimps or prawns on top transforms it into a festive soup.

Spinach soup can be easily made as the above recipe using 2 lb (1 kg) spinach and only 1 lb (450 g) potatoes.

Sorrel soup Sorrel is a perennial, spiky-leaved, wild and cultivated plant which can be picked early in the year when green stuff is in short supply. The leaves have a delicate acid-lemony taste, which quench the thirst, and have done so for many centuries. John Clare in 'The Shepherd's Calendar' writes:

> The mower gladly chews it down
> And slakes his thirst the best he may.

In Elizabethan times it was made into a sauce for fish or chicken (*see* page 105). The sorrel soup I like best is very simply made. First I sweat about 8 oz (250 g) sorrel in a little butter until it is soft but not coloured in any way, then I add this to 2 pints (approx. 1 l) of a good chicken broth. If you want to thicken it, which personally I think is a mistake, then use 3 tablespoons fresh breadcrumbs, and if possible break 2 eggyolks into a warm tureen and pour the boiling soup over, stirring well all the time. This is enough for about 4 people.

Soupe verte is simply 'green soup' and any green vegetables or herbs can go into it, with the possible exception of cabbage as this taste would be too strong. It is a good soup for gardeners who want to use up older peas, beans, cucumber, spinach, all herbs and possibly sorrel or watercress. I have also used turnip, radish and beetroot tops. When you use the latter it becomes a pinky green and so not really a 'green soup'.

Cook a selection of the above herbs and vegetables, even including a few nettles if possible, in a good chicken or meat stock, with seasoning and a good pinch of mace. Do not add more than 3 pints ($1\frac{1}{2}$ l) stock to 2 lb (1 kg) vegetables, and let it all simmer until soft, but not overcooked. Cool, then liquidize, taste for seasoning and add about 1 cup creamy milk, then blend again for about 30 seconds. This soup is equally good hot or cold, but if serving hot add a few fried croûtons as a garnish. The soup relies more on the cook's ingenuity and imagination than on a recipe. I have served it at many a dinner party with acclaim, and the nice thing about it is that each time you make it the taste is different owing to the different balance of ingredients.

Root vegetable soup can be made in the same way as *soupe verte*, using a selection of vegetables such as potatoes, leeks, onions, carrots, turnips, celery, etc., with whatever herbs are available at the time. Sometimes it is good to serve this soup unsieved, with a little cooked pasta or dumplings.

Additions: To make a good hearty and economical meal from soup, use some of the old-fashioned garnishes, such as small balls made from sausagemeat, first lightly fried, then added to pea or vegetable soup: or small dumplings made with half the quantity of margarine to flour with salt and enough water added to make a stiffish dough. (4 oz (115 g) flour makes about 8–10 small dumplings.) Poach these in the soup, or separately if the soup is very thick. Small balls of skirlie (page 35) can also be added. *See also:* 'Soup stews' (pages 134–6), and 'Free foods from Nature' (pages 150–6).

QUICK COLD SOUPS

These are invaluable for both winter and summer use. The following are inexpensive and do not take more than minutes to prepare. None of these can be heated up.

Chachik is the Turkish name for this soup which is called *tarator* in the Balkans. It is exceptionally good in the hot weather, or as a first course before a heavy main course.

1 medium cucumber	Small bunch of mint,
1 large clove garlic	about ½ cup pressed
1 pint (600 ml) natural	well down
yoghurt	Salt

Peel the cucumber and grate it coarsely or chop finely. Cut the garlic and rub it around 4 large soup bowls. Beat the yoghurt a little, then add it to the cucumber. Chop the mint finely, add this to the mixture and salt to taste. Divide between the 4 bowls and serve chilled.

The Persian version of *chachik* includes chopped hard-boiled eggs, and a handful of seedless raisins.

Chicken and lemon soup is a cold Greek soup and extremely refreshing. Combine 1 pint (600 ml) cold chicken broth (de-fatted) with ½ pint (300 ml) plain yoghurt (*see* page 51) and beat well. Gradually add the juice of 1 lemon, beating all the time. Taste for seasoning and garnish with a little chopped parsley and mint mixed. Serves 4–6.

A variation of this is to add 1 teaspoon of curry powder, and to use only half the quantity of lemon.

Polish soup really does defy most people to guess what is in it. It is so simple and yet tastes so complex, as though you had spent hours making it. For 4 people use 1 pint (600 ml) plain yoghurt, and mix it with about half the quantity of tomato juice, beating well. The amount of tomato juice varies with personal taste, but do not use too much. Add salt to taste and serve chilled. If beetroot juice is available, then try that too instead of tomato, for it makes a very acceptable *bortsch*-like soup.

Chilled tomato soup

¾ pint (450 ml) tomato juice	4 level tablespoons instant dried milk powder
¼ pint (150 ml) iced water	Pinch of celery salt
Dash of Worcestershire sauce to taste	

Combine all ingredients except the seasonings and blend in a liquidizer until creamy, then season. Serves 4.
Variations: Use beetroot juice or canned vegetable juice instead of tomato.

Tomato and orange soup

2 oranges
1½ pints (approx. 1 l)
   tomato juice
Juice of ½ lemon
4 tablespoons cider

2 teaspoons sugar
Salt and white pepper
2 medium tomatoes,
   peeled

First finely grate the orange rind from the oranges and reserve, then squeeze them. Mix together the tomato juice, orange and lemon juice, and cider, then add the sugar and finally the salt and pepper. Serve cold with a thin slice of peeled tomato floating in each bowl, and with brown bread spread with butter mixed with the orange peel. Serves 4–6.

2. Egg and cheese dishes

Eggs and cheese are still the cheapest and best form of protein. They are easily stored and can quickly be made into a variety of dishes, from a simple course for a light meal, with perhaps soup first and fruit afterwards, or served for a first or last course. Eggs are best if brought to room temperature before cooking, and cheese should be stored in a cool place, wrapped in greaseproof or transparent silicone paper, and also brought to room temperature before eating or cooking. Stale ends of cheese should be grated and put into a screw-top jar and kept in the fridge. This will prove invaluable for using with pasta, rice or for a topping on fish and other savoury dishes.

TO PRESERVE EGGS

When eggs are plentiful and cheap they can be satisfactorily preserved in the following way. Mix about 4 oz (115 g) lard with about 2 heaped tablespoons borax. A little less or more borax may be required, but it must be well mixed and not powdery. The lard keeps the air from the eggs and the borax stops the lard going rancid. Use fresh, clean and dry eggs about 3 days old, and completely cover each egg with this mixture, candling them in the palms of the hands. Store them broad end uppermost in egg trays in a cool place and lightly covered; they should not be airtight. They will keep well for about 6 months.

To test if an egg is good, put it in a bowl of cold water. If it is fresh it will sink to the bottom; if bad the gas in it will cause it to rise to the top. Preserved eggs are ideal for cooking, but sometimes the yolk breaks if they are boiled or poached.

TO STORE CHEESE

If you don't have a refrigerator, put a lump of sugar in the cheese dish with it, and put the cover on. This draws out the moisture, and keeps the cheese from going mouldy. Replace with a new lump when it starts to liquefy.

EGGS

My grandmother, who had a large family and later also 'adopted' several other children including myself, had a good way of stretching scrambled eggs. Actually, it takes off the 'egginess' which some children dislike and makes 2 eggs go as far as 4. Fortunately for me, she wrote a lot of her tips down in several books, and it is from one of them that I am quoting now.

'Break 2 eggs into a basin and add one cupful of milk and 1 teaspoonful of fine semolina or cornflour. Then beat up and cook in the usual way.'

Spanish omelette makes a very filling meal and is a great receptacle for leftover vegetables, bits of chicken, ham, bacon, sausage, etc. It has the advantage that it is served flat so there is no worry about it going flat.

Allow 2 eggs per person and beat them lightly with seasonings. Then heat about 2 tablespoons oil in a large frying-pan and lightly fry 1 sliced onion, several tomatoes (a tip for getting the skin off is to cut them in half, and fry skin-side down for a minute or so, then turn them and the skin will slide off easily), a little sweet pepper if you have it, or some peas, beans or mushrooms. A little cooked potato cut into dice is traditional in Spain and very good it is too. Cook them until soft but not coloured, then season and add some freshly chopped herbs. Transfer this mixture to a clean pan, and add a fraction more oil if necessary, then pour in the eggs and tip the pan so the eggs run evenly all over. When just golden underneath sprinkle the top with grated cheese and put it all under the grill until the top is puffy and golden brown. Served with a salad afterwards it is a satisfying meal.

Savoy omelette is a French country version from Savoy of the above.

4 level tablespoons butter	6 eggs
2 leeks, chopped	3 tablespoons top of the milk
1 cup cooked potato, cubed	1 tablespoon chopped parsley
1 small onion, grated	3 tablespoons grated cheese
Salt and pepper	

Melt half the butter in a pan and add the chopped white part of the leeks, the potatoes, onion and salt and pepper and cook until the leeks are soft and the potatoes very slightly browned. Heat the rest of the butter in another pan and pour in the eggs, unbeaten, to which have been added the top of the milk and seasoning. Prick the egg-yolks with a fork, and mix gently with the milk, and when the mixture is half cooked add the prepared vegetables and half the parsley. Put the grated cheese on top and put under the grill until cooked and golden. Serves 3.

Irish omelette is very good: light yet full of nourishment.

4 eggs, separated	Salt and pepper
1 large cooked potato	Squeeze of lemon juice
2 teaspoons chopped parsley	1 tablespoon butter

First separate the yolks from the whites of the eggs, then mash the potato very well, and add the eggyolks and parsley. Then season to taste and add the lemon juice. Whisk up the whites stiffly and fold them in while the butter is heating in the pan until it foams. Add the mixture to the pan, cook the bottom until golden, then put under a hot grill to finish the top. Originally the top was finished with a 'brander', which was a heated metal dish, often used in conjunction with the griddle for baking. Makes 2 large portions.

Variation: Scatter a small amount of grated cheese on top before putting under the grill.

Eggs cocotte make a good meal and there are many variations. First you will need some of the small individual ovenproof pots about 2–3 inches (50–75 mm) across. If you have a flat electric hotplate over your grill then start the eggs on top and transfer to the underneath when half cooked. Gas is a little more difficult as you can't put the pots straight onto the burner. Therefore either put the pots in a frying-pan with about 1 inch (25 mm) of water, or on top of a Le Creuset monogrill or something similar, and again when half cooked put under the grill to finish. They can also be cooked in the oven, but I find this more difficult as one can't see the various cooking stages.

First put a little butter or oil in each pot, then let it heat until foaming; tomato, mushrooms, a little chopped ham, or simply herbs can then be added and when these are softened, season, and break the egg on top. Let it cook to halfway through, then transfer to the grill to finish off. One of my favourite ways with either poached or cocotte eggs is to serve them with black butter. Before cooking the eggs, which take only about 10 minutes altogether, heat up 2 tablespoons butter (for 3 eggs) until it is beginning to get brown, then add about 1 tablespoon capers and a little of the caper vinegar. Pour this over the eggs before serving.

Eggs au gratin

Lightly butter an ovenproof dish and break 4 eggs, whole, into it (allow 2 per person). Mix together some top of the milk with salt and a little Tabasco, and spoon over the yolks, then scatter grated cheese over the top. Cook in a moderate oven (350°F/180°C/Gas Mark 4) for about 15 minutes for runny yolks and 5 minutes longer for hard yolks. The milk and cheese makes a good creamy sauce.

Variation: Strew breadcrumbs over the greased bottom of the dish, then a layer of grated cheese, then the eggs, followed by another layer of breadcrumbs and cheese, then the top of the milk over all, and bake as above. This makes a more filling meal and the crisp top is pleasant.

Hardboiled eggs can be served in many sauces, and make a good meal if rice or finely puréed potatoes are served with them (*see risotto con uova*, page 69, for example).

Anglesey eggs are a traditional Welsh method and very similar to the *oeufs à la Bretonne* served in Brittany.

6 medium-sized leeks (green onion tops can be used if leeks are not available)	1 tablespoon flour
	½ pint (300 ml) warm milk
1 lb (450 g) hot mashed potato	2 oz (60 g) grated cheese, plus 2 tablespoons
2 tablespoons butter	8 hard-boiled eggs
Salt and pepper	

Clean the leeks and chop them into small pieces, then cook them in boiling salted water for 10 minutes. Strain very well, and add them to the hot mashed potato. Add half the butter, season to taste and heat until it is a pale green fluff. Arrange around the edge of an oval fireproof dish, and keep warm. Then heat the remaining butter, stir in the flour, and add the warmed milk, stirring well to avoid lumps. Put in the 2 oz (60 g) cheese and mix well. Cut up the eggs and put in the middle of the leek and potato mixture and cover with the cheese sauce. Sprinkle the remaining cheese on top and put into a hot oven (400°F/200°C/Gas Mark 6) until the top is golden brown. Or, if cooked just before serving, brown under the grill. Serves 4.

Variation: Use 1 lb (450 g) spinach instead of the leeks.

SAUCES for serving over hard-boiled eggs are as follows:

Onion sauce

6 small sliced onions	½ pint (300 ml) warm milk
2 tablespoons butter	
1 teaspoon sugar	Salt and pepper
1 heaped tablespoon flour	

Finely slice the onions and then chop them. Heat the butter until foaming, then add the onions, sprinkle the sugar over and let them simmer gently until soft, but do not let them brown. This is easy to do if the flame is low enough and a cover is put on, and the pot shaken from time to time. When they are cooked, stir in the flour and let it cook for 1 minute, then add the warm milk, gradually, stirring all the time. Taste for seasoning (and sometimes a pinch of nutmeg or mace is pleasant) and either liquidize or leave as it is. If the onions are cut finely enough in the first place then the little chunks are crunchy and good. This is particularly good served with spinach and rice. Enough for 4 eggs.

Curry sauce (1) There are several varieties of this sauce: a pleasant summer one is simply to add a teaspoon of curry paste to a ½ pint (300 ml) well-flavoured white sauce, and just before serving to put in about 2 teaspoons of chopped mango chutney. This is also good served over rice.

Curry sauce (2)

2 tablespoons oil	½ teaspoon fennel seeds
1 medium onion, sliced	Pinch ground coriander
1 level tablespoon green masala curry paste	Pinch ground cardamom
	1 teaspoon sugar

Heat the oil and lightly fry the onion in it, then add the

curry paste and the spices. Add 1 pint (600 ml) water and let it bubble up until it boils rapidly and reduces slightly, then reduce the heat. Finally add the sugar and taste for seasoning. Cut the eggs in half lengthways and put them into the sauce. Serve with rice and mango chutney. Cucumber or onion raita is also good with them (see page 109).

Tomato sauce Unless tomatoes are very cheap it is better to use canned tomatoes for this sauce.

2 tablespoons oil	1 medium clove garlic, chopped
1 small green pepper, if available	1 tablespoon chopped parsley
1 small onion, sliced	1 bayleaf
6 mushrooms, chopped	Salt and pepper
1 × 16 oz (450 g) tin tomatoes	Pinch of cayenne

Heat the oil and lightly fry the pepper and onion, then add the mushrooms and cook for a few minutes longer. Then add all the other ingredients, cover and simmer gently until the sauce is quite thick. Remove the bayleaf before using. This sauce can be kept for some time if covered with a layer of oil, and stored in a cold place in an airtight jar. It can also be liquidized. Various spices such as a pinch of cinnamon, clove, allspice, paprika, cumin seed or curry can be added as wished to vary the flavour. It is also very good for serving with chops, sausages, or for baking with fish fillets or chicken pieces. Makes about 1½ pints (approx. 1 l).

Huevos rancheros is a Spanish method of serving eggs, and makes a very substantial meal if served with rice.

1½ pints (approx. 1 l) of tomato sauce	8 eggs

Make the sauce as above and put half into a fireproof dish, then break 8 eggs, whole, on top of it. Cover with the remaining sauce, and bake in a moderate oven (350°F/180°C/Gas Mark 4) for about 15–20 minutes. The eggs should be set, but still a little runny in the middle. Serves 4.

SOUFFLÉS are really very simple: if you can make a thick white sauce and whip up eggwhites, then you are quite capable of making a good soufflé. It has the advantage that it earns you a reputation for being a good cook in double-quick time. There are, however, a few simple rules. First and most important, let the guests wait for the soufflé. Secondly, see that the eggs are properly separated, and don't overbeat the eggwhites. They should be stiff enough to stand in creamy peaks, yet remain adhering to the whisk (much better than an eggbeater) when it is lifted up, not dry and with liquid in the bottom of the bowl.

Cheese soufflé is about the easiest to make, but really it is a marvellous way of using up leftovers of ham, fish, shellfish, or vegetables such as mushrooms or spinach. The filling must be well puréed and dry. For a heavy filling it is advisable to use an extra eggwhite, for it is the air beaten into the eggwhites that makes the soufflé rise.

Cheese soufflé

4 eggs, well separated	2 oz (60 g) hard cheese grated
2 level tablespoons butter	Salt, freshly ground pepper or a pinch of cayenne
2 level tablespoons plain flour	½ teaspoon dry mustard
½ pint (300 ml) warmed milk	

Separate the whites from the yolks, seeing that the

whites are in a large enough bowl to allow for expansion after whipping. Beat the eggyolks well, then heat the butter in a heavy saucepan, stir in the flour and gradually add the warmed milk, stirring until the mixture is quite smooth. Let this sauce cook very slowly, stirring frequently, for about 5 minutes. Then stir in the grated cheese, and pull away from the stove before adding the eggyolks. Stir, off the fire, for a few seconds and season to taste. Now, if you wish, this basic mixture can be left until just before you want to cook the soufflé, but don't beat the eggwhites until just before you want to use them.

When you want to make the soufflé, first preheat the oven to 350–400°F/180–200°C/Gas Mark 6; place the shelf fairly low in the oven and if possible put a baking sheet on the shelf. Then butter an ovenproof dish, 1½ pint (1 l) capacity. Whisk the eggwhites until stiff, then gently fold half into the basic mixture. Take care that this is done gently, with a spatula, seeing that it reaches the sides and bottom. Fold in the remaining half and pour straight away into the buttered dish. Put in the oven on the baking sheet (which will ensure that it starts cooking from the bottom) and 25 minutes later it will be ready, with a liquid centre which is as it should be. If liked dry allow 5 minutes longer.

Variation: Add 3 heaped tablespoons finely ground walnuts, and an extra eggwhite. This gives a really delicious flavour.

HOW TO REPUFF A SOUFFLÉ

If cornflour is used instead of flour for the roux, then it is possible to repuff a soufflé. It doesn't rise quite so spectacularly, but rise it does. Cook as above and leave it in the dish, then when needed stand in 1 inch (25 mm) water in another dish and reheat in a moderate oven (350°F/180°C/Gas Mark 4) for about 25–30 minutes. It is particularly good if the soufflé mixture is baked in a pastry crust instead of a dish. This makes a very filling meal, and can be cooked well ahead of time and repuffed.

Pancakes are a very economical way of serving leftovers. They are cheap, and freeze very well, either plain or filled. They are a trouble to make and serve straight away, but try spending an hour or so on them, and then freezing them (between sheets of greaseproof paper if empty), and they make a most pleasant meal. If stuffed before freezing, then allow them to come to room temperature, cover with a sauce, either cheese, mushroom, tomato or simply melted butter, and heat in a moderate oven for about 25–30 minutes. The following amounts make about 20 small pancakes.

10 oz (280 g) plain flour	1 pint (600 ml) milk
Pinch of salt	A few drops of water
2 eggs	Oil or butter for frying

Sift the flour, add the salt and break the eggs (beaten) into it and mix well, then gradually add the milk, beating all the time. The batter should be quite smooth. Add about 3 teaspoons of cold water and beat again. Leave for at least half an hour to let the air get into it. Beat again before using.

The most important part of making pancakes is the temperature of the pan, and the amount of fat used. The pan should be a heavy one and put on the stove to heat. A very small nut of butter or dribble of oil should be put in to heat up, and the pan tilted so that the grease covers the surface. Put the batter in, using about 1 tablespoon at a time, and *immediately* tilt the pan in a rolling manner so that the pancake spreads evenly to the size you want. This amount will spread to about 6 inches (15 cm). Let it brown underneath, then either toss it or turn with a slice to let the other side cook. Remove to paper to drain and at once put in the next tablespoonful, and repeat the procedure.

You will not need any more butter for about 3 more pancakes and see that it is a very small amount. Do not let the pan get too hot: adjust the heat. Making pancakes is simple so long as you are quick and dexterous, and as the ingredients are cheap it is worth practising.

Sweet pancakes can of course be filled with fruit purées, jam or honey with a few chopped nuts and raisins, or served simply with sugar and lemon juice. To reheat frozen, plain pancakes, let them defrost slightly, then heat in a low oven, covered in foil or with a lid on. Then proceed as usual, or reheat in a pan with a little butter, sugar and either orange juice, about 4 tablespoons for 4 pancakes, or a little spirit, if available, in which case flame them.

Pastella is Italian fritter batter, and it is light and crisp. It is marvellous not only for fruit, but also for small pieces of meat, poultry, fish or shellfish. I also use it for brains (previously blanched, *see* page 137), and sweetbreads when I can find them. If using sharp fruits such as apple, or plums, macerate the slices in sugar and a little lemon juice before dipping them in the batter.

4 oz (115 g) plain flour	4 tablespoons tepid
Pinch of salt	water
1 tablespoon oil	1 eggwhite
	Oil for deep frying

Add the salt to the flour, then pour in the oil, and then the warm water. Mix well so that the consistency is like thick cream. Set aside for ½ hour, at least, and just before

using beat the eggwhite until stiff, and add to the flour mixture, stirring well with a fork so that the white reaches down to the bottom. It will still be quite thick. Heat up a pan of deep oil, but make certain it is not smoking. Dip each piece of food in the batter, drop into the oil and fry until golden on both sides. If the food is not to be used immediately the preliminary frying should be light, the batter hardly coloured, and the food drained on paper. Just before you want to serve, re-fry the pieces in hot oil, and the batter will colour quickly. These little fritters will keep for a little while in a low oven, but do not leave longer than about 20 minutes, or the crispness will go. The above quantity is enough for fritters for about 4 people. Any batter left over can be kept in the fridge, covered for about a day, but it won't be as light and good. *See also* Crempog las (page 33).

CHEESE DISHES

Cheese, bacon and onion savoury is an old country recipe for using up stale cheese and includes a little streaky bacon with an onion. This mixture is most useful as it can be made in advance, and will keep covered in the refrigerator for about a week. It is good as a snack meal, and excellent for serving with drinks.

8 oz (225 g) Cheddar or other hard cheese	1 small onion
	Pepper
About 4 rashers streaky bacon	

Put the cheese, rashers and onion through a mincer, and mix together very thoroughly until it is a well-blended paste. Add pepper to taste, and mix again. When serving, toast bread on one side only, then spread the paste thickly on the untoasted side. Put into a hot oven for about 15 minutes, or under a slow grill (to give the onion and bacon time to cook) until it is cooked and puffed up. It has an original flavour, and tastes as if it had many more ingredients. The above amounts serve 4 for a light meal or about 16 as a canapé.

Cheese crescent is good with a supper dish, a picnic or for packed lunches. It is a cheesy loaf.

4 oz (115 g) grated cheese	½ teaspoon made mustard
4 oz (115 g) cooked, chopped ham or bacon	2 heaped tablespoons softened butter or margarine
8 oz (225 g) SR flour	1 large egg
1 teaspoon salt	Little milk to glaze

Put aside a heaped tablespoon of the cheese, then put all other ingredients into a bowl and mix until well blended. Turn out onto a floured board and shape into a roll about 12 inches (300 mm) long, and make gashes, 1 inch (25 mm) apart down one side. Place on a greased baking tray, curving the roll so that the sides splay out. Brush with milk and sprinkle with the remaining cheese.

Bake for 30 minutes at 400°F/200°C/Gas Mark 6 until risen and golden brown. Either serve straight away, or, when cold cut into wedges, spread with a little butter and keep fresh by wrapping each wedge in foil. Serves 4 as a light meal or about 8 single portions.

Cheese potato cakes make a good supper dish with sausages or bacon, or they are excellent for a picnic.

8 oz (225 g) boiled mashed potato	½ teaspoon salt
4 oz (115 g) cheese, grated	2 eggs
3 tablespoons melted butter or bacon fat, plus 2 extra tablespoons	6 level tablespoons SR flour
	4 tablespoons breadcrumbs
	Oil for frying

Mash the potatoes well and add the cheese, then the 3 tablespoons melted butter or fat, and a little salt. Then add the eggs, well beaten, and the flour, adding enough to make a not too soft dough. Dip in a little melted butter, then in breadcrumbs, and heat up the oil (about ¼ inch, 6 mm) and fry them on both sides, until golden. This amount makes about 12 cakes.

Cheese potato pancakes are traditional in many Celtic countries and are similar to the Jewish *latkes* which are usually made without the cheese. A good supper dish, and excellent with cold meats or sausages.

3 medium-sized raw potatoes	4 level tablespoons grated cheese
1 tablespoon flour	Salt and pepper
1 egg	Oil for frying
1 tablespoon milk	

Peel the potatoes and grate them coarsely, then add all the other ingredients. Mix well. Heat up a little oil (about ¼ inch, 6 mm) in a pan, and drop in spoonfuls of the mixture. Do not cook too quickly as the potato will stay raw in the middle if you do. When golden on one side, turn and cook the other side. They can be kept hot in a low oven for a limited time, but in my experience they are eaten as fast as you can make them. Serves about 4.

Croque Monsieur is a French equivalent of toasted cheese with ham.

2 eggs
1 tablespoon milk
4 crustless slices bread
1 tablespoon butter or margarine

4 slices cold ham or bacon
4 oz (115 g) cheese, grated

Beat the eggs with the milk, trim the bread and dip each slice into the egg mixture on both sides, until it is all well soaked. Heat up the butter and fry each slice until golden on both sides. Put slices of ham on the top, then pile on the grated cheese. Put under the grill until the cheese is bubbling.

Gloucester cheese and ale is a traditional cheese dish of the West Country. It is really delicious served on brown toast with pickles and more beer to drink with it.

8 oz (225 g) cheese, Gloucester for preference although Cheddar can be used
1 tablespoon made English mustard (or according to taste)

½ pint (300 ml) strong ale or dark beer (not Guinness)
6 slices brown toast

Cut the cheese into thick flakes and put into a fireproof dish spread with the mustard. Pour over the ale to cover, then bake in a hot oven for about ½ hour or until it is soft and melted. Have the brown toast ready, moisten it with a little more ale and pour the hot cheese over. Serves 3–6 depending on appetite.

Potted cheese is a very good way of preserving cheese. It has such a good flavour and will keep for some weeks if kept cool, but not too cold. Served with hot toast it can rival a good pâté for a first course, although it was as a savoury course with perhaps a few pickled onions or walnuts that it was originally served.

1 lb (450 g) hard cheese
¼ pint (150 ml) sweet sherry, sweet cider or white wine
¼ teaspoon dry mustard

½ teaspoon powdered mace
Pinch cayenne pepper
4 oz (115 g) butter plus more butter for sealing

Grate the cheese and pound with all the other ingredients very thoroughly, pouring in the wine last and mixing it so that the whole is of a creamy consistency. This can be done in a liquidizer if the wine is added as well. Put into small pots and cover the top with melted butter and when set cover with foil and keep in a cool place.

Old English herb cheese is made in the same way but with the addition of about 2 tablespoons of mixed, chopped fresh herbs, such as chervil, parsley, chives and a very little sage.

Kentish rarebit comes from the nineteenth-century apple pickers of the Kentish orchards and is delicious.

2 heaped tablespoons butter
2 large eating apples

8 oz (225 g) grated hard cheese
Pepper

Melt the butter in a saucepan and gently fry the peeled, cored and sliced apples. Do not let them brown, but just cook until soft through. Add the grated cheese and pepper and mix well. Put on to rounds of toast and brown under a hot grill. This quantity makes enough for 4 large rounds of toast.

Ramkins

From the *Compleat City and Country Cook; or the Accomplished Housewife* by Charles Carter (1736). These ramkins make the most excellent light meal or savoury and use up stale rolls to the best advantage.

8 oz (225 g) grated hard cheese such as Cheddar	Pepper
4 oz (115 g) grated softer cheese such as Cheshire	Pinch of cayenne or mustard powder
4 heaped tablespoons butter	2 eggs
	8 round rolls

Mix up both the grated cheeses, then add the butter, pepper, mustard and eggs. Pound all together very thoroughly. Cut the rolls in half and scoop out most of the crumb, then fill with the cheese mixture. Bake in a hot oven for about 20 minutes: they will rise an inch (25 mm) higher and are best eaten at once. Serves 4 or 8. *See also* the chapter on 'Bread' (pages 39–50).

Welsh cheese pudding *See* the chapter on 'Bread' (page 41.

Welsh rarebit

when well made is a delightful dish. This is a traditional Welsh recipe. 'I am a Welshman. I do love *cause boby* [*sic*], good roasted cheese.' (*First Boke of the Introduction of Knowledge*, Andrew Boorde, 1547.) It was also a great standby in Wales during the days of the great Depression of the 1920s and 30s.

8 oz (225 g) strong cheese, grated	1 tablespoon butter
3 teaspoons flour	Shake of pepper
2 teaspoons Worcestershire sauce	4 tablespoons beer or milk
1 level teaspoon dry mustard	4 slices bread

Put the cheese, flour, Worcestershire sauce, mustard, butter and pepper into a saucepan. Mix well, then add the beer or milk to moisten. Do not make it too wet. Stir over a gentle heat until it is all melted, and when it is a thickish paste stop stirring, and swivel it around the saucepan, which it will do quite easily. Leave to cool a little, and meanwhile toast the bread on one side only. Spread the mixture thickly over the untoasted side and brown under a hot grill. This mixture can be made and kept in the refrigerator for several days if required. Serves 4.

Buck rarebit

is as above with a poached egg on top. The egg is also good on top of the cheese, bacon and onion savoury (page 29).

Whitley goose

is an old Northumberland dish. It's not a goose at all, but a cheese and onion dish. Many similar dishes exist all over Britain and stem from the days when meat was almost as expensive as it is today, relatively speaking.

4 medium onions	tablespoon
2 oz (60 g) grated cheese plus 1 heaped	¼ pint (150 ml) milk
	Pepper

Peel and slice the onions, barely cover them with cold water and bring to the boil, then simmer until tender.

Drain and chop them up, then mix with the 2 oz (60 g) cheese and season to taste. Put the milk into a greased ovenproof dish, add the onion mixture, top with the remaining cheese and bake in a hot oven for about 10 minutes. Serves 2.

Somerset rarebit is the same idea and consists of layers of grated cheese with chopped raw onion, ending with a layer of cheese mixed with breadcrumbs and liberally dotted with butter. This is baked in a medium oven until the onion is cooked.

Swper mam is the Welsh version, and the name means 'Mother's supper'. It is traditionally served either with jacket-baked potatoes or with a Welsh omelette (*see* below).

8 large bacon rashers or ham slices	Pepper and a little salt depending on the taste of the bacon and cheese
2 medium onions, peeled and finely chopped	
4 oz (115 g) grated hard cheese	

Put half the bacon in the bottom of a shallow fireproof dish, then cover with the finely chopped onions, followed by the cheese, seasoning each layer with pepper. Put the remaining rashers on top, and cook in a moderate oven (375°F/190°C/Gas Mark 5) for ½ hour, or until the bacon is crisp and the onion cooked. Serves 3–4.

Crempog las is a Welsh omelette which is more like a pancake, but good with the three last dishes.

8 oz (225 g) plain flour	4 tablespoons milk
Pinch of salt	2 teaspoons chopped parsely
Pinch of grated mace or nutmeg	Small amount of lard or oil for the pan
2 eggs, separated	

Put the flour into a basin and add the salt, mace and the beaten eggyolks. Mix well with a fork, then stir in the milk, beating so that it is smooth. Whip the eggwhites until stiff, add the parsley to the batter and finally fold in the eggwhites, seeing that they mix into the batter at the bottom of the basin.

In Wales this would be fried in a large pan, then cut into 4 for serving, but if preferred 4 separate pancakes can be made. Very lightly grease a heavy pan, let it get very hot, then pour in the batter. When the underneath is golden, turn and cook the other side. Spread with butter before serving. Serves 4.

See also the chapter on 'Milk products' (pages 51–9).

3. Oatmeal and its uses

Oatmeal is one of the most valuable cereals for it contains quite a lot of protein as well as large quantities of minerals and vitamins. It is also remarkably low in calories, 1 oz (25 g) of porridge being only 13 calories as against about 104 calories for cornflakes, which makes it an excellent and filling food for people on diets. The fact that it is reasonable in price only adds to its attraction.

It is traditional to all the Celtic countries, from the oatcakes and bannocks of Ireland and Scotland, to the *Bara ceirch* of Wales and the *Quimperlé* oat loaf of Brittany. It is also popular in the West Riding and the North of England, where the thin oatbread was introduced by the armies of John of Hainault in the twelfth century. Jean Froissart (1338–1410), the French chronicler, attributes the remarkable stamina of the Scottish soldier to the fact that he always carried a wallet of oatmeal with him, which could be mixed with water from the water bottle.

They carry with them not other pervayance [*sic*] but on the horse, between the sadle [*sic*] and the panel, they truss a broad plate of metal, and behind the sadle they will have a little sack full of oatmeal . . . and they lay the plate on the fire, and temper a little of the oatmeal and when the plate is hot they cast the thin paste thereon, and make a little cake, in a manner of a cracknel or biscuit, and that they do eat to the comfort of their stomacs [*sic*] . . . wherfore it is no marvel they make greater journeys than other people do.

This oatcake was also made by Scottish shepherds during their long vigils in the hills.

There are several varieties of oatmeal such as the round ground or flake meal which is best for solid food and is also put into casseroles, and soups; the medium oatmeal is used for bannocks and for mixing with other flours, and the fine oatmeal is usually used for coating fish or meat and for porridge and broths, although it is a matter of taste.

USES FOR OATMEAL

Oatmeal has such a good flavour that it is far superior to flour for coating such fish as herrings or mackerel, especially if the skin is first brushed with some mustard The nuttiness of the oatmeal is delicious with the rich fish. In Scotland the fine river trout is also so treated. A Scottish gourmet of the nineteenth century describes it thus: 'A herring fried in nutty oatmeal and accompanied by a mustard sauce makes a noble supper dish, and never better than when a coarse oatmeal is used and the fish fried in bacon fat. For brown trout, however, I prefer a dusting of the finest oatmeal: and it should of course, be cooked in butter.'

FOR DREDGING MEAT

Lamb or young mutton is particularly good dredged with oatmeal. When the joint is half cooked, cover the skin with a mixture of oatmeal, chopped herbs and a very little oil or water to bind it. Season to taste and then spread this over the top and finish cooking. As a change from herbs, try finely grated orange or lemon peel, or a mixture of both mixed into the oatmeal. It gives an excellent flavour.

FOR STUFFING

Oatmeal makes an unusual and delicious stuffing for chicken, duck, turkey or lamb. For a 4 lb (approx. 2 kg) chicken put about 4 oz (113 g) coarse oatmeal into a bowl, then add a finely chopped small onion, salt and pepper. Add about 2 tablespoons butter or good dripping and some chopped herbs. Mix well and then add about 1 tablespoon of giblet stock, or if the budget runs to it, whisky. Put this into the bird and cook as usual. Small spoonfuls rolled into a ball are often cooked in Scots broth, like dumpling.

The Scottish name for this is 'skirlie', and it is often just turned in a pan, the oatmeal added last when it is served with mince, meats or poultry. If steamed in a greased basin it is called 'mealie pudding' and is good with sausages or bacon. It was known as a 'tightner' during the lean years for it is a great 'filler-upper'.

Mealie pudding was also served with cod poached in milk, with parsley, the milk later being made into a white sauce with the addition of mustard.

1 medium onion	8 oz (225 g) fine
3 heaped tablespoons	oatmeal
good dripping, butter	2 oz (60 g) grated
or margarine	cheese
	Salt and pepper

Parboil the onion and dice it finely, heat the fat, then mix all the ingredients together, put them into a greased basin and steam for 1 hour. Serves 4.

OATMEAL WITH VEGETABLES AND SOUPS

Pratie oaten is an Irish potato and oatmeal cake which is very good with grills, or with sausages, bacon or eggs. This recipe makes about 15 cakes.

Mix together about 2 cups warm mashed potatoes with approximately 1 cup of fine oatmeal until it is a fairly soft dough. Add salt and about ½ cup melted butter or bacon fat to bind it. Roll out on a board sprinkled with oatmeal, cut into shapes, and either fry or cook in the oven.

Cabbage, kale, turnip tops or spring greens are very good if when cooked and drained they are heated up with a little butter and sprinkled with oatmeal before serving. *See also brotchán roy* (page 14), nettle soup (page 154), and oatmeal soup (page 18).

Oatmeal pastry is very good for gooseberry or rhubarb tart or flan, and also with blackberries and apple, or prunes and apple.

1 tablespoon lard	1 level teaspoon sugar
1 tablespoon margarine	About 3 tablespoons
4 level tablespoons SR flour	water
3 level tablespoons fine oatmeal	

Mix the fat into the flour, then add all the other dry ingredients, and enough cold water to make a stiff dough. Turn out onto a floured board and roll out to fit an 8 inch (20 cm) pie dish.

Crumble for the tops of fruit puddings is good made with oatmeal instead of flour. Heat about 2 tablespoons butter or margarine and add 4 tablespoons oatmeal and about the same of brown sugar. Mix it well, then put on the top of the cooked fruit, and heat in the oven (400°F/200°C/Gas Mark 6) for about 15 minutes or until the top is crunchy.

Cranachan or Cream-crowdie

Either lightly toast 4 level tablespoons oatmeal, or toss in a thick-bottomed frying-pan over a gentle heat to give it a nutty flavour. Then whip about ½ pint (300 ml) cream, sweetened to taste, and add the oatmeal to it. Flavour it with rum, vanilla (vanilla sugar can be used) or fresh soft fruit such as raspberries. Vanilla ice-cream can be used instead of cream and the oatmeal gives it a kind of praline flavour.

Oatcakes are very good with fish, especially herrings either smoked or fresh, with butter and raw onions, with soups, sausages, bacon, with jam, honey or marmalade for breakfast. In Scotland they are called bannocks, and *Bara ceirch* in Wales. Traditionally, flour is not used in them, but they are easier to handle if a little flour is added with the oatmeal. They keep well in an airtight container.

2 teaspoons butter or margarine	8 oz (225 g) fine or medium oatmeal, plus extra for rolling
2 teaspoons lard or bacon dripping	*Glaze:*
1½ gills (215 ml) hot water (90°F/32°C)	1 egg beaten with 1 tablespoon milk and
½ tablespoon sugar	1 teaspoon sugar
Pinch of salt	

Melt the butter and lard in the water with the sugar and salt, and whilst still hot add to the oatmeal, kneading it well to a soft dough. Sprinkle oatmeal fairly thickly onto a board and put the dough on it, rolling it in the oatmeal. Break off small balls one at a time and flatten them to the required size (about 3 inches (75 mm) across is easiest). Place onto a moderately hot griddle, or in a heavy pan which has just been wiped with a cloth with a very little grease on it. If there is sufficient oatmeal it will not stick. Then paint on the glaze lightly to give a shiny surface, and bake for about 7 minutes on one side. Leave to harden in a warm place and when needed gently toast the second side under a slow grill. Makes about 12 oatcakes.

An easier method is to use 6 oz (170 g) oatmeal and 2 oz (60 g) flour and to follow the procedure given above.

Car-cakes are fried oatcakes and delicious with bacon or sausages. Mix together 8 level tablespoons oatmeal, a pinch of bicarbonate of soda, a pinch of cream of tartar, salt and pepper. Then add enough milk to make a thickish pouring batter. Heat up some bacon fat or lard, drop spoonfuls into it and turn when browned underneath and brown the other side. Sometimes an egg is added as well as the milk. They used to be eaten on Shrove Tuesday and are mentioned in Sir Walter Scott's *The Bride of Lammermoor*.

Oatmeal biscuits

2 level tablespoons butter	2 teaspoons baking powder
4 oz (115 g) sugar	8 oz (225 g) fine or medium oatmeal
2 eggs	

Beat the butter, sugar and eggs together, then add the baking powder and oatmeal. Drop tablespoon by tablespoon on to a greased baking sheet and bake until golden brown in a moderate oven (350°F/180°C/Gas Mark 4) for about 15–20 minutes.

Oatmeal sausages

Mix together 1 lb (450 g) sausagemeat, 1 medium finely chopped onion, a pinch of chopped sage, 6 tablespoons dried oatmeal (warm it in a moderate oven before using), salt and pepper. When well mixed, shape into sausage shapes with the hands and roll in flour. Heat up some oil or bacon fat and fry slowly on all sides until they are cooked through and brown on the outside. Or, if you have the oven on, bake them for about 30 minutes. Serve with rings of cored, unpeeled apple which have been lightly cooked in butter or margarine. Serves 4.

Parkin is an old Yorkshire oatmeal cake. It should be made at least two or three days before using, and can be kept up to a week before cutting. It is best to do this, as otherwise it tends to be too moist and difficult to cut. It is an oatmeal gingerbread.

12 oz (340 g) medium oatmeal	1 lb (450 g) black treacle
6 oz (170 g) plain flour	4 oz (115 g) butter or margarine
1 tablespoon sugar	$\frac{1}{4}$ pint (150 ml) milk
1 teaspoon ground ginger	1 teaspoon bicarbonate of soda
Pinch of salt	
Pinch of ground allspice	

Mix the oatmeal, flour, sugar, ginger, allspice and salt together. Warm the treacle and the butter together but do not let it get too hot. Warm the milk to blood heat, add the bicarbonate of soda and mix into the dry ingredients with the treacle mixture. Grease a large flat baking tin and sprinkle it with flour. Line the bottom with greased paper and then pour in the mixture. Bake in a moderate oven (350°F/180°C/Gas Mark 4) for about 45 minutes or until it is firm to the touch and a skewer inserted into the middle comes out clean. Leave in the tin to cool. If liked, shredded nuts can be sprinkled over the top after it has been cooking for ½ hour.

When cold, cut into squares and store in a box. In Yorkshire it is often eaten with cheese, and sometimes served, warm, with cooked apple over it.

Inverness gingerbread is a similar cake but has much more flour in it and also candied fruit.

12 oz (340 g) plain flour
1 teaspoon bicarbonate of soda
4 oz (115 g) fine oatmeal
8 oz (225 g) butter or margarine
4 tablespoons top of milk
12 oz (340 g) black treacle
4 oz (115 g) candied lemon peel
1 oz (25 g) shredded green ginger

Mix together the flour, bicarbonate of soda and the oatmeal. Cream the butter, and beat in the flour mixture alternately with the milk. Stir in the warmed treacle, then add the finely chopped peel and ginger. Beat into a light dough, turn out into a well-greased tin and bake in a moderate oven (350°F/180°C/Gas Mark 4) for about ¾ hour, or until firm to the touch. Leave in the tin to cool.

Porridge is still the finest winter breakfast there is and low in calories (*see* page 34).

The following makes a large country portion for one person.

1 cup water
1¼ oz (30 g) medium oatmeal
Pinch of salt

Boil the water in a saucepan, and when it is bubbling add the oatmeal in a constant stream with one hand, stirring all the time with the other. When it is all boiling regularly, pull to the side of the heat, cover and simmer very gently for 10 minutes, then add the salt and stir. Cover again, and simmer very gently for about another 10 minutes; the time cannot be more precise as the quality of the oats varies and thus affects the cooking time. Serve piping hot in cold soup plates, and dip each spoonful into individual bowls of cold milk or cream before eating. This is the method which has been used for centuries. Porridge can also be made in a double boiler, which prevents any fear of burning.

Much thinner porridge is served in Scotland than in Ireland or England, and I think it is better that way. Also the large flake oatmeal used in other countries is nothing like so good as the medium-sized variety in Scotland.

Muesli, the Swiss breakfast food, is easily made at a much more economical price if oatmeal is used.

Mix together 1 lb (450 g) medium or flake oatmeal, 8 oz (225 g) dried skim milk powder, 7 tablespoons wheatgerm powder, 8 oz (225 g) soft brown sugar, or to taste. Add about 8 oz (225 g) dried fruits such as raisins or sultanas, 2 heaped tablespoons ground almonds, and a handful of chopped nuts, either raw peanuts, hazelnuts or split almonds. The exact amounts of the ingredients are really a matter of taste and pocket, and can be adjusted accordingly without any loss of food value or flavour. The mixture keeps well in a tin for some weeks.

4. Bread

There is probably more bread wasted every day, all over these islands, than any other food, and this has been true for some centuries. In 1850 Lord Acton said: 'The waste of bread in England impresses thoughtful observers and foreigners express the most painful astonishment. It is not solely the fragments of it swept daily from the table of the wealthy and thrown away by pampered and careless servants, or those crusts which ill-trained children are allowed to leave at all their meals.'

The quality of bread, and particularly white bread, has seriously deteriorated, even in my lifetime, and it is the white loaf that the majority of people eat. For it is a well proved fact that the poorer and less educated the person, the more he or she will insist on a white loaf. Dorothy Hartley suggests in her excellent book *Food in England* that the preference is due to the thin white wafer of the Mass bread of pre-Reformation days, which was imbued with almost magic properties. In the 1850s Alexis Soyer, the great chef who revolutionized army food in the Crimea and also helped famine victims in Ireland, wrote: 'In Ireland, amongst the poor, it is almost a disgrace to eat brown bread. During the year of the famine, being at Malahide, I saw a female, without shoes or stockings, go into a baker's shop, purchase two loaves, one white, and the other brown; the white she carried in her hand, the brown she hid under her everlasting cloak – her pride would not allow it to be seen.'

Today more and more people are making their own bread, but even so a lot of bought bread is wasted. There are so many uses for stale bread that it is worth listing some of the most useful.

Breadcrumbs are the most obvious choice and are simple to do. Put the bread slices in a low oven until they are completely dried out, and when cool, put them between sheets of greaseproof paper and roll them until quite crushed, with a rolling pin. Then leave again in a warm place to dry out thoroughly before putting them into screwtop jars. A mixture of brown and white bread is quite pleasant for some savoury dishes such as coating for fish or meat, or for stuffings or forcemeats. If the crumbs are lightly tossed in butter or margarine and strewn over vegetables, they are a well-known Polish garnish and used particularly with cauliflower. They are also good mixed with sugar and butter for crunchy tops over stewed fruit.

Brown bread crusts dried in the oven as above are very good for giving to dogs, broken up with their food. White bread is not considered good for animals owing to the additives.

Croûtons are another way of using up stale slices of bread. Fry the slices in oil or butter, sprinkle with garlic or celery salt and then cut into cubes. These are not only very good with soups, but also as a filling for herb omelettes. They give a lovely crunchy taste which is a good foil for the creamy eggs.

Stale sandwiches should be dipped on both sides in a mixture of 1 egg to 2 tablespoons milk (for 3 large sandwiches), then lightly fried in oil or butter until golden on both sides. This is only a variation of *pain perdu* and also of *Croque Monsieur* (*see* page 31). (If Mozzarella or Bel Paese cheese is used it is called *Mozzarella in carozza* in Italy.)

Pain perdu or French toast is very good for children and also liked by some adults. It is simply stale bread dipped in egg and milk as above, then fried in butter and sprinkled either with brown sugar, sometimes mixed with cinnamon, or mixed spice, jam, honey or even puréed fruit. It can also be served as a savoury with fried bacon, sausages or eggs.

Toast Melba is made from stale bread, sliced very thinly and the crusts removed. It should be baked in a slow oven until it is golden brown all over. This can be kept in a tin for some time and is an excellent way of using up stale bread.

Bruschetta is the Italian version of garlic bread. Thick slices of white bread are baked in the oven until crisp and golden. Then they are rubbed liberally with a cut clove of garlic, and a little olive oil is poured over so that it is absorbed. It is a most delicious way of using up stale French or similar-type loaves.

Garlic bread is so well known that I hesitate to mention it. A stale French-type loaf is cut into slices but not right through to the bottom. Butter and pressed garlic to taste are mixed together, then put between the slices. The whole is wrapped in foil and heated in a hot oven.

Paprika bread is less well known but is made the same way, the butter being mixed with paprika to taste, with a few caraway seeds mixed in. It is heated as above.

Crostini di provatura are a Roman dish in which Provolone cheese is used, though Bel Paese, Gruyère, or even stale Cheddar can also be used. Cut 10 rounds about ¼ inch (6 mm) thick from a French-type loaf and put a thick slice of cheese on each. Put them, slightly overlapping, in a long dish, and cook in a fairly hot oven for about 7–10 minutes. The cheese should be just melted, not spread all over. Meanwhile chop up about 6 anchovies and heat them up in a little hot butter, then pour them over the cheese when it is ready. In Siena I had a similar dish spread with chicken liver pâté and it was served with a cup of clear hot broth. Delicious on a cold winter's evening.

Croustade or Surprise loaf is a good way of using up a whole loaf of the 'tin' variety. It is also good used instead of pastry if you are in a hurry. Cut the top off the loaf and scoop out most of the crumb (which can be used for making breadcrumbs or a treacle tart) then fill the middle with drained cooked fresh vegetables, or vegeables mixed with leftover meat or a little cooked mince. Then cover with a white or cheese sauce (about ½ pint, 300 ml), add a squeeze of lemon, then put the buttered crust on top and bake in a moderate oven for about 20 minutes.

If a round loaf is used and trimmed to about 2 inches (50 mm) high it is good for using as a pizza base or for a quiche, made from 2 eggs mixed with ½ pint (300 ml) milk, grated cheese and perhaps a little bacon or chopped ham, all baked for about ½ hour in a moderate oven.

For using stale rolls *see* ramkins (page 32).

Croûte fromage

Dip 8 thin rounds of bread in melted butter, then in grated cheese and put into a hot oven until they are just melted. Then heat 1 heaped tablespoon butter in a saucepan, stir in 1 tablespoon flour, and add ½ pint (300 ml) milk, stirring well until it is smooth, then add a pinch of dry mustard and 4 tablespoons of grated cheese, and cook until melted. Put this between the rounds of bread like a sandwich and serve hot. Serves 4. Bacon, or ham can be used on the bread instead of cheese.

Welsh cheese pudding

4 large slices crustless stale bread	Cayenne pepper or Tabasco
Butter	1 pint (600 ml) milk
8 oz (225 g) grated hard cheese	1 egg

Lightly toast the bread on one side only and butter the untoasted side. Grease an ovenproof dish and lay on it 2 slices, toast side down, and put half the cheese and seasoning on top. Cover with the remaining slices of bread, toast side up, and put the rest of the cheese on top. Bring the milk to just under the boil and let it cool slightly, then add the beaten egg, mix well and pour over the cheese. Let it stand for at least 20 minutes, then bake for 20 minutes in a moderate to hot oven, or until it is puffed up and golden. Serves 4 as a savoury or 2 for a meal.

A FEW PUDDINGS

Bread and butter pudding is also known as Newmarket pudding. It has been popular for several centuries and this version is from Hannah Glasse, the well known eighteenth-century cookery writer.

Grated rind of ½ lemon
½ pint (300 ml) milk
Pinch grated nutmeg or
   ground cinnamon
2 eggs
4 tablespoons sugar

3 tablespoons mixed
   raisins, currants
   and chopped peel
4 thickly buttered slices
   bread

Grate the lemon rind into the milk with a pinch of grated nutmeg, or ground cinnamon. Stir in 2 well-beaten eggs. Butter a fireproof dish, sprinkle the bottom generously with most of the sugar and the raisins, currants and mixed peel. Take the 4 thickly buttered slices of bread, without the crusts, make a layer of 2 slices, sprinkling them with more sugar and fruit before laying on the rest. Pour the egg mixture into the fireproof dish gently and, if possible, leave the pudding to soak for 2 hours before sprinkling the top with the rest of the sugar and baking it for 30 minutes in a preheated moderate oven (350°F/180°C/Gas Mark 4–5). The pudding can also be much improved by the addition of 2 tablespoons sherry or brandy before baking. Serves 4–6.

Gâteau de pain is the French version which a French friend of mine, Monique Guillaume, who is a marvellous cook, always does in the pressure cooker.

Pinch grated nutmeg
½ pint (300 ml) milk
10 crustless slices dry
   bread (sandwich loaf)
4 oz (115 g) raisins

2 tablespoons rum
2 eggs, separated
3 oz (85 g) castor sugar
2 tablespoons butter
Pinch of salt

Put the nutmeg in the milk and let the bread soak in it for at least 10 minutes. During this time put the raisins to soak in the rum. Using a wooden spoon beat together the eggyolks and the sugar until the mixture is frothy. Beat the eggwhites with the salt until stiff. Mix all together and pour into a well-buttered 2-pint (1 litre) mould, not more than ¾ full. Cover the mould with foil and put it in the pressure cooker on a trivet, with 1 pint (600 ml) of boiling water. Close the pressure cooker. Allow 15 minutes to cook after the valve has begun to hiss. Serve this *gâteau* covered with strawberry, apricot or greengage jam, or with *crème anglaise* (egg custard). It is really a delicious pudding made in this way. Serves 4.

If not using a pressure cooker, then bake in a moderate oven for about 35 minutes.

Brown bread ice-cream was a popular Edwardian dish and is best made with crumbs from a homemade wholemeal loaf. It gives the ice-cream a pleasant nutty flavour.

Sprinkle about 8 level tablespoons of brown breadcrumbs with castor sugar and crisp up in a hot oven. Then mix these either into bought vanilla ice-cream or homemade ice-cream with a custard base. Freeze until quite hard. Serves 3–4.

Danish apple cake is not a cake in our sense of the word, but rather like an apple charlotte.

8 level tablespoons
   butter
2 level tablespoons
   sugar
2½ cups breadcrumbs
   (brown or white)

4 cups puréed,
   sweetened apple
   flavoured with cloves
   if liked

Heat the butter and mix in the sugar and brown the crumbs in this mixture until they are crisp. In a shallow dish put alternate layers of crumbs and apple, ending with the crumbs. Either chill, or bake in a 350°F/180°C/ Gas Mark 4 oven for about 30 minutes, then cool and unmould. Rhubarb or gooseberries can also be used. Serves 4.

If finely-grated stale pumpernickel or rye breadcrumbs are used with the apple, then it is called *Bondepige med slør* (veiled country lass). The top is usually decorated with whipped cream and raspberry jam or currant jelly.

Apple dowdy with pumpernickel is a lovely buttery, spicy pudding.

2 tablespoons raisins	2 lb (1 kg) cooking
4 tablespoons milkless tea	apples
Little rum essence	6 oz (170 g) brown sugar
1 lb (450 g) loaf of	3 tablespoons honey
stale pumpernickel or	1½ teaspoons cinnamon
dark rye bread	Pinch of salt
8 level tablespoons butter	

First soak the raisins in the tea with the rum essence added for about ½ hour or longer. Cut the bread into thin slices and remove any crusts, and butter liberally, keeping back about 2 tablespoons of butter. Then spread this remaining butter around a deep pie-dish about 8 inches (20 cm) square or the equivalent rectangle. Mix together the peeled, cored and chopped apples in a basin with 4 oz (115 g) of the sugar, and the honey, cinnamon, salt and raisin mixture. Line the dish with the bread, but retain enough to cover the top, buttered side uppermost. Put the apple mixture in, and cover the top with the rest of the bread, buttered side up. Sprinkle over about 4 tablespoons water and finally sprinkle over the remaining sugar. Bake in a preheated oven (375°F/190°C/ Gas Mark 5) for about 20 minutes, then press the bread top firmly down with a spatula and return to the oven for another 20 minutes or until the top is crusty and the dish juicy. It is extremely good served hot, but very good cold as well. Enough for 4–6.

Queen of puddings

Rind of 1 lemon	Pinch of nutmeg
1 pint (600 ml) hot milk	2 eggs, separated
1 tablespoon soft butter	3 tablespoons warmed
5 tablespoons castor sugar	strawberry or raspberry jam
6 oz (170 g) fresh white breadcrumbs	

Put the whole lemon rind into the milk and infuse it on a warm part of the stove. Strain it into a bowl, add the butter and 1 tablespoon of sugar, and when dissolved add the breadcrumbs and nutmeg. Mix and leave to cool. Add the eggyolks, well beaten, mix thoroughly and turn into a buttered pie dish. Let it stand for 30 minutes and then bake in a moderate oven (350°F/ 180°C/Gas Mark 4) for about 25 minutes. Meanwhile beat up the eggwhites with all but 1 heaped teaspoon of the remaining sugar. Take the pudding from the oven, let it cool slightly and spread the jam over the top, then spread the meringue over the top of this, seeing that it is taken right to the edges. Dust the last teaspoon of sugar over and put back in a slow oven until the meringue is set and the peaks are golden brown. Serves 4.

Snowdon pudding is a good, light steamed pudding made with breadcrumbs which used to be served at the hotel at the foot of Mount Snowdon about the turn of the century. This recipe comes from Alice Corbett, 1887.

Butter to grease basin
  thickly
3 tablespoons seedless
  raisins
4 oz (115 g) butter,
  margarine or grated
  suet
4 oz (115 g) fresh
  white breadcrumbs

2 level tablespoons
  cornflour or ground
  rice
Rind of 1 lemon, grated
3 tablespoons orange or
  lemon marmalade
3 tablespoons brown
  sugar
3 eggs

Take a pudding basin about 6 inches (150 mm) high, butter it well and then press as many of the seedless raisins onto the sides as it will take. Mix together the fat, breadcrumbs, cornflour, then add the grated lemon rind, marmalade and sugar. Beat the eggs well and mix them in with any raisins that might be left over. Spoon the mixture into the basin, taking care not to dislodge the raisins. Cover, and either steam the pudding or simmer in a saucepan with boiling water to halfway up for about 1 hour. Turn out onto a warmed plate and serve with cider sauce. If pressure cooking it will take 30 minutes.

Cider sauce

2 tablespoons sugar
½ lemon rind in one
  piece
2 tablespoons water

1 heaped teaspoon
  cornflour
1 tablespoon butter
¼ pint (150 ml) strong
  cider

Boil the sugar, lemon rind and water for 15 minutes then take out the rind. Mix the cornflour into the butter, then stir into the sugar mixture, then add the cider and let it simmer gently until it has become syrupy, for about 10 minutes. Serve hot, separately. Enough for 4.

Summer pudding is also called hydropathic pudding, because it used to be served in nursing homes to people who couldn't take pastry. It is a lovely fresh summer pudding, but it can also be made with frozen or tinned fruits, thus imparting a taste of summer in the winter.

Slices of stale white
  bread without crusts
A little milk
⅔ of the basin you will
  use of cooked mixed

redcurrants,
raspberries,
strawberries, white- or
  blackcurrants

Cut the slices of bread medium thick and take off the crusts. Moisten them slightly with milk, but do not make them sloppy, and line the sides and bottom of a deep pudding basin with them. They should overlap, so that they will hold together when turned out. Fill the basin to 1 inch (25 mm) of the top with the cooked fruits, then cover the top with more bread slices, and then with greaseproof paper. Put a light weight on top and keep in a cold place overnight. Turn out of the mould by placing a plate on the top and turning it over quickly. Serve with cream or custard. Enough for 4–6.

Treacle tart is a popular dish in the North of England and very easy to make.

8 oz (225 g) shortcrust
  pastry made with 6 oz
  (170 g) plain flour,
  3 oz (85 g) margarine
  or butter, pinch of
  salt and cold water to
  mix

6 level tablespoons
  fresh white
  breadcrumbs
Squeeze of lemon juice
8 tablespoons golden
  syrup

Line a flat, 8–9 inch (200–225 mm) greased tart tin with most of the pastry, leaving enough to make the lattice-work across the top. Crimp the edges and lightly prick the bottom but don't go right through the pastry. Mix the breadcrumbs, lemon juice and warmed syrup together and pour in to within 1 inch (25 mm) of the edge of the pastry. Roll out the strips of pastry, and arrange them across the top, damping the edges to make them stick. Brush over with a little milk and bake in a moderate oven (375°F/190°C/Gas Mark 5) for about 15–20 minutes, or until golden brown. It can be eaten warm or cold.

Zwetschken–Bavesen are Bavarian plum jam fritters made with stale rolls. They are always eaten on the feast-day known as *Kirchweih* (Church Day) held on the third Sunday and Monday in October.

6 stale rolls or thick rounds of bread	2 eggs
	Oil for frying
6 tablespoons plum jam	Sugar
Little milk	Cinnamon

If the rolls are the very crusty kind then trim off any hard crust. Cut them in half and remove a little of the crumb and fill up with plum jam, then put the top on. Soak in cold milk, then dip into beaten egg and fry until golden all over in about 1 inch (25 mm) of hot oil. Serve hot, sprinkled with sugar and a little cinnamon. They are like a very light doughnut.

HOMEMADE BREADS

Making yeast bread intimidates a lot of people, mainly I think because of having to wait some hours for the proving of the dough. Nowadays, when kitchens are not the warm, focal part of the house, it is more difficult to find a convenient warm spot, but the following quick yeast dough does away with all the anxiety. Homemade bread is both cheaper and infinitely better in taste. For those who have deep freezers it is simple to make up a batch, and when cooked to consign it to the freezer for future use. A morning spent doing this will repay in much more than money.

BAKING TIPS

To tell if a loaf is cooked properly, tap it on the bottom and it will sound hollow. If you want the loaf to have a crisp crust then put a pan of boiling water on the lowest rack of the oven during cooking, and when cooked, dry the loaf in a hot place, quickly. If you want a soft crust then wrap it in a clean tea towel while it is warm. To make a shiny crust, brush the top over with a little milk, or sugar and water and return it to the oven for about 5–10 minutes for this to 'set'. For breads covered with poppy seeds, caraway or crushed sugar mixed with spice it is better to put them on about 15 minutes before the bread is cooked. If put on at the beginning they can lose flavour. To achieve a flaky look, sprinkle some flake oatmeal or cracked wheat over about 15 minutes before the loaf is cooked. Always cool bread before putting it away in a bread bin, otherwise it is liable to go mouldy very quickly.

Quick yeast dough It is essential to use fresh yeast which can usually be obtained from cake-shops, or owners of small bakeries. If you get a large quantity and have a deep freezer, the yeast can be stored in that or in a proper freezing compartment of a refrigerator for about 1 week. It also helps to get a good, strong bread flour (which has more gluten in it) and various milling firms can advise on this. However, the usual plain flour can be used if you can't get the other, with 1 fl. oz (25 ml) less water.

For a white loaf:

1 oz (25 g) fresh yeast
14 fl. oz (400 ml) hand-hot water, 13 oz if ordinary flour is used
1 (25 mg) ascorbic acid tablet, obtainable from chemists
1½ lb (675 g) strong plain flour
½ oz (12 g) salt
1 level tablespoon sugar
1 level tablespoon lard
1 large lightly-oiled polythene bag, big enough to take the mixing bowl

Mix the yeast with the tepid water, then add the crushed ascorbic acid tablet and whisk until it is dissolved. Put the flour, salt and sugar into a large mixing bowl and rub in the lard which has been cut into small pieces. Blend in the yeast liquid and work to a firm dough until it leaves the sides of the bowl. (Add a very little more flour if the dough stays sticky.) The sides should be quite clean and the dough elastic.

Turn out on to a lightly floured board or table and knead and stretch the dough by folding it towards you, then pushing away with the palm of your hand. Repeat this, giving it a kind of rocking motion. This should take about 10 minutes until the dough is firm and no longer sticky.

Shape into a ball, put into the mixing bowl and then into the lightly oiled polythene bag. Leave for 15 minutes.

Preheat the oven to 450°F/230°C/Gas Mark 8, and shape the bread as desired, making a deep crease down the middle, or make into rolls if preferred. Brush with beaten egg and water, or milk and water if a glaze is wanted. Bake in the middle of the oven for about 55–60 minutes (lowering the heat to 375°F/175°C/Gas Mark 5 after 10 minutes) for a whole loaf weighing about 1 lb (450 g) or 60–75 minutes for a 2 lb (1 kg) loaf. Rolls will only take about 15 minutes. When cooked the bread will sound hollow when tapped on the bottom. Leave to cool on a wire rack.

Wholemeal bread can be made as above, using wholemeal flour instead of white and slightly increasing the water to about 15 fl. oz (425 ml). Wholemeal dough is given a crisp crust by brushing with salt and water and sprinkling with cracked wheat.

If you can't get fresh yeast then you will have to use the longer proving method. Generally speaking only half the quantity of dried yeast to fresh yeast is used as the raising power is about double. But it is wise to check with the instructions on the tin or package before using. The following Irish recipe using a potato makes very good, moist bread which keeps well. The quantities given below make one large 2 lb (1 kg) loaf or two smaller ones. It also makes very good rolls if formed into shapes about 2 × 3 inches (50 × 75 mm). The baking time for rolls varies slightly: bake in a preheated oven (450°F/230°C/Gas Mark 8) for 10 minutes, then lower the heat to (350°F/180°C/Gas Mark 4) for a further 30 minutes.

White bread

1 large potato	4 level teaspoons sugar
1½ tablespoons butter	¾ pint (450 ml) milk
2 level teaspoons dried yeast	2 level teaspoons salt
Pinch of ginger	1½ lb (675 g) strong plain unbleached flour

Cook the potato, which has been cut into large pieces, in a little water until soft, then drain, reserving about 3 tablespoons of the liquor. Mash it well with a little of the milk and butter until quite smooth. Put the potato water into a bowl and when cooled to tepid sprinkle the yeast, ginger and a teaspoon of sugar over it. Heat up the rest of the milk, then mix it with the rest of the butter, sugar and salt. When cooled to hand-hot stir it, gradually, into the potato and yeast mixture until it is smooth and creamy. When the yeast is foamy mix very well and add, gradually, about 1 lb (450 g) of the flour, stirring well with a wooden spoon. Add more flour, stirring, until it can no longer be stirred with the spoon.

Turn out onto a well-floured surface and knead for about 15 minutes, adding more flour if necessary until the dough is elastic and not sticky. Knock the dough with your knuckles to let out the air bubbles, then knead again. Butter a large bowl and put the dough in, turning over so that it is greased all over, cover with a tea-towel and put in a warm place until it has doubled in size, about 1½ hours. If put into a greased polythene bag the time is cut to about 40 minutes. Punch down again and shape into loaves. Put into buttered loaf tins, cover again, or put into the polythene and leave for about ½ hour, or until almost double in size. Put into a preheated (450°F/230°C/Gas Mark 8) oven and after 10 minutes reduce to 350°F/180°C/Gas Mark 4 for a further 40–45 minutes or until the crust is deep brown and crisp. *See* above for glazing the tops.

Wholemeal bread can be made in the same way using half wholemeal flour and half white. Or you can make the proportion of brown larger if you like, but a little white flour is needed to make it light in texture.

White oatmeal bread is a good variation on the white loaf. It is made in the same way, but 4 oz (115 g) of raw rolled oats is added in place of the same amount of flour. The oats should be added after you mix in the first 1 lb (450 g) of flour.

Herb bread is quick and easy to make. Alas, it doesn't last long for the aroma from it stimulates all palates.

¼ pint (150 ml) milk	¼ pint (150 ml) warm water
1 heaped tablespoon sugar	½ teaspoon fennel or dill seed
2 teaspoons salt	1 teaspoon crushed dried rosemary
1 tablespoon butter	10 oz (300 g) plain white or brown flour
2 level teaspoons dried yeast or 1 oz (25 g) fresh	

Scald the milk with the sugar, salt and butter, then let it cool to tepid. Dissolve the yeast in a large bowl in the warm water, and when it is dissolved add the cooled milk mixture and the herbs. Stir very well with a wooden spoon, then add the flour gradually, and mix until it is smooth and non-sticky. Cover with a cloth (or put into a greased polythene bag) and let the dough rise until about three times the size, approximately 45 minutes to 1 hour. Punch down and stir very well, then turn into a greased bread tin. Let it stand in a warm place for about 15 minutes before baking in a preheated (350°F/ 180°C/Gas Mark 4) oven for about 1 hour.

Yoghurt soda bread is a really delicious variation on Irish soda bread; it can also be made with the same amount of buttermilk, if available. If baked in a loaf tin sized 6 × 3 inches (150 × 75 mm) it makes a good-sized loaf which is easy to cut, but it can of course be made in traditional soda bread shape, i.e. flat round loaves.

8 oz (225 g) white flour	2 teaspoons salt
8 oz (225 g) wholewheat flour	Good pinch ground coriander
1¼ teaspoons bicarbonate of soda (1 teaspoon if using buttermilk)	½ pint (300 ml) plain yoghurt plus ¼ pint (150 ml) water or scant 1 pint buttermilk
3 teaspoons baking powder	1 egg

Sift all dry ingredients together, then beat the yoghurt, water and the egg together and stir into the flour mixture. Turn out onto a floured board and knead for a few minutes only until it is smooth. Then either put into a greased and floured loaf tin, or shape into 2 round cakes, which should be flattened with the hand. Make a deep incision on the top and bake in a preheated oven (375°F/190°C/Gas Mark 5) for 35 minutes. Then take out the bread and paint the top with milk or beaten egg, and put back in the oven for a further 10 minutes. Currants (about 3 tablespoons), raisins or sultanas can be added to the dry ingredients if liked.

The mixture can also be shaped into small scones if preferred, and will only take about 15–20 minutes to cook. All white flour can also be used.

TEABREADS

Banana bread is a favourite of mine from when I lived in Bermuda, where bananas grow like weeds. Once a bunch of bananas starts to ripen you have to think of many ways of using them up quickly. It can also be served as a cake, buttered or spread with cream or cottage cheese.

4 oz (115 g) butter or margarine	8 oz (225 g) plain flour
8 oz (225 g) sugar	1 teaspoon bicarbonate of soda dissolved in about 4 tablespoons cold milk
3 eggs	
4 mashed bananas (about 1 cup)	

Cream the butter and sugar together, then add the eggs and beat thoroughly. Now add the banana pulp and then the flour. Finally stir in the bicarbonate of soda and milk. Put into a greased cake or bread tin and bake in a moderate oven for 30–40 minutes.

Barm brack means 'speckled bread' and is common to all Celtic countries. In Wales it is called *bara brith*; in Scotland Selkirk bannock; *Manx bonnag* in the Isle of Man, and *Morlaix brioche* in Brittany, all countries which have had economic difficulties over the centuries. It is often made with yeast, but it is excellent made with baking powder. The following unyeasted quantities make 3 loaves for tin size 8 × 4 inches (10 × 20 cm) and 3 inches (75 mm) high. It keeps well in a tin and is usually served sliced and spread with butter.

1 lb (450 g) sultanas	3 eggs
1 lb (450 g) raisins	3 level teaspoons baking powder
1 lb (450 g) brown sugar	3 teaspoons mixed spice (optional)
3 cups tea (without milk)	
1 lb (450 g) plain flour	

Soak the fruit and sugar overnight in milkless tea. The next day, add alternately the flour and the eggs. Finally add the baking powder and, if a spiced brack is liked, then add the mixed spice. Mix all together very well and turn into 3 greased loaf tins. Bake for 1½ hours in a moderate oven (350°F/180°C/Gas Mark 4–5). About 5 minutes before they are ready brush the tops with melted honey or warm sweetened milk, put back in the oven to dry out, and they will have a fine glaze.

Date bread

1 lb (450 g) dates
¾ pint (450 ml) boiling water
1½ teaspoons bicarbonate of soda
4 level tablespoons butter
1 lb (450 g) plain flour
8 oz (225 g) sugar
2 eggs

Stone and cut up the dates and then pour over them the boiling water which has had the bicarbonate of soda dissolved in it. Cover and leave until cold. Then rub the butter into the flour and add the sugar. Beat the eggs and add to the flour with the dates and water. Knead well and shape into 2 loaves and put into 2 well-greased tins. Bake in a moderate oven (350°F/180°C/Gas Mark 4–5) for 1½ hours. Cool on a wire rack and leave until quite cold before cutting.

D

Cinnamon teacake

8 oz (225 g) flour
½ teaspoon salt
1½ teaspoons baking powder
6 tablespoons butter
6 level tablespoons castor sugar
1 egg (large)
¼ pint (150 ml) milk
Topping:
2 level tablespoons flour
4 level tablespoons sugar
2 teaspoons cinnamon
2 tablespoons margarine

Sieve the flour, salt and baking powder into the mixing bowl. Cut in the butter and add the sugar. Mix to a soft batter with the beaten egg and milk mixed. Turn out into an 8 inch (20 cm) cake tin, and smooth down the top. Then put the flour, sugar and cinnamon in a bowl and rub the margarine through it until it is like coarse breadcrumbs. Sprinkle over the plain mixture and bake at (375°F/190°C/Gas Mark 5) for 35–40 minutes.

Orange or lemon bread

12 oz (340 g) plain flour
3 level teaspoons baking powder
Pinch of bicarbonate of soda
8 level tablespoons butter
8 level tablespoons sugar
Grated rind of 1 large orange or lemon and the juice made up to ¾ pint (450 ml)
7 tablespoons golden syrup or honey
1 large egg

Mix all the sifted dry ingredients together, then cream together the butter and sugar with the finely grated orange or lemon rind. Mix in the warmed syrup or honey and then add the beaten egg and mix until frothy. Add the flour and orange juice alternately to make a fairly thick dough. Mix well then put into a large loaf tin, smoothing the top. Bake for about 1 hour in a slow to moderate oven (325°F/160°C/Gas Mark 3). Glaze with a little warmed honey or milk and put back in the oven to dry.

Spiced peanut butter loaf

½ pint (300 ml) milk, plus 1 tablespoon instant dried milk
3 tablespoons peanut butter
4 tablespoons honey
½ teaspoon ground ginger
½ teaspoon ground nutmeg
1 teaspoon ground cinnamon
½ teaspoon ground cloves
Pinch of salt
2 teaspoons baking powder
8 oz (225 g) wholewheat flour
2 tablespoons each raisins and chopped raw peanuts (optional)

Mix the milk, peanut butter and honey in a blender if possible, otherwise mix very well with a beater. Then add the spices, salt and baking powder and blend again. Add about a third of this mixture to the flour and mix with a wooden spoon and continue until it is all used up, but stir gently all the time, do not beat vigorously. Add the nuts and raisins if using, and pour into an oiled loaf tin. Bake in a moderate oven (350°F/180°C/Gas Mark 4) for about 1 hour, or until it is a golden colour.

This is good as a savoury bread for lettuce or bacon sandwiches, and with sausages, but it should be kept for at least 24 hours before cutting.

5. Milk products

YOGHURT

Yoghurt is one of the success stories of the last decade. Previously, outside Russia, Turkey, the Balkan countries and the Middle East, it was only eaten by a very small minority of people. Nowadays, it is on every supermarket shelf and almost universally eaten.

For many centuries yoghurt has been used by the Turks and Bulgarians, and all Balkan peoples attribute their longevity to eating it. Some medical observations state that the *Bacillus bulgaricus*, which makes yoghurt, is the only one which remains alive after the passage through the intestines, and this makes it invaluable in cases of stomach or intestinal disorders. I have seen it act successfully on a dog which had been poisoned, and it can be given safely to all ages when no other food is allowed. It is not, as some people think, simply soured milk, but milk cultured with *Bacillus bulgaricus*. This was discovered and isolated in the nineteenth century, by the Russian scientist Ilya Mechnikov, who quickly realized its therapeutic qualities.

History tells us that in the sixteenth century François I of France suffered from an intestinal complaint from which he could not be cured. He heard of a Jewish doctor in Turkey who had a great reputation for curing such complaints with a milk curd. The elderly doctor walked across Europe with his herd of sheep, causing great merriment among the courtiers when he arrived at the French court. The King was cured, and pressed him to divulge the secret. This he refused to do, so he departed, as he had come, taking his little flock with him.

Nowadays, sheep's milk is seldom used outside the Balkans, but both goat's and cow's milk can be used effectively.

However, it can become an expensive item on the housekeeping bill. It is remarkably simple to make and expensive machines are not necessary, so long as it can be kept at an even, warm temperature whilst it is making. For this you will need a wide-mouthed vacuum flask, some milk and a spoonful of yoghurt. The flask can of course be used for other things, so the yoghurt will really only cost you the price of the milk and a little time.

How to make yoghurt

Milk	1 heaped teaspoon
An ordinary clinical	yoghurt (as fresh as
thermometer	possible for each 1
A wide-mouthed vacuum	pint (600 ml) milk
flask	

To make more yoghurt, reserve 1 teaspoon (per pint (600 ml) milk) of this culture when it is made. The culture must be fresh: if sour yoghurt is used, then the result will be sour.

Heat the milk to boiling point and boil for about 1 minute. Have ready a large bowl half-filled with cold water (or use the sink), and put the saucepan into it. Stir from time to time to prevent a skin forming, leave for 5–10 minutes, then plunge the thermometer into the middle of the milk, and when it reads between 105°–108°F (41°–43°C) stir in a heaped teaspoon per pint (600 ml) of milk of yoghurt. Mix it well, pour at once into the flask, cork, and put the top on. Leave undisturbed for 10 hours, or overnight. (If the milk has gone below 105°F (41°C), heat it gently until it reaches the desired heat before adding the yoghurt.) When ready, open the flask and chill to the desired temperature, but cover the top with foil if the flask has a cork and a metal top. Sometimes a small amount of liquid gathers on top: I don't know the reason for this, but it can be drained off with no ill-effects to the yoghurt. I have never had a failure doing it this way, but it must be left undisturbed for the required time. If a flavouring is wanted, such as coffee (1 heaped teaspoon powdered coffee to 1 pint (600 ml) milk), this should be added before the yoghurt culture is stirred in. If you are on a diet, then make it with skim milk, or else remove the layer of cream which will settle on the top when it is made. Do not keep, even in the fridge, for longer than 1 week.

USES FOR YOGHURT

It blends equally well with sweet or savoury flavours, and, in the countries where it is a daily item of diet, yoghurt is used for all courses, and even as a cooling drink called *ayran* in Turkey, when 1 pint (600 ml) is beaten up until frothy, then mixed with a glass of iced water, beaten again, and served garnished with mint leaves. A little orange juice can be added instead of water.

To use yoghurt made from cow's milk in place of sour cream, or for any dish which needs to be boiled up, then the yoghurt must be stabilized to prevent it 'cracking'. This is a simple operation.

To stabilize yoghurt

1 pint (600 ml) yoghurt	Good pinch of salt
½ eggwhite or 2	
teaspoons cornflour	

Whip the yoghurt in a saucepan until it liquefies, then stir in the eggwhite or the cornflour mixed to a smooth paste with a little water or milk, and the salt. Stir well with a wooden spoon and bring to the boil, very slowly, stirring all the time, in one direction only. As soon as it just boils reduce the heat to a low simmer and let the yoghurt barely simmer, uncovered, for about 7 minutes, or until it is thick. On no account cover the pan as even a few drops of steam falling into it can spoil the stabilization. Leave to get cold when it can be used without fear of curdling or cracking.

Yoghurt, whether stabilized or not, is a good tenderizer for all meats as the lactic acid breaks down the tough fibres or tissues. If you are subsequently using the marinade in the cooking, then it is advisable to stabilize it. It is used a lot in the cooking of the north of India as well as in Turkey and Middle Eastern countries.

YOGHURT WITH VEGETABLES

Stabilized yoghurt is excellent for cooking vegetables in, especially stuffed courgettes or aubergines, and I have used it for the old favourite, stuffed marrow. Prepare the vegetable as on page 75, then heat up about 1 tablespoon butter or oil and lightly fry 2 or 3 crushed cloves of garlic with a teaspoon of dried mint and a little salt, then add about 1 pint (600 ml) stabilized yoghurt. Small white turnips are also good, put into this sauce after a preliminary boiling, the whole sprinkled with paprika when it is ready.

Yoghurt, whether stabilized or not, is delicious mixed with cooked spinach with a little chopped garlic added and it is really marvellous served over cooked beetroot, the whole sprinkled with some chopped chives and a little salt. Aubergines cooked in the oven, puréed and beaten with a little olive oil, then with yoghurt, lemon juice, parsley and garlic and salt, is a famous Middle Eastern dish, and is served with fried meatballs spiced with a little cinnamon and ground cumin. The proportions are: 3 aubergines, 3 tablespoons olive oil, ½ pint (300 ml) yoghurt, juice of 1 lemon, 2 cloves garlic.

It can also be used as a salad dressing, mixed with a little oil and herbs.

Cilbir is Turkish for poached eggs, served with a sauce made from about ½ pint (300 ml) yoghurt mixed with salt. This is poured over 4–6 poached eggs, then about 2 tablespoons melted butter flavoured with paprika is trickled over the top before serving. It is such a quick and excellent way of serving an old friend.

See also the chapters on 'Meat' (pages 117–41), and 'Soups' (pages 13–22).

Yoghurt can also be used in place of cream in sweet dishes, and also for cakes (*see* page 148).

COTTAGE CHEESE

This is a very useful food: it is high in protein, therefore important nutritionally, and there are many ways to vary it. The homemade variety has more flavour and is far creamier than the commercial kind. It is simple to make and deep-freezes very well. If anything it becomes a better texture after freezing. Ideally, unpasteurized milk should be used, but this is difficult to obtain in urban districts. It can, however, be made with instant skim milk powder made up according to instructions, and a good mixture is half milk powder and half skim milk. If it is impossible for you to find unpasteurized milk, either whole or skim, then you will have to add rennet to the pasteurized milk, for the milk will go bad before it sours. Rennet, which is made from the stomach lining of calves and also from some plants such as the fig and the thistle, produces a digestive enzyme called rennin which affects the coagulation of milk into curds and whey without souring. The instructions for use are on the bottle, but in fact it is the same as making junket without the sugar or flavouring. Do not use more rennet than is advocated, as if too much is used it produces a metallic taste. For cottage cheese, skimmed milk should be used, but use full cream milk if you want a cream cheese. It is simple to make and needless to say considerably cheaper than the commercial variety.

Cottage (or curd) cheese You will need a flattish bowl big enough to hold the milk, a square of cheesecloth, or very fine nylon net, about 2 foot (70 cm) square or made into a bag to hold the curds, and if possible a cheese drainer, either wicker or a French earthenware one called a *faisselle*, which has holes for draining. (This can be bought from Elizabeth David Ltd, 46 Bourne Street, London SW1.) It is not absolutely essential, but does make it much easier, and since it is not expensive is well worth investing in. You will also find beautiful brown earthenware jugs to go with it to catch the whey, which is very refreshing to drink.

To make a good cup of curds put 1 pint (600 ml) skim milk in a bowl, and put it on top of a warm stove, on a radiator or a convector heater, etc. *The heat must be steady* and not hot enough to crack the dish. Cover to keep out dust, and leave it for at least 24–36 hours. In hot climates it will turn much more quickly: this recipe is for outside temperature of about (50°–60°F 10°–15°C), inside about 68°–70°F (20°–21°C). Do not leave it for longer than 2 days, for if it has not soured naturally by then it means the milk has probably gone bad, and not naturally sour. This sometimes happens with pasteurized milk, but I find that skim milk, rather than whole milk with the cream removed, sours more naturally. You can use rennet, unless you are on a low-salt diet. When it has soured properly the curd will become firm like junket, and will be surrounded by liquid which is called whey. The curd must be firm; do not drain before this happens as it will only drain away and leave very little curd.

If you have a cheese drainer, arrange the cheesecloth or net in the top and carefully pour the curds into it, with a jug or bowl below to catch the liquid. If you have no drainer, put the cheesecloth over a large bowl, and pour in the same way; or put it into a bag made from the cloth. Lift it up quickly, put a clothes peg in the top to secure all ends, and hang it up, with a bowl underneath to catch the drips. Leave for at least 1 day. The curd will have become a soft creamy cheese ready to be used in any way you wish.

It is so simple, and it keeps well in the refrigerator. I always have a supply souring or draining: it has become a nightly routine, to see that there is enough milk left for breakfast, and then to pour the rest into a bowl and stand it on the stove. The secret is the steady heat: it will never become sour or bitter if this method is used.

I've done quite a few experiments with various kinds of milk. The most interesting, to me, was that the instant skim milk powder sours very quickly, and makes a sharp cheese, which is good if mixed with a little yoghurt, salt, pepper and chopped chives, before serving. Make up the milk to the proportion given on the tin, and treat as above. A cheese which tastes like a good Demi-sel or a Boursin is made from half skim milk, and half instant skim milk powder. In a mysterious way, it is more creamy, and the instant powder seems to sour the milk more rapidly. I have more to say about the uses of instant skim milk powder later on.

HOW TO USE COTTAGE CHEESE

What can you do with these cheeses when you have made them? The variations are endless, and these can be used for both sweet and savoury dishes. Apart from the suggestions given below, consult the index of this book.

Just before the curd sets, the milk becomes thick and creamy: this is known as 'clabbered' milk, and is drunk in many Scandinavian countries, Finland, and Ireland as a beverage. The word 'clabbered' comes from the English 'bonny clabber', which is a phonetic rendering of the Irish *bainne clabair*, which means 'thick milk', and was from earliest times the favoured drink of the Irish people. It is known as *viilipiimä* or *piimä* in Finland, and it is served with many meals, especially the cold table or *smörgåsbord*. Sugar and ginger, or sugar and cinnamon, are sometimes added, and then it is whisked before being brought to table, and served in a jug.

Fresh curds can be eaten straight away with a little salt and white pepper, spread thickly on to bread. In France, Italy and Balkan countries it is also sprinkled with castor sugar, and eaten with a spoon. Both ways are simple and good.

In Finland cottage cheese is shaped into small squares or rounds, placed on thick straw or wood, brushed with melted butter, and baked in a very slow oven until golden brown. I do this sometimes, using raw eggwhite: either way, it makes a delectable cheese which keeps for some time. Store it in layers of bayleaves for an aromatic taste.

The fresh cheese can be used in place of margarine or butter for sandwiches; with jacket-baked potatoes; or as a cake filling if mixed with sugar. It will become creamy if whipped, and sometimes a little yoghurt added makes it especially creamy. One stiffly-beaten

eggwhite added to 8 oz (225 g) sweetened cheese makes a French *coeur à la crème*, and is delicious with fresh strawberries or raspberries.

The variations are endless, and must depend on individual taste. Add: tuna, herbs, chopped capers, pickles, pickled walnuts or gherkins, onion juice, a little French mustard, chopped sweet peppers, tomato purée, mushrooms, etc. You will enjoy experimenting with your own choice. It also makes excellent dips (*see* below) and spreads, for which a liquidizer or blender is a help but not essential.

An attractive salad idea is to make the cottage cheese into small balls, and roll them in either grated carrot or grated apple. The fresh crisp vegetable or fruit makes a good foil to the creamy tasting cheese. Or cut the tops off large tomatoes, mix the flesh with low-fat cottage cheese, then replace it in the tomatoes.

Slices of fresh pineapple cut very thinly and shaped into a horn and filled with beaten cottage cheese mixed with a little fresh mint, make a cool summer dish; or use rounds of canned pineapple, and put the minty cheese in the hole in the middle. Canned or fresh pears are good stuffed this way on a hot day. Serve on fresh nasturtium leaves, which have a peppery flavour. Blended with fresh fruits, sugar or honey, and yoghurt, cottage cheese makes delicious sweet desserts or puddings. It can be successfully used with pasta, like ricotta cheese.

The *pièce de résistance* is perhaps cheesecake, always delicious, and an excellent standby for all occasions (*see* page 58).

Liptauer cheese

When the cottage cheese is mixed with fresh chopped chives, onion tops, or fennel or celery seeds its taste is changed completely. This is the Hungarian way.

8 oz (225 g) low-fat cottage cheese	1 small clove garlic, pounded
$\frac{1}{2}$ teaspoon crushed caraway seeds	Salt or salt substitute
1 teaspoon chopped chive or parsley (optional)	1 tablespoon butter or margarine
Freshly ground white pepper	2 mashed anchovies or essence
1 teaspoon paprika	1 heaped teaspoon yoghurt (optional)

Mix all together until thoroughly creamed. Add the yoghurt if the mixture seems too thick. Pat into a shape, and serve with bread, or as a salad.

Cheese and tomato spread (also for mushroom, sweet pepper, etc.)

8 oz (225 g) low-fat cottage cheese	1 medium tomato, peeled, or 1 canned
1 thin slice onion, or 2 tablespoons chives	Salt or salt substitute
	Pepper

If using a blender, put all ingredients into the container. Switch to half speed, and blend until smooth. It will be necessary to switch off machine and scrape down the sides once or twice. Keep cold. If you have no blender, pound all the ingredients together. Small amounts can be mixed with hard-boiled chopped eggwhite, scrambled egg, tuna fish, or fragments of lean ham. This can be used for sandwiches, or rolled into small balls or cakes and served with green salad.

Curry dip

Rather spicy but good with plain toast, etc., or raw vegetables. Best made in a liquidizer.

8 oz (225 g) low-fat cottage cheese	4 tablespoons chopped watercress leaves
1 medium tomato, peeled	2 tablespoons chopped chives or 1 spring onion or 1 small leek
1$\frac{1}{2}$ teaspoons curry powder	Salt
1 tablespoon yoghurt	

Combine all ingredients in container of liquidizer, cover and blend at high speed for 40 seconds, stopping to scrape down the sides if necessary. Makes $\frac{3}{4}$ pint (450 ml).

Herb dip

Can be made without a blender, but the result is less creamy.

1 lb (450 g) cottage cheese	$\frac{1}{2}$ teaspoon lovage or celery seed
$\frac{1}{4}$ pint (150 ml) yoghurt	1 teaspoon tarragon
$\frac{1}{2}$ teaspoon dried or fresh basil	$\frac{1}{2}$ teaspoon dill, or fennel
$\frac{1}{2}$ teaspoon fresh parsley, chopped	2 teaspoons chopped chives
	Salt

First mix the cheese and yoghurt together in the liquidizer container. Then add the herbs and seasoning and blend for 30 seconds. If you do not have a blender beat the cheese and yoghurt together with a rotary egg beater and add the finely chopped herbs last. They will wind round the blades if you attempt to beat them. Makes generous 1 pint (600 ml).

Liptauer dip

Can be made with or without a liquidizer, and used as a cheese.

- 1 lb (450 g) cottage cheese
- 1 teaspoon pounded caraway seeds, or celery seeds or fennel seeds
- 1 pounded or pressed clove garlic
- ¼ pint (150 ml) yoghurt
- 1 rounded teaspoon paprika
- 1 tablespoon chopped chives

Beat all together very well. If using a liquidizer, put all ingredients into container, cover, and blend at high speed for 1 minute. Makes about 1 pint (600 ml).

Sour cream dip

Although an imitation, it does taste very like the real thing. Excellent for serving with jacket-baked potatoes or hot beetroot.

- 8 oz (225 g) cottage cheese
- 2 tablespoons lemon juice
- 1 tablespoon chopped chives
- ¼ pint (150 ml) milk or yoghurt
- ¼ pint (150 ml) oil, preferably safflower or sunflower seed
- Salt

Place all ingredients in blender, cover, and blend for 30 seconds at high speed, until it is quite smooth. If using a rotary beater, do not add chives until you have finished beating. Makes approx. ¾ pint (450 ml).

Yoghurt skordalia

A Greek recipe, very good served with toast or with fish. Can be made with or without a liquidizer.

- 1 medium clove garlic
- 3 walnuts
- 1 teaspoon oil
- 2 tablespoons natural yoghurt
- 8 oz (225 g) cottage cheese
- Salt
- Pepper
- ½ medium cucumber, grated
- Squeeze of lemon juice

Pound the garlic and the walnuts with the oil, then add to the yoghurt and sieved cottage cheese and season to taste. Finally add the grated cucumber and a squeeze of lemon juice (optional) and mix well. If using a liquidizer put the yoghurt and cheese in first, then add all other ingredients, and blend covered at high speed for 1 minute. Makes approx. ¾ pint (450 ml).

Cottage cheese is excellent for making savoury mousse, and also for use in sauces where cream would normally be used.

Smoked salmon mousse is quite inexpensive if made with smoked salmon trimmings which are available at most fish shops. This recipe can also be used for kipper mousse, smoked mackerel or trout, and also for avocado pears which are too ripe for eating with a spoon.

- ½ pint (300 ml) boiling water
- 1 level tablespoon aspic powder or ½ tablespoon gelatine
- 8 oz (225 g) cottage cheese
- 2 oz (60 g) smoked salmon, mackerel or kipper, etc.
- Squeeze of lemon juice
- Few drops of Tabasco or cayenne pepper

Put the boiling water into the liquidizer, then add the aspic powder and blend for 30 seconds, then add all the other ingredients and blend for about 60 seconds. Taste for seasoning, and put at once into a dish or individual dishes and leave in a cold place to set. It sets very quickly, so do not delay in turning it out. It can be served on a bed of lettuce, or in glass dishes. Serves 4.

Sauces

To enrich and thicken sauces whip the cheese so that it is creamy, then add a little of the hot liquid, stirring well, and increase the volume of liquid until you have the consistency you want. This is very good with chicken stock from a poached bird, then seasoned with a good squeeze of lemon and freshly chopped herbs.

Cheese or curd cake

Line a 9 inch 23 cm) flan tin with 8 oz (225 g) shortcrust pastry (page 143). Bake blind, or brush bottom with eggwhite. Fill with the following:

8 oz (225 g) low-fat cottage cheese	2 tablespoons sugar
Grated rind and juice of ½ lemon	1 eggyolk
	1 eggwhite

Mix all the ingredients except the eggwhite well together. Whip up the eggwhite until stiff, and fold in.

Topping: Mix 1 beaten egg with 1 tablespoon each sugar, flour, and melted butter. Pour this evenly over the top. Bake in a moderate oven (350°F/180°C/Gas Mark 4) for 35–40 minutes. Cut when cold.

Cottage (curd) cheese used for a dessert

Serve 2 tablespoons of cottage cheese per person and top each helping with 2 teaspoons of honey or jam (apricot, cherry, strawberry, etc.). 8 oz (225 g) cottage cheese serves 4.

Fluffy cottage cheese dessert

As above, but add 1 stiffly-beaten eggwhite to 8 oz (225 g) cheese, and serve with only 1 teaspoon honey or jam per person. Serves 4.

Iced pineapple and cottage cheese

1 stiffly-beaten eggwhite	4 slices canned pineapple, drained of juice
2 tablespoons yoghurt	
8 oz (225 g) cottage cheese	1 tablespoon castor sugar

Beat the eggwhite until stiff: mix the yoghurt and cheese together. Chop up the pineapple and add it to the yoghurt and cheese, then mix in the sugar. Finally fold in the eggwhite, put into the freezing tray and freeze until firm. Serves 6.

Variation: Omit eggwhite, and mix other ingredients Serves 4.

Cassata cottage cheese

8 oz (225 g) low-fat cottage cheese	3 tablespoons pine-nut kernels (*pinoli*)
2 tablespoons yoghurt	3 slices chopped pineapple, drained if canned
2 tablespoons glacé cherries	
1 tablespoon fine sugar	1 stiffly-beaten eggwhite

Mix all ingredients together, folding in the eggwhite last. Put into freezing tray, and freeze until firm. Serves 6–8.

SKIM MILK POWDER

If for reasons of economy or diet you do not use cream, then a quite satisfactory cream-like sauce can be made with the instant skim milk powder. However, it can only be used if made not more than ½ hour before you want it. If left longer it sometimes separates.

Instant cream sauce

For all classes of diet. Made in minutes, and is eaten just as quickly!

½ cup cold water
Juice ½ lemon

½ cup instant skim milk powder

Put the cold water and lemon juice in a bowl, then add the skim milk powder. Beat with an egg beater (or use a blender for large amounts) for about 3 minutes, or until the 'cream' is like stiffly-beaten eggwhite or marshmallow cream. Chill before using. This cream stays stiff and fluffy for about ½ hour. It can be sweetened to taste if liked. Makes approx. 2 cups.

This cream sauce can be varied as follows:

Cinnamon cream: Add ¼ teaspoon cinnamon and ¼ teaspoon nutmeg before beating.

Orange cream: Add 1 tablespoon grated orange zest before beating.

Coffee cream: Add 1 teaspoon instant coffee powder before beating.

Raspberry or strawberry cream: Add 1 tablespoon puréed fruits before beating.

Chocolate cream: Add 2 teaspoons sugar, and 1 heaped teaspoon cocoa before beating.

Cream sauce (2)

To be kept in a cool place for 24 hours. A liquidizer makes it in 1½–2 minutes, but it can be made with an egg beater.

4 oz (115 g) butter or margarine
½ teaspoon powdered plain gelatine

¼ pint (150 ml) skim milk
Squeeze of lemon juice

Melt the butter or margarine with the gelatine in the milk and lemon juice, and let it cool to blood heat. Put into container of liquidizer, and run at high speed for 1½–2 minutes, or beat with an egg beater until it is stiff. Pour into a clean bowl, and let stand in a cool place for several hours, or overnight. It can then be whipped as ordinary dairy cream.

This is very good for cake fillings. Makes approx. 1 cup cream.

This cream can be beaten or blended in a liquidizer with fruits such as banana, apricots, peaches, etc. to make a fluffy filling or dessert. It can be varied as for instant cream sauce (opposite) which makes the most of the simplest dessert.

6. Pasta and rice

PASTA

Pasta is one of the basic cereal foods for millions of people both in Italy and its original home, China. It is thought that the noodle (which incidentally was also eaten in fourteenth-century Britain) was brought to Italy by the Ostrogoths during their invasion of that country in AD 405. Prince Teodoric made his headquarters in Ravenna, and it is from nearby Bologna that many of the best pasta dishes come, including *ragù Bolognese*, which is a meaty wine stew, not at all like some of the dreadful travesties of that sauce which are served under the same name.

Pasta is perhaps the cheapest food available for a meal. It is both filling and palatable and can be eaten with very little embellishment. The poor of Naples frequently eat it served with small chunks of garlic fried in oil with a little cheese sprinkled over the top. This method (which is in fact one of my favourites) is also delicious when a good tablespoon of cottage cheese (page 56) and some freshly chopped herbs are mixed in. Or to make a dish of more nourishment a raw egg can be mixed well through the hot pasta until it coats each strand. Personally, I prefer the sauces which do not have too much tomato or, worse still, tomato purée. Too much of the latter disguises the fresh, wholesome taste of the pasta and cheese.

Some useful sauces are listed below. They should be mixed into the pasta when it is cooked (in plenty of water, about 12 pints (6.8 l) for 1 lb (450 g) pasta) for not more than about 12–15 minutes. It should be *al dente*, that is not soft but firm to the teeth when cooked, and a strand should be tested first as not all pasta takes the same time to cook. Fresh pasta will take only about 7–10 minutes. If you have to keep pasta warm then put it into a well-oiled dish, cover loosely with a piece of foil and put into a low oven.

If you are a good pastry or bread maker then you will be good at making pasta, which is just as easy as pastry and requires the same touch. In Italy many people make their own pasta, but in country communities, the woman chosen with the finest skill is called a *sfoglina*.

TO MAKE PASTA

A durum or hard flour is the best to use but not easily obtainable in Britain. But if you see a packet labelled '*pura semola di grano duro*' it does not mean semolina but a hard wheat flour, which is the one used in Italy. *Pasta all'uova* means pasta with eggs and although this is the most nourishing kind, it is also possible to make sheet pasta such as is used for ravioli, lasagne or cannelloni without eggs. Both methods are given below. Like all recipes for basic foods, pasta recipes vary enormously as to the number of eggs used. However 2 large or 3 small eggs to 1 lb (450 g) flour is perhaps the most common.

1 lb (450 g) hard, plain flour	2 large or 3 small eggs
1 teaspoon salt	4 fl. oz (100 ml) water

Put the flour and salt on a board and make a well in the centre, then break in the eggs and water. Fold the flour over the top and knead with your hands until a soft dough is formed and it can be rolled into a ball. Flour your hands and the board during this time and put the dough on it and begin kneading. When it has reached an elastic but stiff consistency (add a little more flour if it is sticky, and likewise a little more water if too stiff) hold it with one hand and push it away from you with the other, with your palm. This should take about 10 minutes. Divide the dough in half and roll it very thinly (wrapping it round the floured rolling pin and stretching it from time to time), taking care not to break it. Do this several times, each time flouring the board and the rolling pin. If using a rough table, then spread a clean cloth over it first. It should be tissue-paper thin and like a piece of gauze which you can pick up gently. Leave to dry covered with a cloth on a flat surface and do the same with the other half of dough. Leave the dough to dry for at least 15 minutes and up to 30 minutes.

If you want to shape it into lasagne or sheet pasta, then cut it into rectangles about 5 × 2½ inches (125 × 50–60 mm), but if you want to make noodles, either broad or thin such as tagliatelle or fettuccine, then sprinkle a little flour over the large sheet of pasta and roll it up tightly like a newspaper, then (with a sharp knife) cut across into strips about ¼ inch (6 mm) wide for fettuccine, and slightly less for tagliatelle. Leave the little bundles spread out to dry until you want to cook them, or, if storing when dry, keep them in a tin or jar.

To cook, drop into about 12 pints (6.8 l) boiling water and when boiling, salt it. Stir at once with a perforated ladle and keep stirring until the water boils again to prevent the pieces sticking together. Cook for 7–10 minutes, then drain. They will be delicious if you heat up about 4 tablespoons butter, then add the pasta and a pinch of nutmeg, white pepper and some grated cheese. Lift the pasta very gently with two forks so that they absorb the butter and cheese. Or use any of the sauces given below. For lasagne cook as above and layer with filling given overleaf.

To make pasta and ravioli, etc. without eggs. Ravioli are small filled cushions of pasta.

2 oz (60 g) butter
1 lb (450 g) plain flour
Pinch of salt

Approx. ½ pint (300 ml)
  boiling water
Extra flour for rolling
  out pasta

Mix the butter into the sifted flour and salt until it resembles fine breadcrumbs, then add the boiling water to make a stiff dough. Add either a little more water or flour according to the stiffness of the dough, which should be stiff but elastic. Knead it slightly, then cut into two. It is important to have a space large enough to roll out the dough in one piece; if this is not possible then divide into quarters. Flour the surface well, and also sprinkle the pasta with flour to prevent it sticking. Keep the pasta not being rolled covered with a cloth, and have another one handy to cover the rolled-out piece. Roll as in recipe above, until it is thin but not broken, and leave for at least 15 minutes before filling. Makes about 50 ravioli.

Fillings for ravioli can vary a lot: a popular one is 8 oz (225 g) sieved ricotta or cottage cheese mixed with 3 tablespoons grated Pecorino, Parmesan or other hard cheese, a pinch of nutmeg, 2 eggyolks and a pinch of either basil or marjoram. Mix well, then put about a teaspoon of the filling at a time on the pasta about 1½ inches (38 mm) apart, dampen the edges and lines of filling and place the other sheet of pasta loosely over the top, and then press down well so that the little squares do not come open. Cut down with a sharp knife or pastry cutter and put the prepared ravioli, in one layer only, covered with a cloth until ready for use. They will keep well for 2 days.

Poach a few at a time in 8 pints (4.5 l) boiling, salted water and they will rise to the top when ready: lift out with a slotted spoon and serve with melted butter and grated cheese. Cooked chopped meat, puréed spinach with ricotta or cottage cheese as above, can also be used.

The same fillings can be used for cannelloni. For lasagne *see* below.

To make lasagne al forno, cook the sheets as above, then layer them in a deep dish with the *ragù* given below, alternately with a layer of cooked spinach (either fresh, frozen or tinned), which has been mixed with a pinch of nutmeg, and a layer of good béchamel (white) sauce, ending with a layer of *ragù* with béchamel and a thick coating of grated Parmesan. This can be made some time before it is needed and is baked in a moderate oven for ½ hour, until the top is golden and bubbling.

An alternative filling is to omit the spinach and use 8 oz (225 g) cottage cheese mixed with 4 tablespoons grated hard cheese and a pinch of nutmeg.

Cannelloni can also be stuffed with the above mixture, then put into a fireproof dish with butter, a cupful of chicken stock and grated cheese, then baked for 20 minutes. Or stuffed as below.

Maccheroni ripieni alla Toscana (stuffed macaroni from Tuscany)

Macaroni is said to have got its name from a Neapolitan cardinal, who, when seeing them for the first time, exclaimed '*Ma caroni*' ('my little dears'). Use large macaroni, known as rigatoni.

Mix together 1 lb (450 g) cottage cheese with 3 oz (85 g) grated Parmesan, 1 tablespoon chopped parsley, 1 tablespoon melted butter, a good pinch nutmeg, salt and pepper and 1 eggyolk. Cook the pasta, drain, and stuff this mixture into the wide pipes, or layer it in a casserole. Either cover with a thin cheese sauce or pour over 1 × 16 oz (450 g) tin tomatoes seasoned with basil, and bake for ½ hour in a moderate oven. This is enough for 1½ lb (675 g) pasta, and will serve 6 people.

SAUCES FOR PASTA

Spaghetti torinese

A Turin speciality, which can be used for small shapes, noodles, tagliatelle, etc.

Cook 1 lb (450 g) pasta as above, and drain, put 2 tablespoons oil in the saucepan after draining and let it get hot. Add the pasta and turn quickly so that it gets coated. Then add 2 tablespoons dried basil and the same of grated Parmesan. Mix very thoroughly away from the heat, then put back on a very low flame. Break 2 eggs into the hot pasta and stir rapidly so that the heat of the pasta cooks it and coats every strand. Serve at once, with more grated Parmesan. Serves 2–3.

Variation: The egg can be omitted, and 4 large chopped garlic cloves fried in the oil until brown before adding the pasta. Small pieces of ham finely chopped can also be stirred in, if available.

Pesto is a famous sauce from Genoa. It is used with all kinds of pasta, and as a flavouring for vegetable soups. I use it with jacket-baked potatoes in the winter. It can sometimes be bought at delicatessen shops in small jars, and is made as follows. This sauce will keep in cold place if airtight.

2 medium cloves garlic
2 oz (60 g) fresh or dried basil
3 tablespoons pine-nut kernels *(pinoli)* or

shelled almonds
3 tablespoons grated Parmesan
4 tablespoons olive oil

Squeeze the garlic in a garlic press then pound with the basil and nuts. Add the cheese and mix well. Then add the oil drop by drop, stirring well and steadily, until the sauce resembles green creamed butter. A spoonful is put on top of the hot pasta with a knob of butter and mixed through before eating. Extra grated Parmesan is served separately. This makes enough for 4–6 servings.

Salsa Veronese, a sauce from Verona, also used with poultry or meat. Heat 2 tablespoons oil and fry in it 1 small onion until golden, 2 cloves chopped garlic and 2 tablespoons chopped parsley. Sprinkle with 1 tablespoon flour, then add 8 oz (225 g) sliced mushrooms and 4 tablespoons water. Simmer gently until cooked. It should be thick and chunky.

Ragù Bolognese is served with all kinds of pasta and used in lasagne. Melt 1 tablespoon butter and fry in it 4 oz (115 g) lean and fat chopped bacon; add 1 sliced onion and 1 sliced carrot. When soft add 8 oz (225 g) lean minced beef and brown evenly, and, if available, 4 chicken livers or 4 oz (115 g) chopped pork or veal.

Season well, add a pinch of nutmeg and 1 pint (600 ml) stock or water and ¼ pint (150 ml) white wine. Cover and simmer for 35 minutes. Then mix in 2 tablespoons tomato purée, and simmer again until it is very thick.

Vongole sauce

Clams, cockles or mussels make a very good sauce with pasta. It is usually served with vermicelli or spaghetti, and cheese is not used for this dish.

2 lb (1 kg) clams, cockles or mussels	2 lb (1 kg) tomatoes
¼ pint (150 ml) olive oil	Salt and pepper
1 large clove garlic	1 tablespoon chopped parsley

Wash the shells very well to remove grit, and take out any half-opened shells. Put into a large saucepan with 1 tablespoon oil and 2–3 tablespoons water, cover and place over a high flame, shaking the shells around until they are all open. Cool slightly, then take the flesh from the shells, reserving the juice. If using mussels take off the little beards. Strain the juice and retain.

Put the rest of the oil in a saucepan, add the chopped garlic and brown it, then take it out, and put in the peeled tomatoes, fish juice, pepper, and taste for salt. Simmer gently for about ½ hour and add a little water if it is too thick. Add the chopped shellfish and the parsley, let them just heat up, but not boil and serve over the pasta with plenty of pepper. The tomatoes can be omitted if preferred, but more shellfish should be used, about another 1 lb (450 g), and the sauce should be flavoured with a squeeze of lemon.

Spaghetti all'Amatriciana, spaghetti with bacon and onion.

Spaghetti all'Amatriciana, spaghetti with bacon and onion. This dish comes from Amatrice in the Abruzzi, a large village which supplies Rome with many of its hotel and *trattorie* staff.

1 lb (450 g) spaghetti or noodles, etc.	1 crushed clove garlic
7 oz (195 g) streaky bacon	2 tablespoons grated Pecorino cheese
1 small onion, chopped finely	4 tablespoons Parmesan, or a hard cheese
	Salt, pepper or ginger

Cook pasta as for *alla carbonara*, below, and drain well. While it is cooking cut the bacon into narrow strips, then cook it with the onion and garlic over a medium flame until golden. Then remove the garlic and pour this sauce over the pasta with the cheese, mixing well, add plenty of pepper, and salt if necessary, and serve more cheese separately. Some cooks add 1 lb (425 g) skinned and chopped tomatoes to the sauce, but this is not strictly traditional. Serves 4.

Spaghetti alla carbonara, spaghetti with bacon and egg sauce. *Carbonara* means that it was originally cooked over charcoal. It is one of the best pasta dishes, the eggs coating the long strands of spaghetti so that it is creamy and delicious.

Salt	4 oz (115 g) grated Pecorino, Parmesan
1 tablespoon oil	or hard cheese
1 lb (450 g) spaghetti or tagliatelle	1 tablespoon cream (optional)
6 rashers streaky bacon	
2 eggs	

Put 6 pints (3.4 l) water into a large saucepan and bring to the boil. Add a good tablespoon of salt and the oil (this stops the pasta from clumping together), then when it is on a rolling boil add the spaghetti, broken in two if preferred. Stir at once with a large fork, and lower the heat when it comes to a rolling boil again, but do not turn it too low. Cook for about 10–15 minutes until the pasta is still what the Italians call *al dente*, that is, biteable. When ready strain in a colander.

Meanwhile, chop up the bacon, and beat the eggs. Wash and wipe round the saucepan that the pasta was cooked in, then cook the bacon in it and cook until the fat is melted and it is beginning to crisp. Add the spaghetti, mixing well, and put the flame very, very low. Add the beaten eggs and stir well, then add 4 tablespoons of the grated cheese, and cream if using, and mix that well too. Take off the heat and stir so that all the pasta is coated by the egg and cheese, then serve with more cheese separately. Serves 4.

Spaghetti con fegatini di pollo

Chicken livers make an excellent sauce for pasta of all kinds, not only spaghetti. It is made as follows and this is enough for 1 lb (450 g) pasta.

2 tablespoons oil	2 oz (60 g) grated hard
1 medium onion, finely	cheese
chopped	3–4 tablespoons butter
2 tablespoons tomato	6 oz (170 g) mushrooms
purée	1 lb (450 g) chicken
Salt and pepper	livers

Heat the oil in a pan and fry the onion until softened and golden, but not coloured. Add the tomato purée, salt and pepper, then gradually add half the cheese, stirring after each addition and blending well. Add this to the warm, cooked spaghetti, and keep warm in a low oven in an oiled dish. Then heat the butter and sauté the mushrooms and chicken livers in it, seeing that the mushrooms are just soft and cooked, not crisp, and the chicken livers still slightly pink in the middle. Pour this over the spaghetti and serve with the remaining cheese.

E

SMALL SHAPES OF PASTA, such as frills, baby shells, twists, farfalle, and so on are very useful for making into a lasagne-like dish. Cook them first in the usual way for about 7–10 minutes, then layer them as for lasagne, and cover the whole with a thin cheese sauce. This should then be heated in a moderate oven (350°F/180°C/Gas Mark 4) for about ½ hour. This dish has the advantage, like lasagne, that it can be prepared well in advance and reheated. Leftover scraps of ham, poultry or meat can all be used and it makes a very filling and inexpensive dish which can be served on many occasions. 1 lb (450 g) pasta shapes layered with either spinach or cheese, as for lasagne, and a little meat makes a hearty meal for at least 6 people. The larger shells or macaroni such as rigatoni can be stuffed with cheese or meat and then cooked as for *maccheroni ripieni alla Toscana*, above.

Pasta, especially the smaller shapes, make an excellent salad, cooked and cold. Boil them first for 7–10 minutes, then drain and set aside. As soon as the pasta cools pour a little oil over the top as this will keep it soft, and when it is wanted add one or more of the following: chopped herbs, chopped peeled raw tomatoes, green peppers, cucumber, raw or cooked mushrooms, celery, small chunks of poultry, ham or meat, chopped olives, chopped hard-boiled eggs, flaked cooked fish, and particularly delicious are a few mussels, marinated herrings or mackerel, anchovies, tuna fish, or chopped, cooked kipper. It is really a matter of taste and what you have to hand, as well as what is to accompany it, although if a healthy portion of fish or meat is added it makes a pleasant light meal in itself. Season to taste and if necessary add a very little wine vinegar and possibly a little more oil. A few coked vegetables, such as French beans or cauliflower, can be added, but do not put in too many if it is to be eaten as a main course.

GNOCCHI are delightful little dumplings which can be made from potato or semolina. The potato ones are lighter than the ones made with semolina and easier for the housewife to handle. It is also a great way of using up cold mashed potato.

Potato gnocchi

2 lb (1 kg) potatoes, boiled or baked in their jackets	Salt and pepper
	2 tablespoons butter
8 oz (225 g) flour	3 oz (85 g) dry hard cheese, grated
2 eggs	
1 slice cooked ham or bacon (optional)	

Drain the potatoes well, skin them and mash thoroughly. Add the flour and lightly beaten eggs, also finely chopped ham if using, season, and mix very well to a smooth paste. When it is well mixed, flour the hands and shake a little over the dough, then turn the dough out and roll it lightly. Shape into tiny walnut-sized balls, or small cork shapes. Dent the latter in the middle with the finger to make them roughly crescent-shaped. Leave covered until you want to cook them.

The gnocchi can stay overnight in the refrigerator if wanted.

Heat up to boiling a large pan of water, and when boiling salt it, then drop in several of these balls or corks and cook for about 3 minutes or until they rise to the top. Lift out with a perforated slice or spoon and put into a warmed, ovenproof dish.

The gnocchi can be served simply with melted butter and grated cheese, with *pesto* sauce, *ragù*, chicken liver sauce, or with a sauce made from fresh or canned tomatoes. Serves 4.

Tomato sauce

This sauce can also be served over pasta or with chicken, and is good for cooking fillets of fish in.

2 tablespoons oil	1 lb (450 g) fresh peeled or canned tomatoes
1 medium onion or 2 shallots, chopped	
1 bayleaf	Little thyme or basil
	1 clove garlic, crushed
	Salt and pepper

Heat the oil and lightly fry the onion until soft, then add the bayleaf and all other ingredients. Bring to the boil, and then simmer for about $\frac{1}{2}$ hour, or until the sauce is quite thick. If liked this sauce can be liquidized, and it will keep in a jar if the top has a layer of oil over it. Various spices such as a pinch of nutmeg, cinnamon, clove, allspice, paprika, cumin seed or curry can be added as wished to vary the flavour according to what it is being served with. These amounts make about $1\frac{1}{2}$ pints (approx. 1 l) of sauce, which also freezes well.

Green gnocchi are gnocchi made with spinach and potato, and this is one of the best ways of serving those two vegetables. Gnocchi of all kinds make such a good luncheon dish.

1 lb (450 g) spinach, cooked and well drained	2 tablespoons grated hard cheese
	2 eggs
2 lb (1 kg) potatoes, mashed	Salt and pepper
	Pinch of nutmeg
4 tablespoons ricotta or cottage cheese	2 oz (60 g) butter
	4 tablespoons plain flour

The spinach must be very dry before using. If necessary squeeze it well and purée it. Mix it with the well mashed potatoes, both the cheeses, the beaten eggs and the seasonings. When well blended pour in the melted butter and finally the flour, adding a little more if the mixture is sloppy. Well flour a board or table, roll the dough roughly and cut into shapes as above. Then cook about 8 pieces at a time in boiling, salted water, and serve with melted butter and cheese or fresh tomato sauce, as above. Serves 4.

Cottage cheese gnocchi

These are particularly light and delicious. Sieve about 8 oz (225 g) cottage or cream cheese into a basin, then add about 2 heaped tablespoons melted butter, 4 tablespoons grated hard cheese, 2 beaten eggs and about 4 tablespoons flour. Season with salt, pepper and nutmeg, and then form into shapes as above, with floured hands, and roll in flour. They will appear a bit sloppy, but the flour and eggs will keep them together when cooking. Poach a few at a time in boiling, salted water for about 5 minutes, then lift out and put them in a warmed dish which has a coating of melted butter and a sprinkling of a hard cheese. Serve with more butter and cheese or a *pesto* sauce (page 63).

RICE

Rice is one of the most valuable foods in the world, for at least half the world gets 80 per cent of its calories from this grain, and for some it is the only source of food. Records show that cultivation of this annual grass was known in China as early as 5000 BC. Rice was cultivated in Egypt and Syria from 400 BC and the Greeks later learned of it from the Persians, and the Romans through their Eastern conquests. It is said that the Arabs took the plant to Spain and that its first cultivation in Europe was near Pisa in Italy in 1468. Spanish explorers and settlers introduced rice to America in 1700.

As well as containing high-quality vegetable protein it has some calcium, iron and vitamin B. It is easily digested and one of the few non-allergy-producing foods. Add all these facts to its still reasonable price and you will see why it is an important part of our diet.

There are many different kinds of rice and it is important to use the right one for different dishes. For instance, rice used as a sweet dish should be the short stubby rice, known as short-grain rice; use the medium-grain rice for risottos or croquettes and the long-grain for savoury dishes and curries. There is also brown rice which has only the husk and a small amount of bran removed before processing. This contains most of the natural minerals and vitamins and has a nutty flavour. This rice requires more liquid for cooking than the milled variety, and also takes longer to cook. The different kinds of rice need slightly varying cooking times, and the best way to test is by tasting a few grains. It should be soft, but not mushy unless being used for a pudding when, of course, it is cooked for a much longer time. The pre-cooked or 'instant' rice is only immersed in boiling water until it has absorbed it and is extremely useful for use as a stuffing, or when time is short for a meal.

Rice can be boiled, baked, or cooked with comparatively little liquid on top of the stove so that all the liquid is absorbed. This is probably the simplest way for beginners and is the method used in risottos and paellas. Rice expands a lot in cooking, on average it trebles its volume and weight: 2 oz (60 g) raw rice is usually considered enough for one person, but of course appetites vary. I always cook more rice than I need, for leftover rice is most useful for salads, croquettes, stuffing for courgettes, marrow or poultry, and several other dishes.

Raw rice will keep for months in an airtight container and it is perfect for the hurried or lazy cook for there is no preparation needed, no peelings to throw out and you can make an excellent meal within 20 minutes of coming home with cooked rice, or about half an hour with raw rice. The old method of cooking rice in lots of water, then draining it and putting in a dry, warm place to fluff it up has gone out. The simpler methods given below are generally used, and much easier to do.

METHODS OF COOKING RICE

Top of cooker method

Put 1 cup of raw rice, 2 cups of water and 1 level teaspoon of salt into a saucepan with a tight-fitting lid. Bring to boil and stir once. Lower heat to simmer, cover pan and cook for about 15 minutes without removing lid or stirring. Test rice by biting a few grains and if it is not quite tender or if liquid is not completely absorbed, replace lid and cook for a few minutes longer. Take off the heat, turn into serving dish and fluff lightly with a fork. Serves 2–3.

Oven method

Put rice and salt into a fireproof dish, add boiling water and stir. Cover with lid and cook in a moderate oven (350°F/180°C/Gas Mark 4) for about 40 minutes. Test as above.

Variations: Use chicken or beef stock in place of water or add a cube to the water. Use orange juice instead of water. This is excellent with pork, poultry or fish. Use equal quantities of tomato juice and water.

In place of water use a packet of soup mix made up according to instructions: clear onion or vegetable soups are good. Add a thick slice of lemon while rice is cooking and just before serving remove lemon and fork in 2 tablespoons butter and 1 heaped tablespoon of fresh chopped parsley and chives.

Add a pinch of ground coriander or saffron powder, and when cooked fork in 1 tablespoon of butter and 2 tablespoons of coarsely chopped toasted walnuts or almonds. Fry 1 tablespoon finely chopped onion in 1 tablespoon butter or oil and when soft add 2 teaspoons curry powder. Add water and rice and cook as above. When cooked add a little more butter.

RISOTTO consists of rice cooked slowly in very little liquid and is a speciality of Piedmont and Milan. The basic risotto is called *risotto bianco* and is often served on its own, or in Milan with *osso bucco*. However, fish, cooked chicken, chicken livers, meats, salami, mushrooms, tomatoes, etc. can all be added and cooked with the rice. The risotto then takes the name of the main ingredient.

Risotto bianco and risotto Milanese

1 oz (25 g) butter	1¾ pints (1 l) water or
1 small onion, finely	stock
chopped	Pinch of saffron (for
10 oz (280 g) rice	*Risotto Milanese*)
4 tablespoons white	1 oz (25 g) butter
wine or cider	1 oz (25 g) grated
	Parmesan

Melt the butter in a thick deep pan or metal casserole

and lightly fry the onion until soft and golden. Add the rice and stir until it is impregnated with the butter, but is still white (for *Milanese* chunks of raw beef marrow should be added as well as butter). Add the wine and cook over a medium flame until the wine has almost disappeared, then add the stock or water, 1 cup at a time, stirring each one in, and adding the next one when it has all been almost absorbed. Add the saffron, if using, stir again and cook, very gently, on top of the stove, uncovered, for 20 minutes without stirring. Check to see that the rice is cooked: if it is still firm add a very little water (about 3 tablespoons) and stir gently with a fork until it is ready. For *risotto Milanese* add the butter and Parmesan, stirring lightly with a fork, taking care not to mash the rice. It should be served straight away with more grated cheese, and butter to taste. Enough for about 4.

Risotto con uova is a good dish of risotto served with eggs stuffed with cheese on top.

Risotto con seppie is rice with squid. Mussels, coekles, etc. can also be used.

4 small squid	Salt and pepper
2 tablespoons oil	1 tablespoon tomato
1 medium onion, sliced	purée
1 garlic clove, pressed	1 pint (600 ml) water
4 tablespoons red wine	1 lb (450 g) rice

Clean the squid, removing the bladder and the inside bone. (This can be done for you by the fishmonger.) Chop it all, including tentacles, into small pieces and wash well. Heat up the oil and put in the fish with the onion and garlic and brown all over. Add the wine, taste for salt and cook gently until almost all the wine

has evaporated. Mix the tomato purée with the warmed water and pour that in, cover and cook for about 1 hour over a gentle heat. Then add the rice, and cook for 20–30 minutes or until the rice is ready. Add a little more warm water if it gets too dry. Serves 4–6. Cider, the dry variety, can be used in place of the red wine.

Paella (Spanish rice) is made the same way as the Italian risotto except that olive oil (2 tablespoons) is used instead of butter, the wine is omitted and the water or stock is added gradually, but at the same time stirring constantly until it is boiling again. The dish is then tightly covered, the heat reduced to the lowest point, and it is either simmered for 20–25 minutes or put into a low oven for about 40 minutes, or until almost all the liquid has been absorbed and the rice is soft. It is then fluffed lightly with a fork and tasted for seasoning. If adding shellfish, fish, ham, chicken, etc. put it in after the water is added and do not put on the lid. At no time stir the rice after it has been put in the oven, but when the dish is cooked, bring out and cover with a tea-towel, loosely, for about 7 minutes before serving.

Chopped green peppers make a good addition and sometimes I use a tin of tomatoes with the juice, making up the required amount of liquid with extra water or stock. Curry powder, garam masala, paprika, a pinch of coriander or ground cardamom can all be added according to taste and to make a variation.

Pilaff rice is a good way of using up any scraps of meat, poultry, fish or shellfish. The following method is foolproof.

1½ cups Patna rice
½ sweet pepper, sliced
   and chopped
1 medium onion, sliced
1 teaspoon paprika
   pepper and salt

2½ cups chicken or fish
   stock (depending on
   what is used)
3 tablespoons olive oil

Bring 3 pints (1.7 l) of water to the boil and add the rice, boil for 7 minutes, then drain in a colander and rinse with cold water. Put all ingredients into fireproof dish and bring to the boil, then cover with a clean cloth and a lid, and transfer to a moderate to hot oven (350°F/180°C/Gas Mark 4) for 20 minutes. Take out and add the meat – or whatever you are using – and gently break up the rice with a fork.

By this time almost all the liquid should have evaporated. Work in the meat, poultry or fish carefully. Put the cloth and lid back on and return to the oven for about 10 minutes. Garnish either with wedges of lemon or a little grated Parmesan or, if you have used fish, a few drops of Tabasco. This dish requires only very little meat or fish, for in its country of origin it is often eaten on its own.

A pleasant accompaniment is either mushrooms lightly cooked in butter or oil, a fresh tomato salad, or grated peeled cucumber stirred into plain yoghurt and garnished with freshly chopped mint leaves. If the amounts available are very small, at least it makes a pleasant first course or a light luncheon, equally good hot or cold. Serves 4.

Plain pilau (Indian rice)

Use 1 cup Basmatti rice to 1¾ cups of water. First heat up 4 oz (115 g) butter or margarine, then fry 2 finely chopped medium onions in it until soft and golden. Wash the rice, strain and mix together a pinch each of *whole* black peppercorns, coriander, clove, cardamom and bayleaf, crushed. Add the rice and spices to the onions, then the water, bring to the boil, cover and simmer for about ½ hour or until rice is tender. 1 lb (450 g) rice serves 4–6.

Turmeric (yellow) rice is popular in India.

2 oz (60 g) butter,
   margarine or
   equivalent oil
2 medium onions, thinly
   sliced
1 lb (450 g) long-grain
   rice (Basmatti is best)
1 heaped teaspoon
   turmeric

½ teaspoon cumin
   powder (jeera)
3 cloves
2 tablespoons grated
   unsweetened
   coconut
2 pints (1 l) boiling
   water
1 teaspoon salt

Heat the butter and fry the onions until golden and soft, then add the rice, turmeric, cumin, cloves and coconut and let them fry for 2 minutes. Pour over the boiling salted water and stir well. Cover and either simmer very gently or put into a low to moderate oven until the rice is soft, about ½ hour. Serves 6–8.

Chicken biryani is a dry curry from Pakistan and not unlike a pilaff, for it is a meal on its own and does not require accompaniments. Half-cooked rice is used and any meats, poultry, fish, etc. can be used. Small amounts can utilize leftovers.

1 pint (600 ml) plain yoghurt
4 cloves garlic
½ teaspoon turmeric
Pinch of ground ginger
1 tablespoon ground coriander (dhaniya)
1 large jointed chicken
3 large onions, finely sliced
4 oz (115 g) butter or oil

1 lb (450 g) long-grain rice, cooked for 10 minutes
Salt and pepper
1 tablespoon garam masala

Optional garnishes:
Sliced hard-boiled eggs
Peeled sliced tomatoes
Sliced cucumber
Slivered almonds

Mix the yoghurt, garlic and all the spices together and marinate the chicken joints in this for about 2 hours. Meanwhile brown the onions in butter or oil and mix with the chicken and marinade in a casserole; salt and cook in a moderate oven until the bird is done, about 1 hour. Then take all the meat from the bird and layer it with the rice in the casserole, pouring the sauce over the top. If it seems very dry add not more than ½ cup water, put the lid on and heat up in the oven. Serve on a large hot dish and decorate the top with the sliced eggs, tomatoes, cucumber, nuts, mango chutney or sweet lemon pickle (page 149) and onion *raita* (page 109).

See also Index entry for curries.

Persian chicken with rice

4 tablespoons oil or butter
6 chicken joints
½ pint (300 ml) plain yoghurt
½ teaspoon each ground ginger, turmeric, cumin, coriander, cardamom

½ lb (225 g) Basmatti rice
Salt and pepper
1 tablespoon tomato purée
Grated rind and juice of 1 small lemon

Heat half the butter or oil and sauté the chicken joints until golden, then add water to cover and simmer for 20 minutes and cool. Bone the chicken, and in a large bowl mix the yoghurt with the spices, grated lemon rind and juice and beat well. Add the pieces of chicken and well coat them with the mixture. Meanwhile, heat the remaining oil or butter and cook the rice in it until it is opaque, then add the chicken mixture, with yoghurt and spices, seasoning to taste. Then pour in the stock from the chicken mixed with the tomato purée, adding a further ¼ pint (150 ml) water. Cover and cook very gently either on top of the stove or in the oven for about 20–30 minutes or until the rice is cooked. Serves 6.

Rice with broad beans – leftover poultry, ham or meat can also be added.

4 tablespoons oil
1 large onion
2 cups shelled broad beans
Salt and pepper

2 cloves garlic
1 level teaspoon ground coriander
2 cups long-grain rice

Heat half the oil and lightly fry the sliced onion until soft and golden, then add the beans and just turn them in the oil. Cover with water and simmer until the beans are almost tender, then taste for seasoning.

Heat the remaining oil and fry the chopped garlic and coriander, then add the rice and fry until opaque. Add this mixture to the broad beans, making up the liquid to 1 pint (600 ml). Boil up, and then simmer very gently, with the lid on, for about 20 minutes. Do not stir until after the 20 minutes is up. This dish can be served hot with bacon or ham, poultry or meat, or eaten on its own with leftovers added. Or it is delicious served cold with yoghurt on top as a salad. Serves 4.

Variation: Use 1 lb (450 g) peeled tomatoes, fresh or tinned, instead of the broad beans, but omit the first water, as the tomatoes will juice quite a lot, but make up the liquid when cooking the rice. This is excellent served with small meatballs on top (*see* page 119).

Fresh herbs and small pieces of rhubarb instead of the beans or tomatoes is yet another method.

Risi e bisi is a good Venetian dish using peas and rice, and it is particularly pleasant with young, fresh peas on a summer's evening.

3 tablespoons butter	3 pints (1½ l) chicken
1 small onion	or ham stock
4 oz (115 g) ham or	1 lb (450 g) rice
cooked bacon	2 oz (60 g) grated hard
1 lb (450 g) shelled	cheese
peas	

Heat 2 tablespoons of the butter and add the sliced onion, and when it is soft add the chopped ham or bacon and the shelled peas. Mix well so that they are all coated with the butter, then add ½ pint (300 ml) of the stock and when it is boiling add the rice and mix well. Then add another 1 pint (600 ml) of stock and let it simmer without stirring until it is absorbed, before you add

more. Do this until you have used all the stock. When the rice is cooked, about 20 minutes, stir a little, taste to see that the rice is tender and also for seasoning. It should be more liquid than the usual risotto, but not sloppy. Finally stir in the remaining spoonful of butter and the cheese, and serve a little more cheese separately. Serves 4–6.

Mexican pork chops

If you haven't got an ovenproof dish large enough to take 6 large pork chops, make it in 2 dishes. (Jointed chicken can also be used.)

2 tablespoons oil	2 × 16 oz (450 g) tins
1 large onion, sliced	tomatoes
6 large pork chops	Pinch of chilli powder or
Salt and pepper	cayenne, or few drops
1 sliced green pepper	Tabasco
if available	1 tablespoon chopped
1 lb (450 g) raw rice,	parsley, basil or lovage
preferably long-grain	

Heat up the oil and lightly fry the onion, then brown the chops. Put them into the ovenproof dish or dishes, season to taste, then put the sliced green pepper on top, followed by the raw rice, shaken evenly over. Pour over the tomatoes with their liquid, season again with chilli powder, cayenne or Tabasco, and add the herbs. Cover, and cook in a moderate oven (325°F/160°C/Gas Mark 3) for 1–1¼ hours. During the last 15 minutes check that it is not too dry; if so, add a very little tomato juice. Don't stir the rice but insert a fork into it and separate gently. This is important if making the dish for the first time, as ovens, despite thermostats, do vary. Serves 6.

See also kedgeree (page 101).

COLD RICE OR RICE DISHES can be fried up with mushrooms, tomatoes and leftover scraps of chicken or meat for a quick meal. Or if preferred, the rice can be mixed with cooked beans, diced ham or bacon, or chicken, celery, cucumber, etc. and served cold with an oil and wine vinegar dressing mixed with a little yoghurt or cream. The ratio of oil to vinegar should be 3 oil to 1 vinegar. This salad makes a good first course, a light lunch or a useful vegetable course. Lemon can be used instead of vinegar, or use a good homemade mayonnaise instead of the above dressing.

Cold cooked rice can also be used for sweet dishes.

Honey rice buns

3 heaped tablespoons butter	1½ cups cooked rice
½ cup honey	1¼ cups chopped dates
½ teaspoon grated lemon rind	1¼ cups wholemeal SR flour
2 eggs	½ teaspoon ground cloves

Cream together the butter, honey and grated lemon rind. Beat in eggs thoroughly one at a time. Then mix in the cooked rice and dates. Finally fold in the flour and cloves. Divide mixture between 2 dozen patty tins and bake in a moderate oven (375°F/190°C/Gas Mark 5) for 20 minutes. These buns are delicious eaten as they are, or served warm, split, with butter in between.

Marquis pudding is made from about 2 large cups of cooked rice mixed with 4 tablespoons of the top of the milk. Half the mixture is placed on top of a layer of either apricot jam or purée, and followed by a layer of cooked apple. This is repeated, ending with the rice mixture. The final layer consists of 4 tablespoons castor sugar mixed with 4 tablespoons breadcrumbs and a few drops of almond essence. This topping should be put on roughly so that it stands in peaks. The pudding is baked in a moderate oven (350°F/180°C/Gas Mark 4) for 30 minutes, and is served cold with cider sauce (page 44).

7. Mainly vegetable and vegetarian dishes

The reason for the title of this chapter is that many of the dishes can be cooked with a little fresh or leftover meat, or eaten as a vegetarian meal. Vegetables are an important part of our diet, for not only are they full of vitamins and minerals, but in some cases (especially dried vegetables) they contain quite a lot of protein. The majority are very low in calories and contain no fat, so they are excellent for diets of many kinds. It must also be remembered that although millions of people all over the world live entirely on vegetables (and perhaps eggs and dairy products) without any impairment of physical or intellectual ability, it is quite impossible to live entirely on meat without serious vitamin debility.

Famous vegetarians include Leonardo da Vinci, the poet Shelley, Tolstoy, Gandhi, and nearer our own time, Bernard Shaw, all men of exceptional force and ability, who (apart from Shelley and Gandhi who died unnaturally) continued to do brilliant work until extreme old age.

I do not think that we will ever see cheap meat again in our time, so it is wise to consider other ways of serving attractive and nutritious meals. During the last war many people started to grow vegetables with great success and found that not only was it considerably cheaper to grow than to buy them, but also that there was no comparison in the taste of home-grown and shop-bought vegetables. It is now time to think of gardening again, and even if you don't have a garden but only a small yard or balcony it is quite remarkable what can be achieved in pots, troughs, and particularly the cropping nodules. The latter are large sausage-like bags filled with sterilized peat moss, which only require water to produce the most prolific plants. From personal experience I can vouch for wonderful crops of the more exotic vegetables, such as courgettes, sweet peppers and aubergines, and these bags are also good for tomatoes. They have the great advantage that they can be moved around without too much trouble, so as to get sun, shade or wind-free conditions.

It is for this reason that I am including several recipes for what are the more expensive vegetables to buy; it is also worth remembering that these foods contain very little wastage.

The usual method of cooking vegetables in a lot of water and then throwing away the water (and most of the vitamins) is not to be recommended. In the following recipes I have tried to select the best ways of using all vegetables so that their vitamin content is preserved.

Stuffed aubergine

This method can be used for many vegetables such as cucumber, courgettes, marrow, large mushrooms and sweet peppers. There are many variations of the stuffing and the basis can be cold cooked rice, potato, pasta, breadcrumbs or oatmeal, mixed with a little onion or garlic, chopped herbs and either chopped or minced up leftovers of meat, fish, poultry or cheese. Tomato is pleasant if available and also a few mushrooms, but some of the most successful stuffings are made from available ingredients. If you feel that the stuffing you have prepared is perhaps lacking a little in nourishment, then add either a beaten egg, cheese or a tablespoon of wheatgerm. The following recipe uses a little meat, but this can be replaced with the same amount of cooked rice, pasta or potato, or half the amount of raw oatmeal.

2 medium aubergines	or 4 tablespoons
1 medium onion, chopped	grated cheese
	Salt and pepper
2 medium tomatoes, peeled and chopped	1 tablespoon chopped herbs
1 garlic clove, chopped	1 egg
3 tablespoons oil	1 tablespoon tomato purée, diluted in $\frac{1}{2}$ pint (300 ml) water
8 oz (225 g) minced meat, raw or cooked	

Cut the aubergines in half lengthways and carefully take out the flesh, leaving about $\frac{1}{4}$ inch (6 mm) next to the skin. Prepare and chop the other vegetables, and heat up the oil. Lightly sauté the aubergine flesh, the onion, garlic and finally the tomatoes, but do not let them colour. Take out from the pan, and in the same oil cook the meat until brown if using fresh meat, otherwise mix up the minced leftovers with the vegetable mixture. Season to taste, add the herbs and finally the beaten egg. Put this mixture back into the shells and into a greased baking tin. Dissolve the tomato purée in the water, pour around the aubergines, cover with a piece of foil and bake at 350°F/180°C/Gas Mark 4–5 for about 30 minutes, removing the foil for the last 5 minutes. Serves 4, and can be eaten hot or cold.

Courgettes, marrows and cucumbers are better if steamed or blanched for 5 minutes first: in the case of a large marrow, remove the skin and cut in half across. This makes it easier to get into the steamer and it can be reconstituted into shape with the stuffing. Use the stuffing for Stuffed aubergines (*see* above); about 4 tablespoons cooked rice, oatmeal or potato can also be added to stretch the stuffing, particularly for larger marrows.

Sweet peppers should have the stalk and inner seeds carefully removed from the hole left by the stalk, and they are also better if steamed for 5 minutes first. Peppers can be stuffed with the same mixture as for aubergines, or are exceptionally delicate and good if stuffed with cooked cod's roe. As this is only available around March it should be looked for and frozen for future use. Do not use smoked cod's roe, but the fresh. *See* the chapter on 'Fish' (pages 93–105).

Aubergine casserole is a very good and filling dish. Cauliflower can be used instead of aubergine.

1 large aubergine (about 1½ lb, 675 g)	1 small onion, chopped
1 teaspoon salt	½ teaspoon powdered oregano
2 eggs, beaten	Pepper
2 tablespoons melted butter	2 large tomatoes, peeled and sliced
3 tablespoons dry breadcrumbs, brown if possible	4 oz (115 g) grated hard cheese
	Paprika

Peel and slice the aubergine, then put into a pan with the salt and about 1 inch (25 mm) of boiling water. Cover and cook gently for about 7 minutes, then drain. Mash the aubergine well, and mix with the eggs, melted butter, breadcrumbs, onion, oregano and pepper. Grease a shallow 3 pint (1.7 l) ovenproof dish and put half the sliced tomato on the bottom, then put the aubergine mixture on top and cover with the rest of the tomato. Lay the cheese on top, sprinkle with paprika and bake at (350°F/180°C/Gas Mark 4) for about 40 minutes. Serves 4–6.

Shashlik of aubergines (or cucumber, courgettes, peppers, mushrooms, or a mixture of all the vegetables) makes an attractive and also very filling meal.

1 medium aubergine	8 medium length skewers
8 firm medium mushrooms	8 bay leaves
8 firm small tomatoes	Salt and pepper
8 oz (225 g) Bel Paese, Mozzarella or similar cheese	½ pint (300 ml) milk
	Flour for coating
16 large, thick cubes of bread (crustless French loaf size)	2 beaten eggs
	Approx. ½ pint (300 ml) oil, which can be strained and re-used

Peel the aubergine and cut into slices about ½ inch (12 mm) thick, then cut in half. Remove the stalks from the mushrooms, peel the tomatoes and remove the heel at the top, squeeze slightly and shake out some of the juice. Cut the cheese and bread into slices about the same size as the aubergine. Have the skewers handy and thread each one with a piece of bread, then aubergine, then cheese, mushroom, tomato, and bayleaf, until the skewer is filled, ending with a piece of bread. You can vary the order as you please, but the cheese should be next to the aubergine, bread or the tomato. It is also good next to the courgette or cucumber if using them. Season the filled skewers, then roll them in milk, then into the flour and finally the eggs. Have the oil hot and fry gently until golden brown all over. Do not attempt to fry too many at a time as it will be difficult to turn them. Keep hot in a low oven while cooking the remainder.

They are good served with a green salad or with raw carrots grated and dressed with a little lemon juice. Remove the skewers by first twisting them and then pulling out while serving. An attractive idea is to stick the skewers into half a cut grapefruit set cut-side down in the centre of a surround of rice. Enough for 4. The filled skewers can also be dipped in batter instead of the flour and egg (see *pastella*, page 29).

Artichoke pie is a seventeenth-century recipe and was made originally with globe artichokes which grew like the thistles they are related to, many centuries ago. They do grow easily in most gardens, as does their near relative the cardoon. However, I have found the pie excellent made with Jerusalem artichokes, either on its own, or served as the sole accompaniment to underdone meat, baked ham or bacon.

8 oz (225 g) shortcrust or flaky pastry (see page 143)	1 small bunch white grapes, seedless or seeded
1 lb (450 g) Jerusalem artichokes	10 dates, stoned and halved
1 oz (25 g) butter	Salt and pepper
1 oz (25 g) flour	Pinch of mace
½ pint (300 ml) warm milk	1 hard-boiled egg

First prepare the pastry and leave it to rest in a cool place. Peel and boil the artichokes in salted water for about 10 minutes or until they are almost cooked, then drain them. Heat the butter, stir in the flour and add the warm milk, stirring all the time until it is smooth. Let this sauce simmer gently for a few minutes and make sure it is not too thick; if so add a little more liquid. Add all the other ingredients to the sauce except the egg and put into a deep pie-dish, slice the egg over the top, then moisten the edges and roll out the pastry to the required size. Press down at the edges, brush lightly with milk and bake in a moderate oven (375°F/190°C/Gas Mark 5–6) for about 30 minutes or until golden all over. Serves 4–6. This pie is also good made with small turnips and carrots. *See also* artichoke soup, page 14.

BEETROOT at its best is sweet, tender and deep red in colour. It is easy to grow and both the roots and the tops can be eaten. It is important not to damage the outer skin before cooking as this causes the beetroot to bleed and lose colour. It can be boiled in a lot of salted water, or baked in the oven in water. Try and cook beetroots of the same size together, the cooking time depending on the age and size. Beetroots about the size of a cricket ball are ideal for both taste and tenderness and will take about 35–45 minutes to cook. They can be pricked very lightly to test for tenderness, but don't prick them too hard and lose the juice. Strain the liquid and reserve it for use in a beetroot soup (see *bortsch*, page 15). When the beetroot is cool, rub off the skin and keep in the juice until you want to serve it. The least good way of serving fresh beetroot is dripping in malt vinegar. Remember that the ancient Greeks offered it as a gift to Apollo at his temple at Delphi and treat it with the respect it deserves. It is good food for vegetarians and slimmers as it is low in calories, but high in calcium, ascorbic acid and protein. Beetroot makes a good vegetable, either hot or cold and also a very good first course.

Beetroot with anchovy and yoghurt

Slice 2 cooked medium sized beetroots into a dish and season slightly. Then add 1 small sliced onion or shallot, and about 2 heaped tablespoons of plain yoghurt and mix well, tasting to see if a little more is needed. Add the contents of a drained small can of anchovies, arranged crisscross fashion on top, and finally garnish with a little chopped parsley or chives. Serves 4.

Variation: Pickled chopped herring or mackerel can be used instead of anchovy, and a little chopped, raw apple or celery or chunks of cooked potato can also be added.

Beetroot in orange or lemon sauce is also delicious as a first course or with cold meats, ham or poultry.

1 lb (450 g) cooked beetroot	Salt and pepper
2 tablespoons honey	1 heaped teaspoon finely grated orange or lemon rind
½ pint (300 ml) beet juice	2 teaspoons cornflour
Pinch of crushed cardamom	2 tablespoons plain yoghurt

Combine all ingredients except the cornflour and yoghurt, seeing that the beets are thinly sliced. Let the mixture come to the boil, then add the cornflour, creamed with the yoghurt, stirring well to avoid lumps. Simmer very gently for about 5 minutes. If beetroot juice is not available, milk or cider can be used. The dish can be served hot or cold, and the former makes a pretty dish set in a ring of finely mashed potato, with halves or quarters of warm hard-boiled egg arranged on top. Serves 4–6.

Beetroot and lemon preserve is one of the nicest relishes if you have plenty of beetroots. It is a traditional Jewish preserve and can be served as a sweet or savoury, rather like apple or redcurrant jelly.

2 lb (1 kg) granulated sugar	Pinch of powdered ginger
½ pint (300 ml) water	Salt and pepper
2 lb (1 kg) cooked beetroot	2 tablespoons blanched chopped almonds (if you're feeling rich)
2 small lemons, peeled and sliced	

First make a thick syrup by boiling the sugar and water for about 15 minutes. Then add the beets and cook for 1 hour, then put in the lemons and continue cooking until the beets become opaque. The juice will be brownish in appearance, and should jelly when tested on a plate. Stir in the ginger, salt and pepper and almonds (if using) and a few drops of cochineal if you want it to be a red colour. Pour into warm jars and tie down at once. Makes about 4 lb (approx. 2 kg) of preserve.

BROAD BEANS

Broad beans have a lot of food value and when picked young enough (without the black line around the kidney side of the bean) are a most delectable vegetable. It is worth growing the herb summer savory just to sprinkle over the top of buttered, cooked broad beans when they first come in. They also make a good salad mixed with whole-kernel sweetcorn, dressed with yoghurt or a little mayonnaise. Served with leftover ham, chicken, tongue or a little tuna fish they make a good summer meal.

Broad beans and bacon makes a filling and good casserole dish.

2 lb (1 kg) shelled broad beans	½ pint (300 ml) top of milk
8 rashers bacon or 1 whole Bath chap	2 tablespoons chopped parsley or 1 tablespoon each parsley and savory
1 oz (25 g) butter	
1 oz (25 g) flour	
Salt and pepper	2 cloves garlic

Cook the shelled beans in boiling, salted water for about 10 minutes, then strain but reserve the liquid. Fry the bacon just enough to brown it, and take out. Add the butter to the bacon fat, then stir in the flour and add ½ pint (300 ml) of the bean water, stirring until it thickens and is smooth. Season to taste, then add the top of the milk, seeing that the mixture doesn't get too liquid. Put in half the parsley, then combine with the broad beans, chopped garlic and the bacon or Bath chap. Transfer to a casserole, sprinkle the rest of the herbs on top and bake, covered, in a hot oven (400°F/200°C/ Gas Mark 6) for about 30 minutes. This dish can be prepared in advance and heated up when required. Serves 4–6.

If you have leftovers of cold pork, boiled bacon or ham, they can be used instead of the bacon rashers, but slightly increase the butter for the sauce.

CABBAGE and members of the same family, such as sprouts, kale and broccoli, probably suffer more than any vegetable from being boiled to extinction in a lot of water, but the following Chinese method preserves both taste and vitamin content.

Chinese cabbage

Choose a medium sized cabbage and see that it is well trimmed of stale leaves and a certain amount of the very hard stump is removed. Separate the leaves and crisp them in very cold water. Then roll the leaves up and shred them. Heat about 2 to 3 tablespoons of oil or butter in a large saucepan and when it is hot, put the cabbage in and toss it thoroughly so that every leaf gets covered with the oil. Lower the heat and let it get just softened, but not in any way coloured. This will take about 5 minutes. Then add about 1 large cup water, or stock if available, seasonings and a good pinch of either caraway seeds or a mixture of cumin, fennel or anise. Cover, and let it simmer until the cabbage is tender enough to eat but not mushy, about 10–15 minutes. This is very good with sausages, and a little of the juice is good too. Serves 4–6.

Stuffed cabbage makes a cheap and good meal. You can either remove the larger leaves and stuff them individually, or put the stuffing between the leaves and braise the whole cabbage. The Savoy or loose-leaved cabbage is best, not the tight-hearted York. If the latter is used, then the cabbage should be secured around the outside with string, so that the stuffing does not fall out. The stuffing given for aubergine on page 75 is very acceptable and sausagemeat can be used instead of minced beef if preferred. For the whole cabbage, the very tough outer leaves should be removed, and the tender heart can be taken out and chopped into the stuffing. When secured, put it into a large saucepan with stock to halfway up. A few chopped carrots, turnips or onions can also be added to the stock if wanted. Then put a piece of foil over the top and then the lid. Bring to the boil and simmer for about 45–50 minutes, but test the stump at the bottom to see that it is cooked properly.

Another method is to blanch the large leaves for about 5 minutes in boiling salted water, then to drain and put them in cold water. Put enough stuffing on each leaf and roll up, and tuck the ends in to keep the stuffing secure, then put side by side into an ovenproof dish, and dot with butter. Pour around stock, or tomato purée dissolved in water, to about halfway up, then put cabbage leaves over the top, and cover with foil or a lid. Cook in a moderate oven (350°F/180°C/Gas Mark 4) for about 40 minutes. These are good served with a blob of plain yoghurt, or with *avgolémono* sauce (*see* page 119), or with a little grated cheese. The stuffing can be composed of half-cooked rice or breadcrumbs or oatmeal without the dish being impaired. Allow 2 or 3 stuffed leaves per person.

CARROTS are invaluable for use in many ways. They make an excellent soup (*see* page 16), and can be eaten raw or cooked. A raw carrot, grated and added to the ingredients of a rich fruit cake or Christmas pudding keeps it moist and also darkens it. In the ninth century carrots were referred to in a Gaelic poem as 'honey underground', and they were frequently used in puddings and pies (*see* parsnip tart, page 88). In both Spain and France a delicious jam called *cheveux d'ange* (angel's hair) is made from about 2 lb (1 kg) of shredded carrots with the same amount of sugar, and water to barely cover. It is cooked until only one-third of the liquid is left, and then the finely grated peel of 2 lemons is added, and the juice of one lemon. This conserve is used for filling tarts and tartlets and also served with meringue or whipped cream.

Carrots are very good cooked in the following way with mint, sugar and lemon. Lightly scrape the carrots and cut them into circles if fairly large, but leave whole if small. Put them into boiling water barely to cover, and add a pinch of sugar and very little salt. Let them cook until tender, then drain and reserve the liquid, which is good for stock or casserole dishes. Heat up a good knob of butter in a saucepan and add the carrots, some fresh chopped mint and finally a good squeeze of lemon. Carrots are pleasant mixed with other vegetables such as peas or French beans, but let the carrots cook for some time before adding the green vegetables.

Carrots braised with bacon

1 lb (450 g) young carrots	2 tablespoons butter
1 medium onion	3 tablespoons water or stock
3 rashers bacon	1 tablespoon chopped parsley
Salt and pepper	

Scrape the carrots and cut into thin circles or sticks and peel and slice the onion. Fry the chopped bacon and when the fat has run out, add the onion and carrots. Season to taste, put into a casserole, add the butter and stock, cover and cook very slowly for about 45 minutes or until the carrots are tender. Sprinkle with the parsley before serving. Serves 4.

Carrot salad is simply tender carrots grated coarsely and seasoned with a little salt and lemon juice. It is wonderfully refreshing with a rich meal. Grated apple can also be added and also some sultanas, but do not make it too sweet.

CAULIFLOWER, if it is not overcooked in the first place, makes a good salad mixed with an oil and vinegar dressing. The eighteenth-century Irish way of cooking a cauliflower was to simmer it in milk, then to thicken the milk with cornflour. It gives the cauliflower a creamy flavour, and of course preserves all the vitamins. I don't really see why other vegetables such as celery or salsify shouldn't be cooked in the same way.

The most common way with cauliflower is to serve it in a cheese sauce. This sauce is much improved if a pinch of nutmeg or mace is added and also a few walnuts, which give it a nice crunchy taste. If you want to make it even more of a cheap dish, half cook the cauliflower, drain it, and layer it with cooked rice and tomatoes, then cover it with the sauce and finish cooking it in a hot oven for about 20 minutes. It is also very pleasant to use a large tin of tomatoes mixed with a little basil instead of the cheese sauce. A large cauliflower serves 4–6.

COURGETTES are just small marrows and should always be sliced from the flower end if they are not to be bitter. This also applies to cucumbers. The simplest method of cooking them is to leave them unpeeled, then slice them and fry them until soft in butter or oil. Or they can be dipped in flour and fried in deep oil until crisp and golden. These little crispy flakes are very good mixed with cooked pasta which already has a sauce made from fresh, peeled tomatoes, garlic, and sweet pepper mixed with a little cottage cheese. The crisp courgettes should be added at the last moment, when they taste not unlike nuts.

Courgettes are very good cooked lightly in milk, with the milk then made into a cheese sauce with a hint of nutmeg. Larger marrows can be cooked the same way. They can also be stuffed (*see* stuffed aubergine, page 75), when they are extra good served with *avgolémono* sauce (page 119).

CELERY goes back to the days of the ancient Greeks, and is mentioned in Homer's *Odyssey* which was written about 850 BC. Dioscorides, the Greek medical writer of the first century, recommended eating celery for its sedative effect, and the volatile oil obtained from the ripe seeds is used in medicines today. Wild celery, called 'smallage', was popular in old country gardens, and it is from this that cultivated celery comes. It is eaten raw with cheese, and is good cut into lengths and stuffed with cottage cheese, especially as snacks for people on diets of many kinds. It also makes a pleasant salad, mixed with chopped apple and a few sultanas or raisins, and an oil and vinegar dressing.

Celery cheese makes a good supper dish.

1 large head celery	4 oz (115 g) grated
Little milk	cheese
Salt and pepper	1 egg
	Breadcrumbs

Wash and trim the celery, then grate it on a coarse grater. Put into a saucepan and barely cover with milk. Season to taste and simmer until cooked. Allow to cool. Then mix in the cheese and the beaten egg, sprinkle thickly with breadcrumbs, and bake until brown in a moderate oven (350°F/180°C/Gas Mark 4). Serves 4.

Jugged celery uses up windfall apples and is very cheering on a cold day.

2½ cups apple purée	4 rashers bacon
1 tablespoon sugar	1 large head of celery
4 cloves	Salt and pepper

If possible use a deep dish for cooking, rather like the old-fashioned hotpot. Heat up the apple purée with the sugar and cloves and see that it is fairly dry. Put half the bacon on the bottom of the dish, spread the apple purée on top, then stand as many sticks of celery into it as the pot will hold, and by this time the apple will have risen almost to the top of the celery sticks. Season to taste, put the remaining rashers on top, then a lid, and bake in a moderate oven (350°F/180°C/Gas Mark 4) for about 1½ hours. Serves 4–6.

GIOVECH is a dish common to all the Balkan countries and the name means 'flower-pot'; it is so called from the shape of the original cooking pot. It is simply a mixed

F

vegetable casserole dish, sometimes with chopped fish or meat added. Almost any vegetable can be used and rice can be added if wanted. The following is a typical recipe eaten daily in many country homes. It is called *djuveč* in Yugoslavia, *ghiveciu* in Romania, and *youvetsi* in Greece.

1 lb (450 g) onions	1 pint (600 ml) water or
2 medium carrots	stock
2 large potatoes	2 oz (60 g) raw rice
2 sweet peppers	1 tablespoon chopped
4 oz (115 g) each peas	parsley
and green beans	1 teaspoon paprika
1 clove garlic	Salt and pepper
4 large tomatoes	1 oz (25 g) grated
2 tablespoons oil	cheese
1 lb (450 g) minced	
beef, pork or lamb	
(optional)	

Prepare all the vegetables and skin the tomatoes by placing them in boiling water for a few minutes. Heat the oil in a large frying pan, add the sliced onions and fry until soft but not coloured, then remove. In the same oil lightly brown the meat if using, then add the water or stock and simmer gently for about 10 minutes. In a fireproof casserole layer all ingredients except the cheese, but reserve 2 large tomatoes. Season each layer well. On top put the remaining tomatoes in thick slices and then the cheese. Cover, and bake in a moderate oven (350°F/180°C/Gas Mark 4) for about 1 hour, but remove the lid for the last 10 minutes. Leftover meats or poultry can be used, in which case do not sauté it in the oil. If meat or fish is not used, then 10 minutes before the dish is ready beat up 2 eggs with 1 tablespoon flour and the juice of ½ large lemon. Pour this over the top and put back in the oven for 10 minutes or until the topping is puffed up and golden brown. Serves 4–6.

If sweet peppers are too expensive then use celery, thinly sliced turnips, thick chunks of vegetable marrow or whatever vegetable is cheap and in season.

Plakia is a similar Balkan dish eaten particularly in Bulgaria during Lent. To prepare it sauté 1 lb (450 g) peeled sliced onions and 1½ lb (675 g) peeled, sliced tomatoes in about 6 tablespoons oil or butter. Then add 8 oz (225 g) beans, either green or dried, which have been cooked and drained. Next add ½ pint (300 ml) stock or 1 tablespoon tomato purée diluted to the same quantity. This is all seasoned to taste and 1 teaspoon sugar is added. It is simmered gently for about 30 minutes, and can be eaten hot or cold sprinkled with grated cheese. Serves 4.

LEEKS are a valuable winter vegetable which make a delicious soup as well as a vegetable. Prepare them as for *brotchán roy* (page 14). They can be simmered in a little water and eaten hot with melted butter and lemon as a separate course, or served cold with an oil and vinegar dressing. They also make a delightful flan or tart (*see* below) or pasties. Both dishes are traditional to Wales and Cornwall, areas which have suffered great economic troubles over the years.

Leeks produce a lot of their own liquid when cooking, so the best way to do them is in butter, bacon fat or oil. Chop the cleaned leeks into 1 inch (25 mm) lengths and simmer them very slowly in one of the above fats, shaking the pan from time to time so they do not colour or catch on the bottom. A very little cider (about 3 tablespoons per 1 lb (450 g) of leeks) may be added to make a fine buttery sauce.

Leeks with bacon make a good filling meal. Blanch the leeks after trimming, for about 7 minutes, then wrap each leek in streaky bacon and put them side by side in a fireproof dish. Cover with a cheese sauce and bake in a moderate oven (350°F/180°C/Gas Mark 4) for about ½ hour. Allow at least 2 rolls per person. *See also* Anglesey eggs (page 26).

MARROW: *See* stuffed aubergine (page 75, *and also* courgettes page 80).

MUSHROOMS, especially the large flats, make a good meal and are with us all the year round. They are especially good dipped in batter (*see pastella*, page 29) and deep fried, then sprinkled with salt, pepper and nutmeg, with a squeeze of lemon on each one. If the really large, thick, field mushrooms are used they can taste like a piece of meat. They are also excellent with the stalks removed and the top covered with savoury cooked rice, then baked, covered, in a greased pan with a very little stock for about 20 minutes. Or put raw rice on the bottom, the mushrooms on top with a bread and herb stuffing, mixed if liked with small chopped pieces of meat or poultry, and all baked as above.

Mushrooms with coriander are good as a first course, or with chicken and white meats.

1 rounded teaspoon coriander seeds	3 tablespoons olive oil
8 oz (225 g) mushrooms	2–3 bayleaves
Juice of 1 lemon	Salt and pepper

First crush the coriander well, in a mortar. Trim the mushrooms, wipe them, but do not peel if they are fresh, and cut into quarters. Pour over half the lemon juice. Heat 2 tablespoons olive oil, and when warm add the coriander for 3 seconds, then add the bayleaves,

mushrooms and seasonings. Cover, and cook over a low heat for about 5 minutes, uncover, turn them, then cook again for about 2 minutes. Pour into a shallow dish, with the bayleaves underneath, add the remaining olive oil and the rest of the lemon juice. They can be served hot or cold. Serves 2–4.

Button mushrooms, raw, sprinkled with a little salt and well mixed with yoghurt make a good first course, or a salad with cold foods.

ONIONS are so much a part of cooking that sometimes one forgets that they make an excellent meal on their own. They were worshipped in ancient Egypt and appeared in temple decorations. Perhaps one of the simplest and best ways of cooking them is in their jackets. They should be put into a tin (as the milky juice exudes a little) in a moderate oven like jacket potatoes. A medium to large onion will take about 1 hour and is eaten by peeling off the brown skin, and adding pepper, salt and butter.

Onions with lemon and marjoram sauce

This is delicious on its own, with cheese dishes, or with roast or grilled meats.

6 medium onions	2 tablespoons butter
Bouquet garni of parsley, thyme and bayleaf	2 tablespoons flour
1 teaspoon salt	¼ teaspoon pepper
¾ pint (450 ml) milk	1 tablespoon parsley, chopped
2 fresh marjoram sprigs	1 lemon, cut into wedges
Finely grated rind and juice of 1 lemon	

Put the peeled onions in a large saucepan with the bouquet garni, half the salt, and water barely to cover. Bring to the boil, then reduce the heat and cook for about 20 minutes or until they are tender when pricked. Lift out with a slotted spoon and keep warm. In a small saucepan infuse the milk with the marjoram and lemon rind over a low heat for 10 minutes, being careful not to let the milk boil. Take from the heat and strain the milk into a small bowl and let it cool slightly. Heat the butter until foaming, then mix in the flour and gradually add the milk, stirring until it simmers and is smooth. Season to taste and remove from the heat and add 1 tablespoon of lemon juice. Pour this over the onions, garnish with the parsley and serve with lemon wedges. Serves 4–6.

See also onion tart (page 88) and Whitley goose (page 32).

PARSNIPS are either hated or loved, the former mainly because of bad cooking at schools. However, they are a most versatile vegetable, and can be used for sweet or savoury dishes like the carrot. In the old days when sugar was a luxury parsnips were used with honey for jams, chutneys, sweet pies and tarts, and such a tart is still made in the country and in the South-west region of France. The parsnip, roasted with the meat, was traditionally served with roast beef before the arrival of the sweet potato, which was the first potato to reach Britain. It has an affinity with many foods, especially fish, and there is a dish called Poor man's lobster which is a salad. It doesn't really taste of lobster, although the texture is similar, but mixed with cold flaked fish it is an extremely good dish. It is also a good way of stretching certain fish for a pie or a seafood cocktail. Once it is mixed with the fish it even fools the cat!

Poor man's lobster

3 medium parsnips	1 cup home-made
8 oz (225 g) cooked	mayonnaise with a
white fish	little mustard added
or 2 teaspoons	Lettuce leaves
anchovy essence	Lemon

Cook the finely peeled and sliced parsnips, then cut the rings into halves or quarters and when slightly cooled mix them with the flaked white fish. If not using fish then carefully stir the anchovy essence into the mayonnaise, tasting from time to time to make certain that it is not too fishy and salty. Mix with the mayonnaise and serve on fresh, crisp lettuce with lemon wedges. It makes a good and unusual salad without the fish, too. Serves about 4.

Candied parsnips are extremely good with sausages, bacon or ham. Peel and cook the parsnips as usual, but cut them into rounds. For 1 lb (450 g) heat up 2 tablespoons butter in a large pan, then mix it with 2 tablespoons brown sugar and either 2 tablespoons orange juice or cider. Stir until it is melted, then add the parsnips, turning over constantly, and cook until they are well-glazed and the liquid reduced. Serves about 4.

Carrots or small turnips are good done the same way. *See also* parsnip tart (page 88).

POTATOES have so many uses in the culinary field that it would be possible to write a book just about them. For many centuries they have been the staple diet of the poorer Irish peoples, also of the Dutch, the Romanians and Russians. There are also many Jewish potato dishes, *latkes* being very similar to a variety of Irish potato cakes.

Potato cakes (1) are also known as potato bread and are good with bacon, sausages and so on.

3 tablespoons melted butter or bacon fat	4–5 heaped tablespoons SR flour, depending
½ teaspoon salt	on the flouriness of
8 oz (225 g) boiled mashed potatoes	the potatoes

Add the melted butter and salt to the potatoes, then add as much of the flour as the potatoes will take without becoming too dry. Turn out on to a floured board and roll out to ¼ inch (6 mm) thickness, then cut into circles or triangles. Prick slightly on top with a fork, and put on to a slightly greased pan (or a griddle) and cook for about 3 minutes on each side. These cakes can be eaten hot with butter, honey or syrup, or can be stored in a tin and heated up for savoury dishes. Makes about 12.

Cheese potato cakes can be made as above with the addition of 4 heaped tablespoons grated cheese and 2 well-beaten eggs. Shape into small round cakes, dip in breadcrumbs and fry on both sides until golden. Delicious for supper or for a picnic.

Potato cakes (2)

These cakes have a scone-like appearance and can be used as rolls; the dough can also be used to line a savoury flan.

2 heaped tablespoons butter or bacon fat	1½ cups mashed potato
2 cups SR flour	¼ cup milk
Salt	caraway seeds (optional)

Mix the butter into the flour and add the salt. Then mix in the mashed potato and pour in the milk to make a soft but not slack dough. Roll out on a floured board and cut into rounds about 3 inches (75 mm) across. Sprinkle a few caraway seeds on top of each cake, and bake in a hot oven (400°F/200°C/Gas Mark 6) for 20–30 minutes. Eat them hot, split across the middle and spread with butter. Makes about 9 cakes.

'While I live I shall not forget her potato cakes. They came in hot, and hot from a pot oven, they were speckled with caraway seeds, they swam in butter, and we ate them shamelessly, and greasily and washed them down with hot whiskey and water.' ('The Holy Island', *Experiences of an Irish R.M.*, Somerville and Ross.)

Potato pancakes or latkes

3 medium raw potatoes	1 tablespoon milk
1 tablespoon plain flour	Salt and pepper
1 egg	Oil for frying

Grate the potatoes on a coarse grater and add the other ingredients, except the oil. Mix well, heat up about 1 inch (25 mm) of oil and cook in spoonfuls over a not too fierce heat, to allow the centre to cook through. Turn and cook the other side, and serve hot. A few spoonfuls of grated cheese can be added if liked.

Iahnie de cartofi is a good Romanian dish usually served with fried eggs.

1½ lb (675 g) potatoes	Salt and pepper
2 medium onions	1 bayleaf
2 tablespoons oil	1 tablespoon chopped
2 tablespoons tomato	parsley
purée	
½ pint (300 ml hot water)	

Peel and chop finely the onions and potatoes, heat the oil and lightly brown them both. Mix the tomato purée with the hot water, add salt and pepper and pour over the potatoes and onions. Put in the bayleaf, cover and cook gently on top of the stove until the potatoes are cooked. Garnish with the chopped parsley. This is very similar to the Cornish dish Raw Tattie Fry, but that has streaky bacon in it, the fat from it being used to fry the potato and onion. Serves 4–6.

Russian potatoes are very good indeed, the only trouble being to stop eating them.

6 large potatoes	1 large clove garlic
8 oz (225 g) cottage	Salt
cheese (*see* page 54)	4 oz (115 g) Cheddar
1 tablespoon plain	cheese, grated
yoghurt	Paprika
3 spring onions or onion	
tops or 3 tablespoons	
chopped chives	

Boil the potatoes in their jackets until just barely cooked, and when cooled, peel and cut into cubes. Mix them with the beaten cottage cheese, yoghurt, chopped spring onions, salt and pressed garlic. Put into a greased casserole and sprinkle the Cheddar cheese over the top, then the paprika. Bake in a moderate oven (350°F/180°C/Gas Mark 4–5) for about ½ hour. Serves 4–6.

Variation: Add some anchovy fillets, pickled herring, mackerel, cooked smoked haddock or smoked cod. About 8 oz (225 g) will be enough, but use only half the cheese given above.

Or omit the cottage cheese and yoghurt, layer the potatoes with white or smoked fish, then pour over 2 beaten eggs mixed with 1 cup milk, seasoned according to the fish you have used, then bake as above.

Potatoes are very good for using up leftovers of meat or poultry. This French peasant dish from the Auvergne is particularly good.

6–8 slices cooked lamb,	parsley, chives, thyme,
ham pork, etc	chervil, etc
4 large potatoes	Salt and pepper
1 large onion	1 cup milk
3 fresh peeled or canned	1 level tablespoon
tomatoes	paprika
Little fat bacon	
1 tablespoon mixed	
fresh herbs, e.g.	

See that the meat is carved thinly, then peel the potatoes, onion and tomatoes. Grease a casserole, put a layer of potatoes in the bottom, then onion, chopped bacon, meat, herbs and tomato. Season well. Repeat until the dish is full, ending with potatoes. Warm up the milk, stir in the paprika, then pour over, cover and bake for about 1 hour in a moderate oven (350°F/180°C/Gas Mark 4), removing the cover for the last 15 minutes. Serves 4. Cheese can be used instead of meat if preferred, and other vegetables can be incorporated to taste.

Red cabbage with apples is a lovely winter dish, good with any of the pig family, or with the cheaper game such as pigeon, hare or rabbit. It can be cooked for several hours, and is even better heated up.

1 fat bacon rasher, oil or dripping	3 tablespoons wine vinegar
1 large onion	Salt and pepper
2 cooking apples	1 tablespoon brown sugar
1 medium-sized red cabbage	Good pinch of allspice
1 cup water or stock	2 cloves

If using bacon, fry it, then the sliced onion and apples, just until they soften. Then add all the other ingredients, chopping the cabbage, cover and simmer for at least 2 hours, turning the mixture over from time to time. Taste for seasoning, and also add a little more water, vinegar or sugar if required. It can be made without the apple, but they do give a pleasant tart flavour. Serves at least 6.

SPINACH is such a good vegetable, and there are several varieties which are easy both to grow and to cook in many ways. The seeds come up like grass, and there are winter and summer varieties. An excellent one is seakale spinach, known variously as silver spinach, spinach beet, chard and so on. It has long, thick white stems, which should be removed from the green head and cooked separately in any way suitable for seakale. That is, it can be served with melted butter and lemon, in a cheese sauce, with a vinaigrette dressing or cooked in a casserole with other vegetables. Cooked and mixed with cooked pasta, then covered with cheese sauce makes a filling meal. It has a simple and delicious taste. The green leaves are used in any way suitable for spinach.

Spinach should be well washed and cooked with very little water as it makes liquid. It also boils down considerably so cook at least 1 lb (450 g) for 2–3 people. When cooked it must be well drained, and it can then be heated with a little butter, pepper, salt, a pinch of mace or nutmeg. Chopped garlic, raisins, pine-nuts and a little oil can also be added for special occasions. It makes a most excellent tart (see page 89), and also a delightful ring or crown if baked in a ring mould. The centre can be filled with a macédoine of mixed vegetables, (with poached or hard-boiled eggs on top if liked) creamed mushrooms, chicken in a cream sauce or sausages cooked in cider.

See also lasagne (page 62), and green gnocchi (page 66).

Spinach crown

This is really a 'soufflé without tears'.

8 oz (225 g) cooked, puréed, dry spinach	3 beaten eggs
	1 cup milk
1 tablespoon plain flour	Pinch of nutmeg
1 tablespoon melted butter	Salt and pepper

Mix together all the ingredients very well. Butter a ring or savarin mould, pour the mixture into it, cover with buttered foil, and cook in a dish of water for about 30 minutes in a moderate oven (350°F/180°C/Gas Mark 4). Turn out on to a warmed serving dish and fill the centre with whatever mixture you prefer. Serves 4–6 depending on the filling.

TOMATOES have so many uses that it is difficult to single out special ones. However, perhaps the most simple way, and also one of the best, is to remove the heel at the top and to fill the depression with pulped garlic. Put them on a tray and bake in a moderate oven, near the top for about 20 minutes, or less depending on size. They acquire a most complex flavour. You can also fill large tomatoes with the stuffing given on page 75, under stuffed aubergine, to make a more substantial meal, but the garlic tomatoes served with a savoury rice take a lot of beating. Tomatoes, when very ripe, peeled and served cut in two and marinated in their own juice and sugar, make a very good sweet dish, especially with whipped cream. They are, after all, fruits and not vegetables, and should sometimes be treated as such.

See also tomato flan, both sweet and savoury kinds (page 89).

TURNIPS or SWEDES make a good winter vegetable in casseroles, or as an accompaniment. They also make a good topping instead of potato. They are pleasant boiled, then mashed with plenty of pepper, butter and a discreet pinch of cinnamon. Or the following Balkan method is very good. Peel and dice about 2 lb (1 kg) turnips and put them into a fireproof dish. Then mix 1 tablespoon paprika with 1 cup cider, season the turnips with salt and pepper, then pour the cider over, and dot the top with a little butter. Cover, and simmer for about ½ hour, or until they are tender. Mix 1 cup of cottage cheese with 2 teaspoons paprika and heat, but do not boil, pour over the turnips, mix well and serve. Potatoes are very good done this way, too. Serves 4–6.

VEGETABLE FLANS OR TARTS make exceptionally good meals, and they freeze well for future use. The basis for many of them is similar: for instance, the well-known quiche is an 8–9 inch (200–225 mm) pastry case filled with a little softened onion, and bacon as well if available, with about 2 eggs beaten with ½ pint (300 ml) milk or cream then poured over, the top sometimes sprinkled with grated cheese, and then the whole baked in a moderate oven (375°F/190°C/Gas Mark 5) for about 30 minutes. This can be done with softened onions, leeks (chopped into 2 inch (50 mm) lengths), courgettes cut into thin rings, mushrooms, sweet peppers and many other vegetables. Personally, I do not bake the pastry blind first, but use a tip of my grandmother's, which is to paint the bottom of the uncooked pastry with a little of the beaten egg. This prevents it becoming soggy, and means that the pastry never gets too brown during a double cooking. It is essential to soften the vegetables first in a little oil or butter as they would not be cooked properly if put in raw.

Cottage cheese, about 2 tablespoons, added to the quiche gives a lovely creamy flavour. It should be sieved, and flavoured with a little nutmeg if used with bacon only, and no onion.

Parsnip tart makes a delicate and delicious pudding: it tastes not unlike an ambrosial banana when cooked this way.

4 medium parsnips	Pinch of mixed spice
2 tablespoons honey	Grated rind and juice of
2 tablespoons sugar	1 lemon
Pinch of ground ginger	2 eggs, separated

Boil the parsnips without salt, and drain them well, then purée them. They should make about 2 cups of purée. Mix this with the honey, 1 tablespoon sugar, the ginger, spice, lemon rind and juice, and the 2 eggyolks, and beat well. Put this into a flan case lined with pastry and straighten the top. Put into a moderate oven (375°F/190°C/Gas Mark 5) and bake for about 20 minutes or until the pastry is beginning to colour. Meanwhile beat up the eggwhites with the remaining sugar until stiff and put on top of the tart. Return to the oven for about 10 minutes or until the meringue is set, and the peaks are golden brown. Serve warm or cold. Or use only 1 whole egg in the purée, and put the pastry trimmings lattice fashion across the top, brush with egg or milk and bake as above. Serves 4–6.

Spinach tart is one of my favourite dishes. It can be made in one large tart, or in several smaller ones. I have often used these tarts for a cold buffet for they not only look attractive but are quite delicious with cold meats or poultry. Shortcrust or flaky pastry can be used, and the filling for an 8–9 inch (200–225 mm) dish is made as follows.

8 oz (225 g) cottage cheese	2 eggs
8 oz (225 g) cooked, puréed spinach, squeezed fairly dry	1 tablespoon butter, melted
2 tablespoons grated hard cheese	Pinch of mace or nutmeg
	Salt and pepper

Mix all ingredients together and put into the pastry case and bake in a moderate oven (350°F/180°C/Gas Mark 4) for about ½ hour, or until the filling is springy when touched. Serve warm or cold. Enough for 4.

Tomato flan is a Scottish speciality. It need not be put in a pastry case but can be cooked in a fireproof dish.

4 rashers bacon	Salt and pepper
2 tablespoons oatmeal	2 eggs
4 large tomatoes, peeled	

If using pastry, roll it out and cover an 8 inch (20 cm) flan dish, then paint the bottom over with a little beaten egg. Trim the rashers and cut into large pieces and put on top. Then sprinkle with oatmeal, add a layer of tomatoes, and season to taste. Repeat this, ending with tomatoes. Pour over the beaten eggs, and bake as above in a moderate oven. Serve warm or cold.

Tomato flan (sweet)

Proceed as above with the pastry, then sprinkle with oatmeal and put in a layer of peeled tomatoes (green ones are very good), a squeeze of lemon and a sprinkle of sugar. Repeat this and pour over 1 egg beaten with ¼ pint (150 ml) top of the milk. Sprinkle over the top 2 tablespoons coarse oatmeal mixed with the same of brown sugar, and 1 tablespoon butter or margarine and bake as above.

DRIED VEGETABLES such as lentils, dried peas and all the wondrous varieties of dried beans are a very important part of our diet. They are full of protein, they keep well, and are cheap. With a pressure cooker you can have a very substantial meal in about half an hour once the beans have been soaked for several hours. It is not necessary to soak dried split peas or lentils with a pressure cooker, but if you have time it cuts down on the cooking.

Basically the following recipes for beans, dried peas or lentils are interchangeable; it is a question of what particular flavour you want to stress. They can be served as a meal on their own, or with small amounts of meat, leftover poultry joints, or sausages added, or all of these in the case of the French cassoulet.

In the nineteenth century hot pease pudding was sold in the streets of London and Dublin, and served with boiled pickled pork, salt beef or bacon. It certainly cuts down dramatically on the amount of meat eaten, and is so delicious that it is the meat that is the adjunct.

Boston baked beans make a wonderful winter dish.

1 lb (450 g) dried white beans, soaked	1 tablespoon brown sugar
8 oz (225 g) streaky pork or bacon	Pepper
2 tablespoons black treacle	1 pint (600 ml) water
1 teaspoon dry mustard	Salt
2 tablespoons tomato purée	1 onion
	Sprig of thyme and leaf of sage

Do not salt beans until they have been cooking for at least ½ hour as this can toughen them. First of all cover the beans with water, boil for 10 minutes, then drain. Put half the beans in a casserole or pressure cooker, then put the pork in one piece on the top and cover with the remaining beans. Mix together the treacle, mustard, tomato purée, sugar, pepper and water, then pour it over. (If pressure cooking them see that the water covers the beans. Pressure cooking time is 30 minutes after pressure is reached. If you prefer you can half cook the beans, then transfer them to a casserole and finish them in the oven.) Cover and bring to just under boiling point, then transfer to a low oven (225°F/110°C/Gas Mark ½) and cook for about 3 hours. Every hour stir the beans and if they seem dry add a little more hot water. An hour before serving take off the lid and bring the pork to the top to brown. Serves about 8.

Cassoulet de Toulouse is similar to the American dish, but it is not sweet and contains more meat.

If using a pressure cooker half cook the beans in water for 15 minutes, then proceed with the recipe. Otherwise cook the soaked beans with garlic cloves, bouquet garni and the rind from the salt pork, with water to cover, for about 1½ hours. Then drain, but reserve the liquid.

1 lb (450 g) medium haricot beans	8 oz (225 g) sausages, preferably continental ones, or a piece of salami
2 cloves garlic	
1 large onion	
Bouquet of herbs	Salt and pepper
8 oz (225) g) salt pork or bacon	2 peeled tomatoes
1 lb (450 g) breast or shoulder lamb, boned or boned neck chops	2 heaped tablespoons breadcrumbs

Prepare the beans as given above, making certain to boil them first and throw away that water. After that, and during the second boiling, add the salt and pepper; then roast the pork and the lamb in a moderate oven, also the sausages if the ordinary type, but boil them with the beans if they are a continental kind. When the beans are ready and you have drained them but reserved the juice, throw out the onion and herbs, then put a layer of beans at the bottom of a deep fireproof dish, then the sliced tomatoes, chopped meat and sausages. Cover with the rest of the beans and add a large cupful of the reserved liquid. Sprinkle the breadcrumbs over the top and cook in a low oven (225°F/100°C/Gas Mark ½) for about 1–1½ hours. The breadcrumbs should have formed a crust and some cooks stir that crust in and add a second one halfway through cooking. When checking on the first crust, see that the beans are not too dry, if so add a little more of the bean stock.

The fine smell will sharpen most appetites and it is a hearty meal for about 6 people. If you have wings or legs of cold duck or goose they can be added with the other meats, likewise a meaty ham-bone, but don't add odd pieces of meat and destroy the fine flavour.

Beans soaked and cooked as in the pre-cooking above, for 1½ hours, or in a pressure cooker for ½ hour, are very good used as a salad when drained and mixed with a little oil. They can also be cooked with onion and herbs until they are tender, then short macaroni or other small pasta is added, and the dish is cooked for a further 20–30 minutes. It is well seasoned to taste and some chopped parsley and grated cheese are added. This is called *fagioli e pasta*, and is popular all over Italy.

Lentil casserole uses the brown or green lentils and can be served as given, or it is quite delicious if an additional 1 lb (450 g) of chopped lean lamb or pork is added.

4 tablespoons oil	3 fresh peeled or tinned tomatoes
1 large onion	Sprig of thyme
2 carrots	Salt and pepper
3 stalks celery — all sliced	1 tablespoon parsley
1 large clove garlic	8 oz (225 g) bacon, pork or lamb (optional)
1 lb (450 g) lentils, soaked	

Heat the oil and lightly fry the onion, carrots, celery, and garlic until just soft but not coloured. Then add the lentils and turn them well in the oil. Add the tomatoes, the thyme and seasonings. Cover with water, bring to the boil, then simmer, covered for about 1½ hours, or until the lentils are tender. Add a little more water if it looks dry, but don't make it soupy. Sprinkle lavishly with parsley before serving. If using the meat, chop it into cubes and brown it first of all in the oil, then add the onion and so on. To give it an authentic touch pour over a trickle of olive oil just before serving, and if you like garlic add about 1 large pressed clove and mix it in. Serves about 8 people.

See also lentil soup (page 17).

Pease pudding is one of the oldest English dishes and used to be sold on little barrows in the streets. It can be served with boiled salt pork, bacon or salt beef. Any left over is easily made into soup with the addition of more water, stock or milk.

1 lb (450 g) yellow or green split peas	Salt and pepper
1 large onion	1 tablespoon butter
1 diced rasher of bacon or a ham bone	1 teaspoon Worcestershire sauce

Soak the peas for at least 4 hours, slice the onion, dice the bacon and mix with the peas and add enough water or ham stock to come about 1 inch (25 mm) over the top. Cover and simmer for about 1½–2 hours, or until the peas are quite soft and can be mashed with a fork. Stir from time to time to prevent burning. Before serving, season and beat in the butter and add Worcestershire sauce to taste. Pressure cooking time is 30 minutes. Serves at least 6.

Dahl is the Indian lentil or split pea soup and sauce. It is good either as an accompaniment to rice, with a curry, or with hard-boiled eggs, as a soup, or even as an vegetable served with Western-style food.

1 lb (450 g) orange lentils or split peas	Oriental shops)
6 large bayleaves	3 teaspoons salt
16 whole black peppercorns	2 heaped teaspoons sugar
2 small chillies or pinch of chilli powder	2 level teaspoons turmeric
1 heaped teaspoon garam masala (obtainable from	6 inch (15 cm) piece of cinnamon bark
	1 medium onion
	Little oil

Put the lentils in a large saucepan and shake them out until they cover the bottom evenly, then pour over cold water to a depth above the lentils of five times the depth of the lentil layer. Heat to boiling and stir from time to time to prevent them clumping together as the water heats. While it is doing so, add all the other ingredients except the onion and oil. Simmer gently, stirring periodically to prevent sticking, and when the lentils swell and the liquid is much reduced, which will take about 1½ hours, prepare the garnish. (If the lentils are still too liquid, then raise the heat slightly to reduce.) Heat the oil until hot in a frying pan, then add the thinly sliced onion and fry until quite dark brown. Drain on kitchen paper and just before serving add two-thirds of the onions to the *dahl*, keeping the rest to scatter on top. Serves at least 6 people.

See also the chapter on 'Free foods from Nature' (pages 150–6).

8. The cheaper kinds of fish

Apart from herrings and mackerel in season, fish is no longer the cheap food that it was a few years ago. However, it is important for its food value as it not only contains protein and vitamins but is easily digested. It is perfect summer food, for it is light yet satisfying, and extremely good in winter.

Fish and chips, now a national dish, do not appear in any cookery books until the late nineteenth century. Fried fish to take away was brought to England by the many Italian immigrants who came to Britain at the time of the *Risorgimento* (1860), some of whom made a living selling ice-cream and others selling an anglicized form of *fritto misto de mare* from their brightly painted carts in the streets. Chips first appeared in Dundee about 1870, sold by the Belgian Edward de Gurnier and his wife, who had a stall providing them with hot, boiled peas, as they had been used to doing in Belgium. Who could have thought that such a felicitous marriage was in the offing?

So many fish dishes are spoilt by overcooking: apart from very large fish, cooked either whole or in steaks, fish requires very gentle and quick cooking to achieve perfection. When poaching fish, never let the water or stock (which you have made from the bones and skin) reach more than a slow simmer. If you live near the sea, then try steaming or poaching your fish between layers of seaweed. It will give it a beautiful taste and prevent it drying out. River fish can likewise be poached with wild herbs, such as wild mint, sorrel, wild thyme, young nettle tops and even a few pine needles. Make a bed of these fragrant leaves and put the cleaned fish on the top. Incidentally, new potatoes are excellent cooked in sea-water, the skins left on and removed after cooking. Remember to try it when on a camping or caravan holiday.

The Portuguese and the Japanese, both peoples who consume large quantities of fish, always prepare fish first by covering it well with coarse salt for a few hours before cooking. The Portuguese also add a few coriander seeds. The fish should be drained before being cooked in whichever way you choose.

Herbs probably make more difference to fish cookery than to any other. Do try and use sprigs of fresh fennel (which grows so easily once established), lemon balm, lemon thyme, burnet and dill, even a pinch of sage with fatty fishes such as mackerel is good. If you feel you really must have a more expensive fish dish from time to time, then choose a recipe which stretches it, or use cider instead of wine and stabilized yoghurt or cottage cheese instead of cream.

FISHES TO TRY

ANGLER FISH

Don't ignore a fish such as angler or monkfish if you see it on sale: it is an ugly fish and therefore usually sold without its head, but the flesh is solid, milky and well-flavoured. It has no bones but only a cartilaginous spine. The texture is firm, almost like a lobster, and it needs longer cooking than most fish. I usually marinate it in lemon juice, a little oil, herbs and salt for a couple of hours before cooking. It is very good when cut into

chunks and threaded on to skewers with chunks of tomato, mushrooms, bacon and chunks of bread soaked in oil and rubbed with garlic. Add a bayleaf or two as well if you like, then grill them on all sides, not too fast, so that the middle gets cooked through. 2 lb (1 kg) fish makes a good meal for about 6 people done in this way. Kebabs are a good way of stretching expensive fish or shellfish such as scallops. They can be mixed with other fish such as angler.

Baked angler

Marinate the fish as above, then bake it in the marinade with a little water or stock for at least 40 minutes in a moderate oven (350°F/180°C/Gas Mark 4). You can add tomatoes, mushrooms or thick slices of half-cooked potato if you like, and sometimes I sprinkle the potato with cheese. The potatoes are a good idea as they thicken the sauce. It can also be baked in tomato sauce (page 27), and it is good poached, then served cold with mayonnaise. Dogfish, coley and cod can be cooked as above.

GURNARD or GURNET

There are three species of gurnard, grey, yellow and red. All are quite acceptable as they have a firm, white flesh which is good for baking. They are best served in a sauce with the bones removed first. Or select one of the sauces given below.

Baked gurnard

Also good for a whole small bass.

1 large gurnard (at least 4 lb (2 kg) – the head is large)	3 tablespoons olive oil
	1 pint (600 ml) water mixed with 1 tablespoon tomato
Salt and pepper	purée or use equal
½ teaspoon crushed coriander seeds	quantities water and cider
Bunch of parsley	
1 lemon	

Rub the fish with salt, pepper and crushed coriander and put into a fireproof dish. Sprinkle with plenty of chopped parsley, and arrange the whole lemon, sliced, along the backbone. Pour over the oil, then surround with the water. Cover with foil and bake for ¾ hour in a moderate oven (350°F/180°C/Gas Mark 4), basting with the liquid at least once during cooking. It can be eaten hot, of course, but in either case carve it along the spine as if carving a duck. This way you will avoid the worst of the bones, and as it is a cheap fish you can afford to waste a bit. If serving cold, make a good mayonnaise and mix it with the juice of ½ lemon and 1 tablespoon grated horseradish. Serves 6.

SMALL FILLETS of fish such as lemon or witch sole, whiting, pollock or plaice can be very pleasant if the fillets comprise the whole side of the fish. My way is as follows.

Sprinkle each fillet with salt and lemon juice, then spread over 1 fillet about 2 teaspoons cottage cheese. Add a good spoonful of mixed herbs and a tiny nut of butter. Put the other side on top and put on to a grilling pan with the black side up. Pour over a very little oil and a sprinkle of salt, then grill until the skin blisters slightly. Turn over and do the other side. The 'sandwich' of fish and buttery, herby cottage cheese is quite delicious. Or if you prefer you can roll up each fillet singly, then put them side by side into an ovenproof dish and cover with 3–4 tablespoons cider and a nut of butter on each roll. Then bake in a moderate oven (350°F/180°C/Gas Mark 4) for not longer than ½ hour.

Variation: Add a pinch of curry powder and a little chopped apple or pineapple to the stuffing.

Gratin of fish

This is good for small fillets which don't have a lot of taste on their own. Or haddock, hake, cod, etc. can all be used, but they should be free of bones.

Approx. 1 tablespoon butter	Salt and pepper
2 large tomatoes, peeled	6 tablespoons fresh breadcrumbs
2 lb (1 kg) white fish, filleted	1 tablespoon mixed chopped herbs
1 lemon	

Lightly butter an ovenproof dish, then arrange the sliced tomatoes on the bottom. Put the fish fillets on top, add half the lemon juice and salt and pepper. Then mix the grated rind of the lemon with the breadcrumbs and herbs and arrange over the top. Dot with the remaining butter and bake for ½ hour in a moderate oven (350°F/180°C/Gas Mark 4). Serves 4–6.

WHITE FISH steaks such as cod, pollock, bass, whiting, hake or even chunks of angler are good cooked as I once had snapper done in America. The fruit-tasting butter is exquisite. It is also a marvellous way of cooking skate or ray.

Salt	orange and grapefruit
4 fish steaks	peel and 1 tablespoon
4 tablespoons butter	juice from each fruit
1 tablespoon each grated	Good pinch of nutmeg

Salt the fish then lightly grease an ovenproof dish. Put the steaks into it and pour over the rest of the butter, melted. Put some orange and grapefruit peel on each fillet, sprinkle on the nutmeg and finally trickle the juices over. Then cover and bake for about ½ hour in a moderate oven (350°F/180°C/Gas Mark 4). Serves 4.

Italian baked fish cutlets

Almost any white fish can be used, such as cod, hake, haddock, brill, etc., and the sweet-sour sauce, beloved of the Italians, gives an excellent flavour.

4 fish cutlets or steaks	Pinch of dried fennel
1 × 15 oz (425 g) tin	seeds or marjoram
tomatoes	1 small onion, sliced
2 tablespoons clear	1 green pepper, cut into
honey or brown sugar	rings
Juice of 1 lemon	1 bayleaf
1 teaspoon tomato	
purée	

Put the cutlets into a lightly greased ovenproof dish. Pour the juice from the tomatoes into a bowl and add the honey, lemon juice, tomato purée and the herbs. Cover the fish with the sliced onion, pepper rings and the tomatoes, then pour over the prepared sauce, finally adding the crumbled bayleaf. Cover and bake for 30 minutes at (375°F/190°C/Gas Mark 5). Serves 4.

Smoked haddock with tomatoes makes a good meal full of flavour, and any leftovers can be mixed with mashed potato, bound with an egg, then rolled in flour and fried as fishcakes the following day.

1 lb (450 g) smoked	Few drops of Tabasco
haddock or cod	1 × 7 oz (195 g) tin
½ pint (300 ml) milk	tomatoes
1 tablespoon cornflour	Little grated cheese
2 cloves garlic	
2 tablespoons chopped	
parsley	

First poach the fish in the milk, then remove but reserve the stock. Break the fish into flakes, removing the bones, and put into an ovenproof dish. Thicken the stock with the creamed cornflour, stirring all the time to avoid lumps, then add the chopped garlic, parsley, Tabasco and the tomatoes, seeing that the juice is not making the sauce too thin. Mix the fish with this sauce and scatter the grated cheese over the top. Bake at (350°F/180°C/Gas Mark 4,) for 30 minutes. Serves 4, or 2 and fishcakes the next day.

HERRING

The nineteenth-century naturalist Lacépède said that 'Herring is one of those productions which decide the destiny of empires' and this was certainly true of many of the Baltic and Northern ports where, in medieval times, many cities prospered enormously from the sales of the herring shoals in the North Sea.

The delicacy of flavour of the fresh herring is famous throughout the Western world today and we are indeed fortunate to be able to procure these excellent fish at moderate prices.

Bones are often off-putting with regard to herrings; it is simple to remove the backbone, but often the tickly little rib bones remain. However, if you really do dislike them then run your fingers over the side flaps and if you feel bones there, then snip them off with the scissors, or remove them with a sharp knife. The black skin of fish too, is disliked by many people, although they don't mind the white skin. If you find it difficult to remove, then try my method. Put the fish, skin-side down, into a really hot, non-stick pan, without adding anything else. Leave it for a few minutes, then take out and you will find the black skin peels off easily. If you prefer you can put it, skin-side towards the heat, under a hot grill for a few minutes, and it will have the same effect. It only needs a few minutes so don't leave it too long or the fish cooks and dries up.

My favourite way of serving herring fillets is still with mustard and medium oatmeal, and it is done as follows.

Herring with mustard and oatmeal

8 herring fillets	Salt and pepper
Approx. 1 tablespoon made French mustard (*blanc de Dijon* if possible)	4 tablespoons medium or fine oatmeal
	1 lemon

First line the grilling pan with foil, then put the fillets on top, skin-side up. Grill for a few minutes until the skin blisters slightly. Take away from the grill and peel off the skin. Paint the flesh with mustard and sprinkle over a little salt, pepper and oatmeal, then grill again until the oatmeal is crisp, about two minutes. Turn with a slice and do the same to the other side. When ready, about 10 minutes in all, serve with lemon wedges. Serves 4.

Variation: Instead of mustard and oatmeal, use pounded peanuts mixed with pounded cornflakes.

G

Potted or **soused** herrings are still a popular dish, but have you tried them baked in tea? It is a Cornish recipe, and unbelievably good. It can also be used for mackerel.

8 cleaned herrings	½ pint (300 ml) of equal parts of white vinegar and cold milkless tea
8 bayleaves	
20 black peppercorns	
1 tablespoon brown sugar	

Remove the black skin as above, if preferred, then lay the cleaned and filleted fish, with a bayleaf inside each one, side by side in an ovenproof dish. Sprinkle over the peppercorns and brown sugar evenly, and finally pour over the mixed vinegar and tea. Cover with foil or a lid, and bake in a moderate oven (350°F/180°C/Gas Mark 4) for about ½ hour (or for a longer time at a lower heat). Leave to get cold in the juice, when it will be slightly jellied. Serve cold with a salad made from potato, beetroot, onion and apple, covered with oil and vinegar or lemon juice.

Variation: Use either cider or a light beer instead of tea. One sliced onion can be added with these liquids, but not with the tea. Also a few cloves or a piece of mace is a good idea.

Herrings can also be stuffed and baked. The simplest stuffing is to use 1 heaped tablespoon breadcrumbs per fish mixed with fresh herbs, a pinch of mace, the grated rind of a lemon and either a little knob of butter or, if there is enough stuffing, an egg. If the fish have roes, then chop and add them as well. Roll up the fillets, put into an ovenproof dish and add enough light beer or cider to come to halfway up, then cover and bake in a moderate oven (350°F/180°C/Gas Mark 4) for about 35 minutes.

On the sea coasts of Scotland, where this dish comes from, about ½ inch (12 mm) of sea-water is used instead of the cider.

MACKEREL

Cape Cod mackerel

1 tin concentrated orange juice (frozen)	1 tablespoon butter or margarine
1 tablespoon soft brown sugar	4 large mackerel, either filleted or cleaned and left on the bone
1 tablespoon soy sauce	

Unfreeze the orange juice then add the sugar, soy sauce and butter and heat up to boiling point. Put the fish in a baking tin, pour over the sauce, cover with foil and bake in a moderate to hot oven (375°–400°F/190°–200°C/Gas Mark 5–6) for about ½ hour. This recipe is also very good for thick white fish, such as cod steaks.

Baked mackerel with orange stuffing

1 large orange	1 small apple
2 tablespoons fresh breadcrumbs	Salt and pepper
1 small onion	4 mackerel, cleaned
1 tablespoon chopped parsley	½ pint (300 ml) cider

First, finely grate the zest of the orange on to a large plate, then quarter it, carve out the flesh and coarsely chop it. Mix with the breadcrumbs, finely chopped onion, parsley and the peeled and grated apple. Season well, then fill the fish with this stuffing. Put into a fire-proof dish, pour the cider around, cover with foil and bake for about 25–30 minutes in a moderate oven (350°F/180°C/Gas Mark 4). Serve with a little of the juice when hot, or leave to get cold and serve drained, with lettuce salad and slices of fresh orange. Serves 4.

Mackerel en papillotes

Clean the fish and put a small wedge of lemon and some chopped herbs (fennel if possible) in the gullet, lay on a largish piece of foil, then paint the fish with oil and season with salt, pepper and a pinch of ginger and mace. Wrap the foil up, securing it well so that the juices don't escape, then put into a baking tin and bake for about 25 minutes in a moderate oven (350°F/180°C/Gas Mark 4). Serve each fish in its foil, 1 per person, with some extra lemon. This way of cooking fish stops any odour going through the house. Baked, fried or grilled mackerel is excellent with gooseberry sauce or rhubarb sauce (page 105).

Mackerel pâté

4 mackerel, either fresh or smoked	2 tablespoons plain yoghurt or cottage cheese
4 tablespoons dry breadcrumbs slightly toasted	Salt, pepper and a good pinch of mace
Juice of 1 lemon	2 stiffly beaten eggwhites

If the mackerel is fresh cook it in foil as above (smoked mackerel is already cooked), then take all the fish from the bones, also the skin. Mash it up very well so that it is a paste, then add the breadcrumbs and lemon juice, mixing very well. Stir in the yoghurt or cottage cheese, beating well, and season to taste (if you have a liquidizer this will all only take about 1 minute). Meanwhile beat up the eggwhites and gently fold them in. Shape into a mound, or put into a dish and chill very thoroughly before serving. This pâté has a delicate flavour and the mackerel does not taste at all fatty. Makes enough for about 6–8 people.

Variation: Kipper and smoked cod's roe can also be used instead of mackerel.

Herrings and mackerel can be potted in Guinness to great advantage. Roll 8 filleted fish from head to tail and place together in a fireproof dish. Scatter a finely chopped onion and a small chopped carrot around, also 2 bayleaves and about 12 black peppercorns. Season lightly, then pour over ½ pint (300 ml) Guinness. Cover and bake in a moderate oven (350°F/180°C/Gas Mark 4) for about 35 minutes. Serve either warm or cold.

KIPPERS can be used in many ways, not simply as a breakfast dish. They are good served with scrambled eggs, and they can also be used for a kedgeree (*see* page 101). They are also pleasant grilled and filleted, then served with boiled rice and a wedge of lemon. A sort of coarse smoked salmon can also be made with them.

Marinated kippers

Soak raw boneless kippers completely in lemon juice for at least 6 hours, preferably overnight, turning them at least once. Drain (but reserve the juice as it can be used again), carve very thinly, and serve with brown bread and butter. Some cooks add an oil and vinegar dressing, but in my opinion this rather spoils the taste.

COD'S ROE used to be a traditional breakfast dish in Ireland, served crisp and golden alongside rashers of bacon. It is at the height of its season in the spring and there are many ways of preparing this succulent food, for all courses and many occasions. It can be bought ready cooked, but usually I prefer to buy it raw and cook it myself. Do not choose too large a roe; the smaller ones have a more delicate flavour. It has the added advantage of being not only nutritious but also cheap.

Many young housewives today have never tasted it, and the salmon-pink floppy balloons of roe give no hint of its delightful taste. I tried it out on three young people, in very small quantities, and before I knew what had happened it had all gone in second helpings. If bought raw, it is cooked in the following way. It freezes very well either raw or cooked.

To cook raw cod's roe

Put on a medium-sized saucepan of salted water, with an added dash of white vinegar, and let it heat. Wrap the roe either in a piece of cheesecloth or in foil, and put it into the hot water. Let it cook very gently – the water should just bubble and no more – for about 30 minutes. When cool, remove from the water and let it get cold before further preparation. Take off the outer membrane before using, but leave it on until you use the roe as it keeps it moist.

Cod's roe fritters (1)

1 lb (450 g) cooked cod's roe cut into circular slices about ¼ inch (6mm) thick	2 tablespoons flour
	2 tablespoons oil
	Wedges of lemon or Tabasco
1 egg	

Remove the skin from the roe slices, then beat the egg in a flat soup-plate. Dip the rounds of roe in flour, and then in the egg. Heat up the oil until hot but not smoking, and drop in the fritters. Fry on both sides until golden. Serve on toast or on French toast, with grilled rashers or tomatoes or mushrooms, etc., and garnish with lemon wedges or Tabasco. 1 lb (450 g) cod's roe makes at least 16–20 fritters.

Cod's roe fritters (2)

1 cooked cod's roe, cut into circular slices as above	2 tablespoons SR flour
2 eggs	Salt and cayenne pepper
¼ pint (150 ml) milk	Approx. ¼ pint (150 ml) oil

Prepare the rounds of cod's roe as in the preceding recipe, then make a batter from the beaten eggs, milk, flour and seasonings until it has a soft texture like sponge dough. Have the oil almost smoking hot, dip the roe in the batter so that both sides are coated, then drop into the oil, and fry until golden brown on both sides. Drain on kitchen paper before serving and keep warm. They puff up well, and make about 30 fritters.

Variation: If preferred about 8 oz (225 g) roe can be skinned, mashed up and added to the above batter before frying in spoonfuls as given above.

Cod's roe pâté (1) is excellent for smoked cod's roe, also for smoked mackerel or trout. Best made in a liquidizer, but can be made without.

1 lb (450 g) cooked cod's roe	2 tablespoons lemon juice
2 eggwhites	1 tablespoon olive oil
1 clove pulped garlic	Salt
8 oz (225 g) cottage cheese	Dash of Tabasco or cayenne pepper
¼ pint (150 ml) plain yoghurt	

Skin the roe, and mash it up thoroughly if not using a liquidizer. Beat the eggwhites until stiff. Combine all the ingredients, leaving the eggwhites until last, and season to taste. If using a liquidizer put it all (except eggwhites) on high speed for 1 minute; otherwise beat well until it is thoroughly amalgamated, and fold in the eggwhites last. Chill and serve with toast. Serves at least 6 people.

Cod's roe pâté (2) is like the Greek *taramasalata* except that cod's roe is used instead of grey mullet roe.

8 oz (225 g) cooked cod's roe	2 tablespoons olive oil
2 slices crustless white bread, about ½ inch (12 mm) thick	Juice of 1 lemon
	Pinch of mace to taste
	Freshly-ground white pepper
Approx. 4 tablespoons milk	1 clove pulped garlic (optional)

Remove the skin from the roe, and mash it up well. Soak the bread slices in the milk (you may need a little more to make it soft, but do not make it sloppy) and leave it until absorbed, about 10 minutes. Combine the bread and roe and beat well. Add the oil gradually, beating all the time, then the lemon juice, and finally season to taste, putting in the mace first, so that you can see how much pepper you require. It may need a little salt, but do taste it, for some seems to be more salty than others. Chill and serve with thin toast. Serves 6.

Cod's roe also makes a very good soufflé-type dish, which was popular in the last century.

Cod's roe ramkins

12 oz (338 g) cooked cod's roe	1 tablespoon chopped parsley
2 cups loosely packed fresh white breadcrumbs	Juice of ½ lemon
½ teaspoon mace	2 eggs, separated
Salt and pepper	4 tablespoons cream or top of milk

Mash the roe (with the outer skin removed) with the breadcrumbs, mace and seasonings. Add the parsley, lemon juice, and the beaten eggyolks mixed with the cream. Leave for about 10 minutes, until the breadcrumbs have absorbed all the moisture, then fold in the stiffly beaten eggwhites. Put the mixture either into individual greased fireproof dishes or into 1 large one, and cook in a hot oven (400°F/200°C/Gas Mark 6) for about 15 minutes for the small ones or 30 minutes for the large one, or until it is puffed up and golden brown. Serves 4.

This is served hot, but is excellent cold, especially if when cool it is covered with either aspic or about 4 tablespoons consommé which will jelly when cold.

Variation: The above mixture is very good put (well mixed and before cooking) into a pastry case. The top is sprinkled with a little grated Parmesan cheese, and it is baked for ½ hour in a moderate oven (350°F/180°C/Gas Mark 4). Can be served hot or cold.

The fritters given above make an excellent garnish for all kinds of fried or grilled fish. Cod's roe also makes an excellent filling for pancakes or an omelette, or for green peppers.

Green peppers stuffed with cod's roe

6 green or red peppers	water mixed with 3 teaspoons tomato purée
1 lb (450 g) cod's roe	
1 pint (600 ml) stock or	

Remove the seeds from the peppers by cutting a circle at the top and spooning out the seeds and stalk. Then steam them, standing up, for about 10 minutes. Cool slightly, then fill them with cooked, mashed, seasoned cod's roe. Put into a fireproof dish and pour the liquid around, and then bake gently in a moderate oven (350°F/180°C/Gas Mark 4) for about 20 minutes. Serve either hot or cold. Serves 3–6 depending on whether you use them for a first or main course.

WAYS OF MAKING FISH GO FURTHER

Kebabs (mentioned on page 128) are a very good way of stretching fish and particularly shellfish. There are days when one longs for the taste of a large scallop, and if it is cut into chunks and then skewered with other cheaper fish, vegetables and pieces of bread, it goes considerably further. Not only that but the other fish becomes impregnated with the scallop's distinctive taste.

Kedgeree is a well-known dish which originated in India. The word comes from the Indian word *khicharhi* and originally the dish consisted of rice, onion, cooked lentils, spices, fresh lime or lemon, butterfat and fish. In fact this makes an excellent dish and is worth trying if you have some lentils left over. Kedgeree is best made with a strong tasting fish. Smoked haddock is very good, and when salmon is at its cheapest do try it using a little salmon instead. It makes a dish worthy of a good summer luncheon.

2 hard-boiled eggs
2 large cups cooked boned fish
8 oz (225 g) cooked rice
2 heaped tablespoons butter
Salt and pepper
Pinch of ground coriander and nutmeg
Squeeze of lemon juice
2 tablespoons plain yoghurt
Parsley or chives for garnish

Cut up the eggs and combine with all the other ingredients except the yoghurt and herbs. Put into a buttered fireproof dish, cover with a piece of foil, then bake in a hot oven (400°F/200°C/Gas Mark 6) for about 15–20 minutes. Just before serving, spoon over the cold yoghurt and garnish with the fresh herbs. The cold yoghurt with the hot rice and fish is very good. Serves 4.

Try it with flaked crabmeat, and add 2 peeled tomatoes as well.

Pasta makes an interesting dish if mixed with the kedgeree ingredients, omitting the rice. Pasta is good mixed with small shellfish such as mussels, cockles or clams, then garnished with fresh herbs and mixed with an oil and vinegar dressing. Small chunks of fish such as angler can be used too. *See also* pasta with vongole sauce (page 64), for which mussels can be used instead of clams.

Couliabyaka is a marvellous Russian way of serving an expensive fish such as salmon, as very little is needed to make an impressive dish for about 6 people. It can be served hot or cold, and the fish inside can be a mixture of cheap and more expensive fish without the dish losing flavour.

1 lb (450 g) salmon, angler, turbot, halibut, hake, etc.
2 oz (60 g) butter
2 cups cooked rice
2 hard-boiled eggs
1 tablespoon chopped fresh herbs, e.g. parsley, fennel, dill, chives
Salt and pepper
8 oz (225 g) puff or shortcrust pastry (*see* page 143)
1 cup sour cream or whipped cottage cheese

Fillet the fish, then either lightly fry chunks of it in the butter, or poach it whole very lightly and then cube it. Mix it with the rice, sliced eggs, herbs and seasoning and shape into an oblong. Roll out the pastry to a large sheet about 12 × 10 inches (30 × 35 cm) and put the fish mixture along it. If you haven't used the butter then dot it along the mixture and also the thick sour cream or cheese. Wrap the pastry up and secure at the top, first dampening the edges with egg or milk. Paint the top with beaten egg, then put on to a baking sheet and bake until golden brown in a moderate oven. Serves about 6.

Pasties made from similiar ingredients to the *couliabyaka* make good picnic or packed lunch fare.

SHELLFISH have in general become too pricey for the average housewife to use in any great amounts. However, some of the dishes suggested above can be used, and shellfish such as mussels are still within the reach of most pockets. Cockles and clams are too, but, except in Wales, they are hardly ever seen in fishmongers' shops. All shellfish of the bivalve class must have the shells well scrubbed before cooking, and any which are half open should be discarded. They should be put into a large saucepan with a little water, wine or cider, a little chopped shallot or onion and some herbs.

Mussels

For 2 lb (1 kg) of mussels use only about 2 cups of liquid. Bring to the boil, with the lid on, and shake gently while it is coming to the boil. The bottom shells will have opened, so turn them round so that the top ones are at the bottom. They will take only about 5 minutes to cook. Strain, but reserve the juice which is of exquisite flavour. Open the mussels and remove the small beards with a knife. It is by these little fibres that the mussel adheres to the rocks. Discard any mussels which you can't open, and serve the others in a large soup-plate with the strained juice to which you have added a knob of butter worked with flour, then simmered in the stock. This will thicken it slightly. Add more fresh parsley and you have one of the finest dishes in the world.

Mussels make a good garnish to white fish, not only for their taste, but also for the colour contrast. It is worth reserving a few to add to a sauce or to add to a soup such as potato.

SAUCES FOR FISH

Butter sauce is the simplest, and also one of the best.

Heat 1 tablespoon butter per person until foaming, then add a good squeeze of lemon juice, or a few drops of wine vinegar. If using with a coarse fish such as skate or ray or cod steaks, then about 2 teaspoons (per person) picked capers and a little of the juice can also be added. Or add a few fennel or anise seeds.

In Denmark a small jug of melted butter and also a small jug of very thin made mustard (of pouring consistency) is served with large cod steaks. I have also had the melted butter mixed with a very little anchovy essence, and this goes well with fish such as whiting.

Beurre blanc is the French version of drawn butter and very good with poached, baked or braised fish, from either sea or river.

2 finely chopped shallots	Salt and white pepper
3 tablespoons white wine vinegar	8 oz (225 g) unsalted butter, cut into small pieces and chilled
2 tablespoons fish stock from the dish being cooked	

Put the shallots into a saucepan with the vinegar and the fish stock, season, and cook over a fairly high flame until the liquid is reduced by three quarters and the shallots are soft. Remove from the heat and cool. Then leave it until you want to serve the fish. Then heat up the shallot mixture until lukewarm, and rapidly whisk in the butter pieces with a fork. Lift the pan from the heat from time to time so that it does not become overhot and keep whisking in the butter until it turns to a whitish cream, not unlike a thin mayonnaise. Don't let it become oily and transparent – if it does plunge the saucepan into iced water and beat well. This makes enough for about 4 servings.

Sauce aurore is good with fish which have been poached or baked in milk, when you can use the milk to make the béchamel sauce, by adding it (warm) to 1 heaped table-spoon butter, heated and mixed with 1 level tablespoon flour, per ½ pint (300 ml) milk. When it is smooth and creamy after stirring constantly, add to it a purée made from 4 large peeled tomatoes cooked in butter with a garlic clove and 1 teaspoon onion, all well seasoned. The purée must not be watery, and should be added to the white sauce to your taste. A teaspoon of tomato purée can be added for colour.

Just before serving add a nut of butter and, if available, some fresh, chopped herbs such as parsley, fennel, chives or tarragon. Makes enough for about 4. It is done very easily in a liquidizer.

Béchamel sauce made from the stock used to cook the fish, can be the basis for many sauces.

Cheese sauce: The most usual is made by adding about 2 tablespoons grated cheese to the sauce, which is then poured over the warm fish and glazed under the grill.

Capers can be added, fresh, chopped herbs, or chopped sorrel.

Sauce Chivry is another lovely sauce, especially in the summer. To ½ pint (300 ml) béchamel, add the following. Chop 1 tablespoon each of parsley, chives and chervil, and simmer them in a glass of white wine (or cider) until only about 1 tablespoon of liquid is left. Add the liquid to the béchamel and let it simmer gently. Then cook about a handful of spinach with the herbs and when cooked, drain very well, and mash with 1 heaped table-spoon butter, or put into a blender. Just before serving mix in the spinach and butter mixture, but taste as you add it, for it should not be too aggressive in flavour. Keep the sauce warm but do not let it boil. Do not use dried herbs for this sauce.

Egg and sultana sauce: To the béchamel given above add 2 tablespoons sultanas and 2 hard-boiled eggs, sliced with a squeeze of lemon. Pour over the fish and brown under the grill. Green grapes, seeded, can be used in place of the sultanas when in season.

Gooseberry sauce is traditionally served with mackerel or herrings in Ireland. The fish can either be stuffed and baked (*see* page 97) or poached in water with salt and a little lemon juice.

8 oz (225 g) gooseberries	1 tablespoon chopped fresh fennel, if available
2 tablespoons sugar	
1 tablespoon butter	

Cook the trimmed gooseberries in ¼ cup water with the other ingredients. Do not let them overcook, but just burst open. Serve hot.

Variation: Add 1 handful of sorrel leaves instead of the fennel and 1 tablespoon more of sugar.

Mustard sauce

Mustard sauce, if it is to accompany herrings or cod, should be fairly strong. Somehow just the use of various mustards doesn't seem to be quite right, so I usually add some juice from mustard pickles.

1 heaped tablespoon butter, oil or margarine	made French mustard
1 heaped tablespoon flour	½ pint (300 ml) warm milk
1 teaspoon each dry English mustard and	Approx. 1 tablespoon mustard pickle juice

Heat the fat, then mix in the flour and dry mustard

powder, then add the warmed milk, stirring to avoid lumps. Then add the made mustard and pickle juice and mix well until smooth. Enough for 4 herrings. *See also* butter sauce (page 103).

Rhubarb sauce is a traditional sauce used in the West Country for serving with baked or grilled mackerel. It can also be served with herrings, and I have used it with success for John Dory. It is served in Poland with chicken or pork.

1 lb (450 g) chopped rhubarb	4 tablespoons brown sugar
8 tablespoons cider	Pinch of mace or nutmeg
Squeeze of lemon	

Cook all ingredients over a gentle heat until the mixture is quite soft and like a purée. It should be fairly dry, and can be liquidized if liked. Serve separately, hot with the fish. Enough for 8–10 large fish.

Sorrel sauce has a flavour like lemon and is a delicious spring or early summer sauce with white fish, mackerel, salmon and some river fish such as pike or perch.

1 heaped tablespoon butter	2–3 tablespoons stock from cooking the fish
4 oz (113 g) sorrel leaves	2 tablespoons beaten cottage cheese
½ pint (300 ml) thin cream or stabilized yoghurt (page 52)	Salt and pepper

Heat the butter until foaming, then purée the sorrel in it. This only takes a few minutes, and in fact can be made well ahead of time. As sorrel has only a short season I make up small quantities of this chiffonade and freeze it for use in the winter. Heat up the cream or the yoghurt, add the sorrel and also the fish stock and finally gradually add the beaten cottage cheese, season to taste and stir until it is all creamy and well mixed. This makes enough for about 4 servings.

Tomato sauce (page 27) is invaluable for baking fish in, and also as a basis for making fish stews or soups. Dilute it with some fish stock and then add small chunks of fish, and mussels, cockles or clams too if you have them. It can be seasoned according to taste, and with fish a dash of Tabasco is sometimes pleasant. Stalks of celery, sweet peppers and herbs can all be added to advantage. If grilled or baked fish is served with rice, then this sauce is useful as an accompaniment.

See also fish chowder (page 16) and Index entries for fish with pasta or rice.

9. Poultry and game

POULTRY

All poultry is expensive if taken solely by the weight of meat, for the carcass bones often weigh more than the flesh on them. When I was young, chicken was a luxury for high days and holidays, then it became much cheaper, but now a free-range bird is almost in the luxury class again. However, it is good meat for people who have a fat intolerance or bad digestion, or for convalescents. It is light and can easily be digested. Also it is very good served cold, and there are a myriad ways of cooking it.

The old days of the boiling fowl are almost gone. Occasionally one sees some scrawny, yellow-skinned birds, but they are not the fat, broody, second-year birds of my youth, who were killed off because they had stopped laying. My grandmother, who was Cornish, would hang them for a day or so, then rub inside and out with lemon. Then a good stuffing would be made from oatmeal or breadcrumbs, redolent with onion and herbs, and the bird was rubbed liberally with chicken fat and the whole wrapped in well-greased greaseproof paper and tied up with string.

The large steamer usually kept for Christmas puddings would be got out from the top shelf of the larder, and the fowl would be steamed, very gently, for about 4 hours or even longer if it was a right good-sized bird. Then the dampers would be pulled out of the old stove to get the oven as hot as possible, and the steaming parcel of chicken would be opened, and our lips would smack at the gorgeous smell. She then dredged the bird thickly with flour, a good shake of pepper and salt, then quickly into the roasting tin and into the oven. 'Go up and wash your hands, quickly,' she would say, and we would hurry up, then rush down the stairs and wait perhaps five minutes before the bird was dished up, golden, crisp and juicy, just as if it had been roasted all along. The roasting part never took longer than about 20 minutes, and sometimes less. The chicken fell to pieces when carved, and the taste was almost like that of pheasant, something one never finds today with factory-bred birds. You can achieve a similar effect by simmering, with water to cover, very, very slowly for about the same time.

My grandmother also used to joint a boiling bird, then layer it with thick slices of streaky bacon and all sorts of root vegetables, herbs and lots of seasoning so that every part of the pot was packed. It was covered with stock made from the body carcass and the giblets, the lid was put on the earthenware pot and all would be cooked very, very slowly in the oven for about 3–4 hours, or until the fine three-pronged steel fork, which I still have today, went into the drumstick, and it was pronounced tender.

Therefore, if you want to economize, and can't find good boiling birds but still serve poultry, it is wise to use recipes which get all the nourishment from the carcass, and also leave you with a good stock for soups. In that way, the bird is not so expensive after all. Another method is to serve chicken in curries or rice dishes, ones in which only a little chicken is used, but the flavour is so good that the little can satisfy quite a number of people.

If you feel you must roast the bird, then see that you make a good stuffing: the skirlie given on page 35 is excellent, for it has a nutty taste and is filling. I'm sure you all have ways of cooking birds which you enjoy, so I will give just a few that you may not know, yet are simple to do and also economical to make.

Chinese boiled chicken

This is a remarkable recipe, given to me by a Chinese cook we once had in India, for not only is the chicken always cooked perfectly, and the stock superb, but it saves considerably on fuel. It might sound odd to you, but once you have tried you will find it magical, for it never seems to matter what size the chicken (or duck or turkey) is, for it to be cooked to perfection.

1 large chicken	1 or 2 stock cubes
Salt	Pepper
½ lemon	*And, most important, 3*
Herbs of your choice	*silver or plate dessert*
4 pints (2¼ l) water	*spoons or forks*

Wash the bird thoroughly, then sprinkle salt inside and rub outside with half the cut lemon. Put the spoons or forks *inside* the body of the bird, and place it in a large saucepan. Add all the other ingredients, seeing that the water comes up to barely cover the bird. Cover and bring to the boil, then boil for 15 minutes only. Turn out the flame, keep the lid tightly on, and leave in a cool place until it gets completely cold. This usually takes about 4–6 hours, or do it so it rests overnight.

You will have a chicken cooked to serve cold, or, in some mysterious way, if you want to reheat it to make a chicken paprika, curry or something similar, providing you cook it gently for not more than ½ hour, it will still not be overcooked.

Before using the stock, de-fat it, then heat up and strain. You will find the stock is very good too, and often a thick jelly when cold. I often serve this chicken cold, skinned first, then coated with the following lemon sauce. It can also be reheated and served with this sauce, hot.

2 tablespoons butter	2 tablespoons chopped
2 tablespoons flour	parsley
1 pint (600 ml) warm	
chicken stock	*Garnish:*
Juice and peel of 1	About 12 prunes, stoned
lemon	Wedges of lemon

Lemon sauce

Before cutting the lemon, grate off the peel finely, and reserve for the garnish. Heat the butter, stir in the flour, then add the warm chicken stock and stir until it boils and is thick. Add the lemon juice and taste for seasoning. Let it cool slightly, then cover the bird with it. On top sprinkle the parsley and grated lemon peel, and serve on a large dish surrounded by halved, cooked, stoned prunes and lemon wedges. This is an adaptation of Hindle Wakes chicken, which is also stuffed with 1½ cups breadcrumbs, herbs, onion, 1 cup prunes, 1 tablespoon grated suet, lemon juice, a pinch of cinnamon and 1 tablespoon brown sugar. However, you would have to stuff the chicken and boil in the usual way.

Hindle Wakes is a corruption of 'Hen de la Wake', a dish first brought to Britain, by refugee Flemish weavers in the fourteenth century. It is still served during Wakes Week, particularly at Wakefield in Yorkshire.

Chicken paprika is simply made by using the 15-minute boiled chicken. Joint the bird and remove the skin, then take out about 1 pint (600 ml) of de-fatted stock. Heat about 2 tablespoons of oil and lightly sauté a finely sliced onion until it is soft, but not coloured. Pour off any excess oil, then stir 1 tablespoon paprika and 1 heaped tablespoon flour, and cook for 1 minute. Gradually add the stock until the sauce is the consistency you like, stirring all the time. Then put in the chicken joints, and let them simmer for about 5 minutes. Taste for seasoning, then add, just before serving, 1 cup of stabilized yoghurt, stir lightly, and simmer for about 1 minute. Unstabilized yoghurt can be used, but in that case do not let it reboil. Serve with rice, noodles or potatoes.

Curry sauce is good for making a chicken curry from the boiled bird: hard-boiled eggs, fish or meat can also be cooked in this curry sauce. It is not a hot curry, but full of flavour. If a hot curry is liked then add a little more chilli powder. Instead of the spices you can use a good curry paste, but the fresh spices keep well in an airtight jar, and can be used individually in other dishes. All these spices can be bought at an Oriental grocer.

2 tablespoons oil or	1 teaspoon paprika
clarified butter	½ teaspoon chilli powder
2 medium onions, finely	Pinch of ground ginger
chopped	1 small stick cinnamon
2 finely chopped garlic	(about ½ inch, 12 mm)
cloves or ¼ teaspoon	2–3 whole cloves
garlic powder	2 whole peeled tomatoes
2 teaspoons ground	or 2 teaspoons tomato
dhaniya (coriander)	purée
1 teaspoon turmeric	Salt
1 teaspoon ground jeera	Approx. 1 cup chicken
(cumin)	stock
2–3 green cardamom	
pods, peeled and	
ground, or 1 teaspoon	
ground cardamom	

Heat the fat, then lightly fry the onions and garlic until golden. Then add the spices and tomatoes and cook gently for 5 minutes. Then add the chicken joints, boned chicken or eggs, fish, etc. and fry with the spices for about 3 minutes, and add salt to taste. Add the stock, bring to the boil, then cover and simmer gently for about 20–30 minutes. If using fresh chicken joints or raw meat, sauté them first all over and increase cooking time to about 45 minutes or until tender. If liked, 1 or 2 table-spoons yoghurt can be stirred in just before serving. Enough for 4 servings. *See also* chicken *biryani* (page 71).

This makes a large dish served with boiled rice and *dahl* (page 91), and a cucumber, banana, or onion *raita* is delicious as an accompaniment.

Raita is almost any vegetable or fruit, such as banana, sliced and served in yoghurt which has been mixed with salt. Sometimes a pinch of cumin is added, and with cooked sliced potato, raw onion, cooked cauliflower, a little chopped fresh mint can be added.

Pachadi is similar to *raita*, but usually has some un-sweetened, grated coconut added – about 1 tablespoon to ½ pint (300 ml) yoghurt.

Chicken Korma can be made as lamb Korma (page 128).

Turkish chicken is another variation of using the 15-minute boiled chicken. Take the chicken from the bones, and reboil the bones in the stock. Let it get cold and remove the fat. Fry 2 medium onions in a little oil until golden, then add the contents of a 16 oz (450 g) tin of tomatoes, a bouquet garni of herbs, salt and pepper, and 8 oz (225 g) raw rice. Let it simmer for 1 minute, then pour in 1 pint (600 ml) chicken stock and the chicken. Cover, and simmer very gently for about ½ hour, or until the rice is cooked. Check halfway through cooking time to make certain it is not running dry, if so add a very little more stock. Just before serving add ½ cup blanched sliced almonds, or, if they are too expensive, then add, with the stock, 2 tablespoons sultanas or raisins, and 1 teaspoon grated orange peel. Serves about 4.

Chicken pie can be made with the 15-minute boiled chicken, and personally I prefer it taken from the bone. A Cornish method uses a thick bed of parsley at the bottom, then the chicken, a minced shallot or small onion and a few chopped pieces of bacon, all seasoned and with a pinch of ground mace or nutmeg. Add some of the stock, then put on the pastry crust and bake in a moderately hot oven (400°F/200°C/Gas Mark 6) for about ½ hour or until the pastry is golden.

Welsh chicken pie uses a thick layer of chopped leeks instead of parsley.

Chinese recipes use very little chicken in them, but often the accompanying vegetables such as bean sprouts, etc. can be expensive. However it is not essential to use them, for finely chopped white cabbage, celery, onions, mushrooms can all be used to advantage. When in season, Jerusalem artichokes, sliced thinly, can almost pass for water chestnuts.

Chicken Chow Mein can be made in the following way. Other vegetables can be used according to availability. Remove about 8 oz (225 g) chicken from the bird and take off the skin and any bones. Slice it into small strips and roll them in cornflour. Finely slice 1 small onion or green onion tops, 2 tender celery stalks, about 1 cup white cabbage and 6 mushrooms. Heat up a little oil and quickly fry them until coated in oil but not coloured. Drain any excess oil off, then add the chicken strips, and sprinkle liberally with soy sauce. Add about 1 cup of de-fatted chicken stock, and simmer for not longer than 5–7 minutes. About 6 drained chopped pineapple pieces can be added if liked. Serve with cooked egg noodles or add a few to the dish. Sometimes it can be served with a very thin omelette, made from 1 egg beaten with 1 teaspoon soy sauce, and 1 teaspoon water and a few chopped chives or parsley. Fry this quickly on both sides in oil, then cut into large strips and scatter over the top of the chicken dish. Serves 2, or 4 with other dishes.

Chicken livers are very good value when they can be found. They are excellent threaded onto skewers as for a kebab with tomatoes, mushrooms, etc. or quickly fried in butter or oil, sprinkled with parsley and seasonings then moistened with a little stock or cider and served with a bed of fluffy rice. They can also be used in any way that lamb's or calf's liver is used, but do not cook them too much. *See also spaghetti con fegatini di pollo* (page 65).

Chinese chicken livers and mushrooms

1 lb (450 g) chicken livers	4 oz (115 g) mushrooms
2 tablespoons cornflour	3 large cabbage leaves, finely sliced
4 tablespoons oil	2 tablespoons soy sauce
1 large onion	

Well clean the livers, removing any yellow pieces for they will be bitter, then slice them thinly and roll them in seasoned cornflour. Heat half the oil and lightly turn the sliced vegetables in it for about 5 minutes and remove from the pan. Add the rest of the oil and cook the livers quickly, pour off excess oil and add the soy sauce. Then combine the 2 mixtures and cook for 3 minutes. Serve with rice. Enough for 4.

Chicken and liver paste is an old country dish which is very good for using up leftovers of chicken, or you can use the whole 15-minute chicken. It is the English equivalent of a terrine.

8 oz (225 g) chicken livers	½ pint (300 ml) chicken stock
4 rashers streaky bacon	8 oz (225 g) cooked boned chicken
2 tablespoons butter	
1 shallot or small onion, chopped	Pinch of ground cloves and allspice
1 tablespoon parsley	Melted butter to seal
Salt and pepper	

Trim and cut the livers into small pieces, also the bacon. Heat the butter and lightly fry the shallot, then the liver and bacon for 2 minutes, then add the parsley and season to taste. Pour off the excess fat and then transfer the mixture to a liquidizer, add 2 tablespoons chicken stock and blend for 1 minute. Cut the chicken into small pieces, season and add the spices. Butter a deep dish then put in a layer of the liver mixture, then chicken and so on till the dish is full, ending with the liver. Pour over the rest of the stock, cover, and steam for 2 hours. When cooked, cool, then press down with the back of a spoon, and when cold cover with melted butter. Serve cold, cut into slices with hot toast. Enough for 4–6.

Quick liver pâté can be made in minutes in a liquidizer.

1 lb (450 g) chicken livers	1–2 cloves garlic
Oil	¼ pint (150 ml) jellied stock or use equal amounts stock and red wine
Salt and pepper	
Chopped herbs	
2 teaspoons flour	

Trim the livers and fry them quickly in a little oil, so that the outside is browned and the middles are still pinkish. Season, sprinkle with the herb of your choice, the flour and garlic. Pour into the container of the liquidizer with the stock, cover and blend for 1 minute, or until it is creamy and without lumps. Transfer to a dish and press down. If not using at once cover with a layer of melted butter.

See also the chapter on 'Pasta and rice' (pages 60–73).

GAME

Game falls into two classes: furred and feathered. Generally speaking, feathered game is too expensive for the average family unless you live in the country and can sometimes bag the odd pheasant, partridge or grouse for yourself. In which case, if the bird is young, then roasting is the best way to serve it after hanging it for several days. In a book such as this, which centres around economical dishes, pigeon is the best buy in feathered game, although if you come across some elderly game birds the braising recipe given opposite produces a succulent meal.

Pigeons braised and stuffed in beer or cider

This is an eighteenth-century recipe from Worcestershire, and really does make a festive dish from a few pigeons. The stuffing not only enhances but makes them go much further. Allow 1 pigeon per person.

4 pigeons
2 tablespoons oil
Little flour
1 large onion, sliced
4 medium mushrooms
Sprig each of marjoram, thyme and lovage
Salt and pepper
1 pint (600 ml) dark draught beer or dry cider

Stuffing:
8 prunes
2 heaped tablespoons breadcrumbs
Salt and pepper
1 large eating apple, chopped
1 egg, beaten

Garnish:
Few chopped gherkins
Few pickled walnuts (if available)

Pour boiling water over the prunes and let them stand 10 minutes. Then drain and stone them, and chop them finely. Add the breadcrumbs, seasonings, chopped apple and finally the egg. Stuff the birds with this mixture and secure. Heat the oil, brown the birds all over, then sprinkle with flour. Put into the casserole and cover with the onion, mushrooms and chopped herbs. Season and pour the beer or cider over, cover and cook in a moderate oven (350°F/180°C/Gas Mark 4) for about 1½–2 hours. When serving, garnish with the chopped gherkins and pickled walnuts. This dish is excellent served with braised red cabbage (page 86), or braised celery. Serves 4.

Braised game birds

This is an excellent way of treating not-so-young game. It can be done with any elderly game birds, or a combination of several. If using birds of different sizes, then cut the larger ones in half, or joint them.

1 large onion	and thyme
2 carrots	½ teaspoon chopped
2 turnips	rosemary
2 leeks (if available)	1 bayleaf
1 parsnip	Salt and pepper
2–3 game birds with	½ pint (300 ml) cider
their giblets	2 tablespoons butter
Sprig each of parsley	1 tablespoon flour

Make a bed of the peeled and coarsely cut vegetables at the bottom of a heavy casserole, then add the game giblets, herbs and seasonings. Add cider, mixed with water, to cover the vegetable bed, and let it simmer gently. Meanwhile, heat the butter and lightly fry the birds, and put them on top. Retain the butter. Cover the casserole with foil and a lid and simmer gently for 2 hours or until the birds are tender. Since they are out of the liquor they steam gently and do not break up. When they are cooked, heat up the butter in a saucepan, add the flour and pour over ½ pint (300 ml) of the stock, strained from the casserole, and bring to boiling point, stirring all the time. Add a little more cider if it is too thick. Reduce over a high flame, then serve over the carved portions of game. Serves 4–6.

RABBITS are a speciality of mine, for as a young girl during the last war I became very inventive about cooking them. They were not rationed, so my girlfriend, with whom I shared a small flat in Chelsea, and I vied with each other to find ways of changing the taste. One very successful method we called Normandy rabbit, mainly I think because it had cider in it. I published it in my first cookery book, and I often see it reproduced in other works. It was made with what we could get, and very good it was too.

Normandy rabbit

1 rabbit, jointed	1 tablespoon tomato
Salt and pepper	purée or 2 large
2 oz (60 g) butter or	puréed tomatoes
the equivalent amount	½ pint (300 ml) cider
of oil	1 tablespoon finely
4 cloves garlic, chopped	chopped parsley

Simmer the jointed and marinated rabbit in water barely to cover with a little salt and pepper for about ½ hour, reserving the liquid. Let it cool, then remove the joints and take all the meat from the bones and cut it into pieces about the same size. Heat the oil or butter and lightly fry the chopped garlic until golden, then add the rabbit pieces and sauté until cooked.

Heat up about ½ pint (300 ml) of the rabbit stock and dissolve the tomato purée in it, then pour it over the rabbit and season to taste. Let it boil fairly quickly so that the sauce reduces and thickens a little, then pour in the cider quickly, so that it 'quenches' the sauce. Boil rapidly for 2–3 minutes, then serve garnished with the parsley and very finely mashed potatoes. Serves 4.

If possible pick a white-fleshed rabbit for they have a better and milder flavour. Get the poulterer to chop it up for you, as it's easier to sauté and also to get into the pan. First of all, soak it for about 1–2 hours in salted water. This will whiten it and also cleanse it. Then marinate it for a day and a night to get the best flavour. It needn't be an elaborate marinade, simply oil and either a little red or white wine, or cider, with some herbs, a small sliced onion or shallot, a bayleaf, a few allspice berries or cloves and black pepper. The marinade should come to about halfway up the rabbit and the joints can be turned a couple of times to ensure they are soaked in the marinade.

(350°F/180°C/Gas Mark 4) for about ½ hour, then lower the heat to (300°F/150°C/Gas Mark 2) for a further 1½ hours or until the rabbit is tender. Sometimes I add a few carrots, but in general I prefer freshly-cooked vegetables with this rabbit dish.

Garlic can be added with the onion, or in the marinade if liked. Also the rabbit joints can be sautéed in the fat from bacon. This makes delicious rabbit pie as well. Serves 4.

Braised rabbit is the simplest recipe which uses the marinade. Sometimes I do this dish in the pressure cooker and the time is 20 minutes.

1 rabbit, jointed and marinated as above	½ pint (300 ml) stock (½ cube will do)
3 tablespoons oil	Salt and pepper
1 large onion, sliced	1 cup red or white wine or cider, according to the marinade used
Little flour	
Pinch of powdered marjoram	

Take the joints from the marinade and pat them dry, then heat up the oil in a frying pan and fry the joints all over. Lift them out and put them either into the pressure cooker or into a casserole. In the same oil, lightly fry the onion until it is soft but not coloured, then shake over about 1 tablespoon flour and the marjoram. Mix well and then pour over the stock and stir until it is all quite smooth. Gradually add the marinade, stirring all the time, and, when well mixed and slightly thickened, taste for seasoning, and then pour over the rabbit. Top up with the wine or cider, cover and cook in a moderate oven

Rabbit in mustard sauce is an excellent way with rabbit.

2 oz (60 g) butter or margarine	English mustard – it is too hot)
8 oz (225 g) streaky bacon, diced	1 bayleaf
1–2 large onions, coarsely chopped	Little thyme or parsley
1 rabbit, jointed	Salt and pepper
3–4 tablespoons Dijon mustard (do not attempt to use the same amount of	½ cup white wine or cider
	Garnish:
	Button mushrooms, fried whole
	Fried bread

Heat the fat in a large pan, add the bacon, and when it has run out a bit add the onions let them colour slightly, then add the rabbit joints and brown them. Pour off any excess fat, add the mustard and stir well, then the herbs and salt and pepper.

Now put this mixture into a casserole, with the wine, cover tightly and cook in a moderate oven (350°F/180°C/ Gas Mark 4) (or on top of the stove) for about 1 hour, but test that the rabbit is tender. Remove the bayleaf and sprig of thyme before serving and garnish with the lightly-fried mushrooms and fried bread. Serves 4.

Variation: After the herbs have been removed, add 4 tablespoons of stabilized yoghurt, stir well, then reheat.

Elizabethan rabbit is a seventeenth-century recipe, full of flavour. It can also be used for a boneless joint of pork, and sometimes I make it with a mixture of the two, when the flavour has to be tasted to be believed.

1 rabbit, jointed	4 Jerusalem artichokes
1 lb (450 g) lean pork (optional)	2 oz (60 g) mushrooms
2 tablespoons oil	2 carrots
Little flour	2 apples
½ bottle red wine or cider	Salt and pepper
	½ orange
1 large onion	½ cup grapes
1 clove garlic	2 tablespoons raisins
	Bouquet of herbs

Soak the rabbit joints 1–2 hours in salted water, then remove and pat them dry, heat up the oil and fry the joints until brown on both sides. If using the pork then cut it into large pieces and brown them too. Shake over about 1 tablespoon flour and then add a little of the wine first, then add it all gradually, and stir well. Put it all into a casserole, add the vegetables and apples, peeled and cut up, also the herbs, and season well. Peel the orange and remove the pips, likewise the grapes. Slice the orange peel very thinly and see that the pith is removed from the orange sections. Add the sections to the casserole with the raisins, and add a little more liquid, either stock or water, so that it comes level with the meats and vegetables. Cover and cook in a moderate oven (350°F/180°C/Gas Mark 4) for about ½ hour, then lower the heat to about (275°F/140°C/Gas Mark 1), for a further 1½ hours. Test that the rabbit is quite tender before taking from the oven. If using the pork as well, it will make a marvellous meal for about 8 people.

German rabbit is an excellent method and succeeds in making a rabbit taste almost like pheasant.

2 tablespoons oil	2 large onions, sliced
1 rabbit, jointed	12 prunes, soaked
1 heaped tablespoon flour	Salt and pepper
½ pint (300 ml) Guinness or dark beer	

Heat the oil and fry the joints on all sides until they are brown, then sprinkle the flour over and let it cook for about a minute. Transfer to a casserole, pour the beer and water over, add the sliced onions, prunes which have been soaked for at least 1 hour and drained of the water, salt and pepper. Cover and cook in a moderate to slow oven (325°F/160°C/Gas Mark 3) for about 1½ hours. Serves 4.

HARE is still quite inexpensive, and unless you are a large family, it is almost too much if you cook the whole animal. The best way to deal with it is to cut off the legs and head and to roast the saddle or body first.

Roast saddle of hare

To find out if the hare is a young one, test by splitting the ear: if it splits easily it is young and can be roasted without any fear of its being tough. Remove the legs and head and roast the saddle as follows.

Before roasting, the saddle can be stuffed with bread stuffing, mixed with a small grated onion and chopped herbs, also with finely chopped liver or sausagemeat mixed with a few chopped prunes, but this is a matter of taste. Wrap the saddle in rashers of streaky bacon, pour a little oil over all and roast in a moderate oven (350°F/180°C/Gas Mark 4–5) for not longer than 1½ hours, and possibly a little less if the hare was a small, young one. It should be carved along the backbone like a duck, and the pan juices boiled up with a little red wine, salt and freshly ground black pepper. Hand redcurrant jelly separately. Braised celery goes well with hare, but cooked, hot red cabbage is the perfect accompaniment (*see* page 86). Serves 3–4.

Meanwhile the hare legs should be in the following marinade, where they can be left quite well in a cool place for several days. They should, however, be turned from time to time so that they are covered by the liquid. They can then be used for jugged hare.

Marinade for hare

½ bottle red wine or cider, or red wine vinegar mixed with half water	6 tablespoons olive oil Peppercorns Bayleaf Sprig of rosemary

Jugged hare

A hare too old for roasting can still be jugged successfully but should first be marinated overnight in the above marinade.

1 hare or legs from saddle	and thyme
4 tablespoons oil	1 bayleaf
4 oz (115 g) bacon in the piece, cubed	4 cloves
1 large onion	Salt and black pepper
1 celery heart	2 tablespoons flour
1 large carrot	½ pint (300 ml) marinade (*see* above)
1 clove garlic	3 tablespoons redcurrant jelly
Juice and chopped rind of 1 lemon	¼ pint (150 ml) port or red wine
Sprig each of parsley	

Dry the joints of the hare slightly when taken from the marinade, heat the oil and fry the bacon cubes and the hare until brown all over. Transfer to a fireproof casserole with a lid, and add the chopped vegetables, chopped garlic, lemon peel and juice, herbs and spices. Shake the flour over and see that everything is coated with it. Then add the marinade, and enough water barely to cover. See that the lid fits well, and cook in a slow to moderate oven (325°F/160°C/Gas Mark 3) for about 2½ hours. Half an hour before it is ready add the redcurrant jelly and the port. If a thicker sauce is required work 1 tablespoon flour into a walnut of butter and add this. (Classically the sauce should be thickened with about ¼ pint (150 ml) of the blood of the hare, but this is not always available.) Finish cooking and serve. Serves 6.

Stuffed and roasted hare or rabbit

1 young hare or rabbit		*Stuffing:*
4 rashers bacon		8 oz (225 g) sausage meat
3 tablespoons oil		6 prunes simmered in cider, stoned and pounded
2 sprigs of rosemary		Pinch of cinnamon, ginger and nutmeg
Marinade:		Salt and pepper
1 glass white wine vinegar or white wine, or cider		
1 onion, sliced		
2 bayleaves		
Salt and papper		

Marinate the hare or rabbit for at least 4 hours in the above marinade – turning it over at least once.

Mix all the stuffing ingredients together, take the hare from the marinade, wipe it dry and stuff with the above mixture. Secure with a skewer, season well, then wrap the hare in the rashers of bacon. Put into a baking tin with the oil, and rosemary tucked in the side, cover with a piece of foil, and bake in a moderate oven (350°F/180°C/Gas Mark 4) for 1½–2 hours. (If using a hare it will probably take a full 2 hours, but test for tenderness at the end of that time.) Baste it at least twice with a little of the marinade (about ½ pint, 300 ml), which will make a delicious gravy if it is reduced by boiling rapidly on top of the stove. Carve along the backbone as you would for a duck. Serves about 4–6.

Hare pâté can be made either with the legs of the hare if just the saddle was roasted, or with any meat left over from a jugged hare, plus the liver. Also for raw rabbit, game birds or venison.

Any leftover pieces from saddle or the legs (about 8 oz, 225 g)
8 oz (225 g) pickled belly pork
1 bayleaf
Salt and pepper
3 cloves garlic, chopped (optional)
2 tablespoons medium sherry
1 egg

Mince all the leftover meat and the pork, add the other ingredients, put into a greased loaf tin, cover with foil and bake, standing in a tin of water to halfway up, in a moderate oven (350°F/180°C/Gas Mark 4) for 1½ hours. When cold it should be weighted on top, and served the next day cut in slices, with toast. If not using it at once, cover the top with melted butter. It also freezes well.

10. Making the most of the cheaper cuts of meat

Meat is an expensive item for every household, but many good and nourishing dishes can be made from the the cheaper cuts. In the days when the majority of people had less money, one had to be inventive, and nothing was ever wasted. Price, however, is not always the best guide to meat. The practice of wrapping up joints and pieces of meat in trays and cellophane is not a good one, for often when the packet is opened it is found that fat, gristle or other inedible parts are underneath. Examine meat before you buy it, even if it means breaking open the packets, for in that way you will get the best value. Minced meat is another case in point: the cheapest has the highest fat content and, as you know, fat does not contain the protein that lean meat does. It is really better to buy a piece of stewing beef and have it minced, or do it yourself at home. The fat in mince produces a disgusting greasy taste, which quite destroys flavour.

Roasting is an expensive way of cooking meat, for not only do you need a better cut, but it also shrinks in cooking. I realize that it is difficult to restrict oneself to casserole-type dishes, but there are cheaper cuts, such as topside of beef, and they go much further with the addition of vegetables, Yorkshire pudding and so on. Chops and cutlets are, if weighed purely by the meat content, a fantastic price, but the succulent little neck or shoulder chops roast very well and can also be used for dishes such as Irish stew or Lancashire hot-pot, both dishes which are now world-famous and which stem from days of great economic depression. The addition of a few kidneys to the latter dish give it added flavour, and they are not all that expensive for they are solid meat and have good food value. Lamb shoulders and breast both roast well (for dredging with oatmeal *see* page 35).

Belly of pork roasts into a delicious little joint and also boils well, especially if it has been slightly salted, when it is known as pickled pork. Boned shoulder of pork can be extremely good, likewise shoulder of veal. Veal is always an expensive meat, but it is just possible to use the economical cuts of breast, shoulder and shin.

For many years these were the staple joints of country people, for even if they were farmers, the more expensive joints went to market. Nothing was ever wasted; heads, feet, tails, ears of pigs were all simmered down with herbs to flavour, to make good brawn or galantines, the fat rendered down to make lard, and even the blood was used to make black puddings, still popular in Ireland. The lesser cuts of beef were used to make good steak and kidney puddings and pies, which are still made all over the country. Sheep's head broth is traditional in the Isles of Scotland, but that is too greasy for my taste, although I frequently buy the brains and the small lamb's tongues which make a good meal.

If you are buying cheaper cuts, then marinate them in cider, which can afterwards be used in place of wine to cook them, or a little oil and wine vinegar with some herbs can make an enormous difference to a beef or lamb casserole, or for a roast breast of lamb. Yoghurt, too, is a marinade which should not be forgotten, for the lactic acid in it breaks down tough fibres in the meat. For this reason it is used as a marinade in the North

of India, where the meat is not hung to our taste, and therefore can be tough (*see* lamb Korma, page 128, for this use).

MEATBALLS

Unquestionably, I would say that most households today use minced beef when they want to lower the household bills. It is a curious thing but no English, or even British, recipe for meatballs exists. There are rissoles (which come from 'risshe shewes', the fifteenth-century English for 're-show'), generally made from cold meat, shepherd's pie and so on, but none of the almost poetically named meatballs which exist all over the world are to be found in our traditional food. In India they are called *koftés*, in Russia *bitki*, *youvarlakia* or *kefthedes* in Greece, *bitterballen* in Holland and *köttbullar* in Scandinavia.

Meatballs are the best way I know of using mince: the basic method for making them differs very little from country to country, but the sauces they are served in, or with, are very varied. The balls should not be too large (about the size of a medium plum or greengage) and 1 lb (450 g) of mince will make about 20 of this size.

In many of the countries already mentioned they are served in a very thick soup-like sauce; sometimes they are fried first and then added and heated up in the sauce, but often they are dropped straight into the boiling soup and cooked gently, so that they do not come apart, for about 30–40 minutes. Either way, they are quite excellent, and have the added virtue that they can be made hours ahead, or even in two parts.

With regard to the latter statement, I quite regularly find that when attempting a new recipe, it is much simpler to do it in several stages. That is, if a sauce is required, make it first if it is one that will keep; if it entails paring vegetables, do those and then have a breather. In this way, it doesn't become a chore; also, as I said earlier, the method seems to sink in and become more familiar. For instance, if you are making something as ordinary as a shepherd's pie, you usually either mince the meat, or boil the potatoes at quite different times, not to mention making the gravy. If you did it for the first time, it would seem a complicated business doing it all at once.

The basic preparation to make about 20 small meatballs is:

1 lb (450 g) lean mince	Salt, pepper, pinch of
3 small slices of crustless	mace or nutmeg
bread, moistened in	Little flour or fine
milk	semolina for rolling
1 medium minced shallot	them (I prefer the
or finely chopped onion	latter, as it thickens
1 egg	the soup and has more
Pinch of lovage or basil	flavour)
or parsley, etc.	Oil for frying

Everything except the flour and oil is mixed together, and with floured hands you shape the mixture into small balls.

Variations in different countries are: in India a flat tablespoon of curry powder is added, also a pinch of fennel seeds, or crushed cardamom seeds; in Yugoslavia a pinch of paprika; in the Balkans a teaspoon of lovage; in Russia and Germany sometimes two mashed anchovy fillets are added, and in Greece they often add a dash of ouzo, a sort of aniseed brandy. In fact, you can take your pick, or even add a flavouring of your own. Once made, they are either first fried (deep oil with a basket is the quickest and easiest) or kept for poaching in a thick soup or sauce, either on top of the stove, or put in a casserole in the oven, for about 30–40 minutes.

Sauces

The simplest is undoubtedly the Russian one of pouring plain yoghurt or sour cream over them after frying, and putting them in the oven. Next, the Russian and Greek one of first frying and then reheating them in a casserole with a 16 oz (450 g) tin of tomatoes, a scattering of basil, a chopped stalk of celery or green pepper if you have them, but neither of the latter is essential. In Greece, too, they are poached in stock for about 30 minutes, and served with *avgolémono* sauce.

Avgolémono sauce

2 eggs	1 pint (600 ml) stock
1 tablespoon cornflour	(vegetable, meat or a
Juice of 1 large lemon	stock cube)

Beat the eggs in a saucepan and mix in the cornflour, then add the lemon juice. Bring the stock to the boil, and pour it over the egg mixture, beating with an egg-beater all the time until it is frothy and slightly thick. It will keep warm over hot, not boiling, water to the side of the stove. Whisk it again before serving.

This sauce is also good with boiled chicken, fish, ham, kebabs, and vegetables such as cauliflower.

Koftés

The method I find very popular is the Indian one with the curry added. I first make a vegetable soup to which I add curry powder to taste, turmeric and a pinch of cinnamon, and either cardamom or crushed coriander, or I use curry sauce (page 26). Then, after frying the meatballs, I pour this over, and heat it up in the oven. Strangely enough, mashed potato seems to go very well with these *koftés*, although you can serve rice and chutney if you prefer. Incidentally, these little balls, served dry, make a marvellous snack with drinks, and a change from the eternal chipolata sausages.

Another method is to thread the raw meatballs on skewers, interspersed with chunks of tomato, mushroom, bayleaves, etc., or to mould the mixture around the whole skewer, without additions, and to grill them. They are good served with boiled rice or spaghetti, sauerkraut, grilled or fried mushrooms, hot red cabbage – the list of accompaniments is endless.

It is well worth experimenting for yourself, but whatever method you prefer, your friends and family will find it hard to recognize the pound of mince.

Meatballs with sweet and sour sauce

1 lb (450 g) lean minced meat
1 large onion
2 teaspoons Worcestershire sauce
Salt and pepper
1 egg, beaten

2 tablespoons soy sauce
Pinch of paprika or cayenne pepper
1 level tablespoon sugar or honey
2 tablespoons cornflour
2 tablespoons vinegar

Sauce:
1 × 16 oz (450 g) tin pineapple cubes

Mix together the meat, finely sliced or grated onion, Worcestershire sauce and seasoning, then finally add the egg and shape the mixture into about 12–18 balls, then either fry or grill them, or bake them in a hot oven (400°F/200°C/Gas Mark 6) for 15 minutes or until well cooked. Meanwhile, make the sauce with the pineapple cubes, their juice made up to 1 pint (600 ml) with water, and all the other ingredients except the vinegar and cornflour. Let it simmer for about 4 minutes then cream the cornflour with the vinegar and add to the sauce. Bring to the boil, stirring all the time, and simmer for a few minutes. Put the meatballs on a warm dish and pour the sauce over the top. Serves 4.

Or you can serve the mince in a curry as follows:

Keema curry

2 tablespoons oil
1 large onion, finely chopped
¼ teaspoon garlic powder or 2 cloves garlic
1 teaspoon ground jeera (cumin)
3 ground cardamoms
½ tablespoon ground dhaniya (coriander)
½ teaspoon turmeric

Pinch of ginger
1 teaspoon garam masala
2 fresh peeled tomatoes or 1 teaspoon tomato purée
1 lb (450 g) minced meat
1 cup beef stock or plain yoghurt
Salt

Heat the oil and lightly fry the onions and garlic, then add the spices and tomatoes, coarsely chopped. (You can use 1 tablespoon of good Indian curry paste instead of the spices.) Mix well and cook on a high flame for 2 minutes. Then add the meat, stock or yoghurt, and salt to taste, mix, and cook slowly for about 1 hour. The curry should only be slightly moist and served with rice. (*See* Index for other curries.)

OTHER USES FOR MINCED MEAT

Meat loaf is such a good dish: it can be eaten hot, when it is very succulent, or prepared in advance and eaten cold. Both are good.

1½ lb (675 g) minced beef or 1 lb (450 g) beef and 8 oz (225 g) sausagemeat	1 level teaspoon salt
	1 tablespoon chopped parsley
1 small onion, grated	Pinch of powdered sage or thyme
1 clove garlic, pulped (optional)	2 crustless slices brown or white bread, grated to crumbs
Pinch of ground allspice or cinnamon and cloves	4–5 tablespoons stock or cider
Freshly-ground black pepper	1 beaten egg

Mix all ingredients together, adding the stock or cider and egg last, and see that the mixture is soft but not sloppy in texture. Oil a loaf tin or a baking dish, put in the mixture and bake in a slow to moderate oven (325°F/120°C/Gas Mark 3) for 1–1¼ hours. Check that it is not drying up after 45 minutes; if so baste with a few tablespoons of warmed wine, stock or cider. Serves 6–8.

Meat loaf is very appetizing served with a sauce made from a tin of tomatoes, simmered down and mashed, with salt, a pinch of sugar, pepper, a crushed bayleaf, a little garlic powder and a pinch of thyme. Or add 1 tablespoon mustard or a dash of curry powder to a white sauce. A dash of Worcestershire sauce or tomato pickle is also good if a piquant flavour is liked. The loaf freezes very well.

Moussaka is a Greek dish made with either minced lamb (more popular in Greece) or beef. This dish freezes very well and makes a good party dish.

2 medium aubergines (if available) or use 1 lb (450 g) cauliflower	Salt and pepper
	1 × 8 oz (225 g) tin tomatoes
3 tablespoons oil	¼ pint (150 ml) stock or ½ pint (300 ml) white sauce
1 lb (450 g) minced meat	
2 medium onions, sliced	1 egg
1 teaspoon parsley	¼ pint (150 ml) milk
Pinch of ground marjoram	

First slice the aubergines crosswise, sprinkle with salt and leave for 1 hour. If using cauliflower, then break it into flowerlets and half cook them, then chop to a convenient size. Meanwhile heat up the oil and fry the meat and onions, then add the chopped and ground herbs and seasoning. Drain the aubergines, and put a layer in the bottom of an ovenproof dish, then meat and onions, then tomatoes. Repeat this until the dish is full, then gently pour over either the stock or the white sauce, seeing that it gets down to the bottom. Cook in a moderate oven (350°F/180°C/Gas Mark 4) for 30 minutes. Then beat up the egg with the milk and pour over the top and continue cooking until the top is puffy and golden brown, about ½ hour. Sometimes grated cheese is sprinkled over the top. The aubergine gives it the characteristic flavour, but it is very pleasant made with the cheaper cauliflower. Serves 4.

The cheaper cuts of beef lend themselves to many excellent ways of cooking. Many are of Continental origin, from countries where they are used as a matter of course. I have written about some of these inexpensive methods of cooking on pages 10–11.

PRESSURE COOKING

This is not only a very good way of saving fuel, but also a way of making foods which need hours of cooking taste better in a fraction of the time. Often in long, slow cooking the delicious gravy boils away, but this never happens with pressure cooking, for the speed at which it cooks retains all the juices.

Pressure cookers are far from being a new idea: they were invented in about 1678 by a Frenchman called Denis Papin, who came to London to work with the Irish scientist, Sir Robert Boyle. He was made a member of the Royal Society, but, alas, died in poor straits in 1712. His contraption was called a 'digester' and was made to soften bones to make nutritious jellies for invalids. Stock made in a pressure cooker is superb and can nearly always be relied upon to jelly when cold.

I have had a pressure cooker now for many years and have formed certain conclusions on how to get the best out of it. First, with the exception of vegetables and sweet dishes, I hardly ever use my cooker for speed. That is, I don't necessarily use it if I'm in a hurry, for I would prefer to open a tin or have an omelette or pasta. I have found that dishes which normally require long, slow cooking are far better if cooked in the pressure cooker, then allowed to get completely cold, and then gently reheated. Whether or not it is that all the flavours have time to amalgamate, I simply don't know, but try it, and you will find there is no comparison in the flavour. Incidentally, if buying a pressure cooker, I find that the high-dome kind are exceptionally useful for dealing with whole chickens or odd-shaped hams.

Pot roast

2 tablespoons oil
2 bayleaves
4 lb (2 kg) joint of beef (topside, brisket or rib roast), boned and rolled
1 large onion, sliced
6 medium carrots, sliced
Pinch of rosemary or marjoram
4 whole cloves
6 whole allspice
Approx. 1 tablespoon flour
1 pint (600 ml) stock (a cube will do)
Salt and pepper

Heat up the oil and put the bayleaves in, so that they split and crackle, then add the meat and let it brown on all sides. Add the vegetables and let the onion just soften, but not brown, then put in the herbs and spices, but first pour off any excess oil there may be in the pan if the meat is inclined to be fat. Shake over the flour, sprinkling it on both sides of the meat, then let it brown for a minute and pour over the stock. Season to taste and put the lid on. Let the steam come out of the small vent at the top in an even flow before adding the weight valve, then cook at 15 lb pressure for 12 minutes to the pound (450 kg), allowing the pressure cooker to cool naturally. It will take 2–3 hours cooked on top of the stove without a pressure cooker.

Now, I would let it get completely cold, removing any fat from the top, before reheating, either in the cooker or transferred into a casserole which can be heated on top of the stove, very gently, or in a low oven. Serves 6–8.

CASSEROLES

Beef casserole with cider and oranges

This is also good for pork or chicken. Pressure cooking time is 25 minutes.

2 lb (1 kg) stewing steak	1 clove garlic, chopped
1 tablespoon seasoned cornflour	2 medium carrots, cut matchstick thin
Salt and pepper	2 small oranges
2 tablespoons oil	¼ pint (150 ml) cider
2 medium onions, sliced	1½ beef stock cubes

Trim the meat, cut into cubes and roll in the seasoned cornflour. Heat the oil and sauté the cubes, then put them into a casserole and sauté the vegetables lightly. Add them to the meat and mix well. Peel the oranges and remove the pith (to do this easily, stand them in boiling water for a few minutes), finely cut the peel into strips and squeeze out the juice. Add half the peel to the casserole. Mix the orange juice, cider and dissolved stock cubes (to make 2 pints (approx. 1 l) in all) and pour over. Cover and cook at (325°F/160°C/Gas Mark 3–4) for 1¼–2 hours. Serve with the remaining orange peel over the top as a garnish. Serves 4.

Carbonnade flamande

2 oz (60 g) butter	stock
4 medium onions, sliced	Salt and pepper
3 lb (1½ kg) stewing steak	1 level tablespoon brown sugar
2 bayleaves	Pinch or sprig of thyme
1 heaped tablespoon flour	1 teaspoon French mustard
½ pint (300 ml) beer	1 tablespoon vinegar
½ pint (300 ml) beef	

Melt the butter in a frying pan, and fry the sliced onions until golden, then put into a casserole; add the beef, cut into cubes, to the pan and brown very well with the bayleaves, sprinkle the flour over, and add the beer and stock. Season well to taste, then add the sugar, herbs and mustard, and combine with the onions in the casserole. Cover and cook in a slow oven for 1½–2 hours, and just before serving add the vinegar. Serve with boiled potatoes and a salad. It improves with reheating, if you want to cook it beforehand. Pressure cooking time is 25 minutes. Serves 4–6.

Beef and green ginger casserole

2 lb (1 kg) lean stewing steak	1 pint (600 ml) beef stock (dissolved stock cube will do)
2 tablespoons oil	4 pieces of green ginger (walnut size) – this can be bought fresh or in tins at Oriental grocers'
1 large onion, sliced	
4 bayleaves	
Salt and pepper	
1 tablespoon flour	
Pinch of powdered marjoram	

Trim and cut the beef into serving pieces, heat the oil, put in the bayleaves, covering the pan lest they spatter the oil. Add the beef when they are brown, and let that brown on all sides, then add the onion and fry until golden. Season, shake over the flour and marjoram, then add the stock and the peeled and finely sliced ginger. Let it bubble up, then cover and transfer to a slow to moderate oven (275°F/140°C/Gas Mark 1) and cook for 1½–2 hours. Check at least once that the liquid is not drying up; if it is, add a little more water. Half red wine (or cider) and half water can also be used in place of stock, if preferred. It can be cooked ahead of time and reheated in a moderate oven for ½ hour. Pressure-cooking time is 25 minutes. Serves 4.

Goulash

2 tablespoons oil	2 large carrots, sliced
2 lb (1 kg) shin of beef, chopped into cubes	1 clove garlic
2 large onions	1 tablespoon tomato purée
1 chunk of marrow bone (if possible – not essential)	1 bayleaf
	1 teaspoon powdered marjoram
1 heaped tablespoon flour	2 tablespoons paprika
1 glass red wine or cider	2 teaspoons caraway seeds
1 pint (600 ml) water	Salt and pepper
	Yoghurt

Heat the oil and fry the meat and onions in it until they are soft and brown, then add the marrow bone and brown on both sides. Shake the flour over, add the wine and water, stir well and add all other ingredients except the yoghurt. Cover, and cook in a moderate oven (350°F/180°C/Gas Mark 4) for about 2½ hours, checking that it does not run dry of liquid. Just before serving dig the marrow from the bone if you have used it, stir it in, and add about 4 tablespoons plain yoghurt. Serve with boiled potatoes, or buttered boiled noodles. Sometimes in Hungary the potatoes are added to the stew about ½ hour before it is ready. Pressure cooking time is 25 minutes. Serves 4.

Pressed beef flank

3 lb (1½ kg) flank of beef	Salt
8 oz (225 g) bacon rashers or 1 lb (450 g) pork sausagemeat	1 teaspoon black peppercorns
2 bayleaves	½ pint (300 ml) stock
	½ pint (300 ml) water

Remove any superfluous fat from the meat and lay it out flat, line it with the bacon or sausagemeat, bayleaves and seasonings, then roll it up and tie securely. Put into a large saucepan or casserole, cover with the stock and water, and simmer slowly for about 4 hours or until the meat is so soft it will shred with a fork. Take out the meat and put into a dish which just fits it, add a little of the stock, cover with foil and weight the top, then put into a cold place overnight. Serve cold, cut into thin slices with a sauce made from 3 parts oil to 1 of wine vinegar, with chopped capers and chopped fresh herbs in it. Pressure cooking time is 55 minutes. Serves 6–8.

Sjomansbiff (Sailor's beef)

2 lb (1 kg) chuck or round beef, trimmed of bone and gristle	2 teaspoons salt
	1 cup water
5–6 medium potatoes	Freshly-ground pepper
2 medium to large onions	1 cup beer or stout
2 tablespoons butter or margarine	1 tablespoon chopped parsley

Cut the meat in thick slices, about ½ inch (12 mm), and then pound them until they are thin. Peel the potatoes and cut into thick slices, and also peel and thinly slice the onions. Heat the fat in a saucepan, add the meat and brown quickly, and when brown sprinkle with 1 teaspoon of salt. Remove the meat and cook the onions in the same pan until they are just gently golden, then remove them. Add the water to the pan and boil up for a few minutes, scraping down the sides.

Put the meat, onions and potatoes in alternate layers in a 4 pint (2.2 l) casserole, seasoning each layer with the remaining salt and pepper. Finally pour over the pan liquid and the beer.

Cover and bake in a moderate oven (375°F/190°C/Gas Mark 5) for about 1½ hours. The lid can be removed 20 minutes before the end of the cooking time to let the potatoes brown on top. Sprinkle with chopped parsley before serving. Pressure cooking time is 25 minutes. Serves 4.

Beef curry using chopped, lean shin or chuck beef can be made with the curry sauce given on page 108, and, if the meat is inclined to be tough, then make it in the pressure cooker, where it will take 25–30 minutes, but leave to cool, and then reheat before serving.

Oxtail makes a wonderfully succulent meal and is very cheap. For more than 2 people it is necessary to use 2 oxtails.

2 oxtails, chopped and trimmed	1 tablespoon paprika
Little cooking oil	1 tablespoon tomato purée
1 large onion	Approx. 1 pint (600 ml) stock, water or cider
1 bayleaf	Salt and freshly-ground pepper
1 rounded tablespoon seasoned flour	
Pinch of rosemary	
½ teaspoon powdered marjoram	

Trim as much of the fat from the tails as possible, and leave on the thin ends as they make good stock. In a large pan, heat the oil and quickly fry the meat on all sides and put into a casserole, then soften the chopped onion, adding the bayleaf as well. Put these with the meat and shake over the flour, the herbs and paprika, mixing it well. Add the tomato purée and liquid to the pan and boil it up, season, and pour over the meat and onion, mixing well.

Bring this to the boil, and see that the liquid comes to at least three-quarters of the way up the meat. If not, add a little more. Cover, and cook in a slow oven (275°F/140°C/Gas Mark 1–2) for about 3–3½ hours or until the meat is very tender. Unless the oxtail is almost falling from the bones it will be disappointing. It is best to let it get quite cold and remove all fat from the top before reheating and serving. This dish can be beautifully cooked in a pressure cooker in 35 minutes, but make certain you do the frying in a separate pan first, otherwise it can cause sticking on the bottom. Serves 4–6.

Dumplings added to any of the above casseroles are economical and good. They can either be poached separately and served with it, or put on top of the casserole about 20 minutes before it is ready. For recipe *see* page 20.

LAMB

Lamb or mutton (a word never used today, although the meat exists for it is only a two-year-old animal) is on the whole cheaper than beef, and certain cuts such as shoulder, shoulder chops, neck and breast are very good buys. The middle of the animal is expensive, and the leg is dearer than the shoulder, but it is very lean so there is little waste. However, there are several parts of a sheep that deserve mention, the first being lamb shanks which is the joint between the trotter and the shoulder. They are quite meaty and have a good flavour. They are also cheap.

Roast lamb shanks

4 lamb shanks	Parsley
2 medium onions or shallots	Butter or oil
4 oz (115 g) mushrooms	2 oz (60 g) grated hard cheese
Salt and pepper	

Take 4 pieces of foil large enough to wrap up each shank securely, then put 1 shank on each piece, add a little chopped onion, mushrooms, seasoning, and parsley. Either rub with butter or pour a little oil over, sprinkle each one with cheese and wrap up well. Put into a baking tin and cook in a moderate to hot oven (375°F/190°C/Gas Mark 5) and roast for about 1 hour. Serve each shank in its foil with a jacket-baked potato, sprinkled with fresh herbs and served with ice-cold plain yoghurt. Serves 4.

Crown roast is a pretty joint consisting of the whole of neck of lamb or mutton cutlets in one piece. This is cut almost down to the thick end, but the spindly fatty tail-ends of the cutlets are trimmed of fat. Spread it in a circle like a crown (the eye of the cutlet being spread out) and secure the thin ends by joining together with skewers. Invert the joint, thick end downwards, in a roasting pan, brush with oil and roast in a hot oven for 1 hour. Meanwhile, cook at least 2 lb (1 kg) of green peas with mint and seasoning, and $\frac{1}{4}$ hour before serving, drain off the excess fat, put the peas in the middle of the 'crown' and add 1 cup water or stock to the pan juices. Put back in the oven to continue cooking. Or fill the 'crown' with herb or oatmeal stuffing (skirlie – see page 35) and omit the peas. Serves 4–6, allowing 2 cutlets per person.

Best end of neck chops left in one piece are called a rack, and include the rib chops. If left in one piece this makes a good roast, but see that the tails of the chops are not too fatty, in which case trim them slightly. You can cut them in half if you like and cook them with the bone ends arched over the middle. This is called a Guard of Honour.

First marinate the meat in a little oil (about 3 tablespoons) with just a dash of wine vinegar and some chopped rosemary or thyme for about 1 hour, turning at least once so that it gets coated all over. Use this marinade to cook the meat.

2 best ends of neck (about 12–14 chops left together)	Pinch of chopped rosemary and thyme
1 tablespoon butter or margarine	2 tablespoons fresh chopped parsley
Slightly over $\frac{1}{4}$ pint (150 ml) cider	5 tablespoons fresh breadcrumbs
3 cloves garlic	Salt and freshly-ground pepper

Trim the chops of any gristle and fat then butter the roasting tin and put them in fat-side upwards. Butter a double piece of foil and cover with this, then put into a moderate oven (375°F/190°C/Gas Mark 5) for 15 minutes. Meanwhile, warm the cider with the marinade, chopped garlic, rosemary and thyme and let it boil, then reduce it to just over half. Remove the joint from the oven and pour this over, and replace foil. Continue cooking for 45 minutes, basting at least twice more.

While it is cooking, mix together the parsley and breadcrumbs, then mix in about 2 tablespoons of the pan juices, and season well. When the lamb is cooked, put on to a fireproof dish, heap the breadcrumb mixture on top and either brown in the oven or under a hot grill. Serves 4–6.

Braised breast of lamb

1 breast of lamb	Stock to cover
1 medium onion	3 oz (85 g) melted
2 carrots	butter
Thyme	Breadcrumbs
Salt and pepper	

Roll the breast and tie with some string. Put into a saucepan with the sliced carrots and onion, thyme, salt and pepper, cover with stock or water and simmer for 1½ hours.

Remove from the stock when cooked, untie it and pull all the bones out. If they do not pull out easily the breast should be returned to the saucepan for further cooking. Place the boned meat on a flat meat dish and cover with another. Put a weight on top and leave to get completely cold.

When it is cold, cut it into oblong pieces and trim off all extra fat. Season well, and dip each piece into melted butter and then into the breadcrumbs. Grill under a hot grill on both sides until they are a light brown, and serve with piquante sauce (below). Serves about 4, depending on size of breast.

Piquante sauce

Chop a shallot or small onion very finely and put into a pan with 2 tablespoons of wine vinegar. Let it reduce to half, then add 4 chopped gherkins, 1 cup thickened stock, 1 tablespoon redcurrant jelly, 1 tablespoon chopped mint and parsley, and seasonings. Boil up to reduce slightly and add a squeeze of lemon before serving.

Stuffed breast of lamb

Choose a lean breast and ask the butcher to remove as many bones as possible. Then make up a bread stuffing with herbs, onion and garlic, binding with an egg, and stuff the breast with this, roll up and secure. Roast in a moderate oven (350°F/180°C/Gas Mark 4) for 20 minutes to the pound (450 g) and serve with tomato sauce (page 27).

China cholla is an economical dish, especially in the season of fresh peas, lettuce and cucumbers. It is an Anglo-Indian dish, pleasant on a summer's evening.

2 lb (1 kg) neck of lamb chops	2 oz (60 g) butter or margarine
2 small lettuces	½ pint (300 ml) stock
1 lb (450 g) shelled green peas	Salt and pepper
4 spring onions or equivalent of chives	½ small cucumber
	2 oz (60 g) button mushrooms

Trim the meat of fat, bone, gristle, etc., and cut into very small pieces. Put into a casserole and add the lettuces, finely shredded, the peas, chopped spring onions, butter, stock, salt and pepper. Cover and cook gently on top of the stove for 2 hours. Half an hour before serving, add the chopped cucumber and the mushrooms, cover and continue cooking. Serve with fluffy boiled rice, well sprinkled with chopped fresh mint. Serves 4.

Lamb Korma

3 medium onions	1 teaspoon cardamom
Little oil	1 teaspoon garam masala
5 oz (140 g) yoghurt	3 lb (1½ kg) lamb,
3 cloves garlic	trimmed and cubed
Small piece of chopped	2 tablespoons tomato
green ginger or ½	purée
teaspoon ground ginger	1 teaspoon chilli powder
1 teaspoon ground jeera	2 bayleaves
(cumin)	Salt
1 teaspoon ground	1 teaspoon mixed
dhaniya (coriander)	ground cardamom
1 teaspoon cloves	and jaiphal (nutmeg)

Fry the finely chopped onions in oil until soft and golden. Meanwhile mix together the yoghurt with the chopped garlic, a piece of chopped green ginger about size of 5p piece, a teaspoon each of ground jeera, ground dhaniya, cloves, cardamom, and garam masala. Rub the trimmed, cubed lamb in this and leave until blood and water come out of the meat. Then put straight away into the hot onions and let it bubble away with a lid on a medium heat. After ½ hour add tomato purée, chilli powder, bayleaves and salt. Mix well with a wooden spoon and let it bubble away over a medium heat until the oil separates from the spices. This means they are properly cooked. Then add about ¾ pint (450 ml) of cold water and simmer slowly until the meat is tender. Before serving sprinkle with mixed ground cardamom and jaiphal. Serves 6–8. This recipe can also be used for beef or chicken.

For other curries *see* Index.

See also moussaka (page 121), lentil casserole (page 91) and Soup-stews and hot-pots (pages 134–6).

KEBABS

Kebabs are just about the most economical way of serving the more expensive meats, fish or shellfish so that they taste and look good, yet don't give the appearance that you are being skimpy with them. A Turkish dish originally, kebabs are now common all over Greece and many Balkan countries as well as in Asia.

They are an excellent way of serving food to everyone's taste, for the little chunks of meat can be absolutely without fat, for those who like it, or with a little rim of it around, which gets crunchy after cooking. Once the main ingredient and the vegetables or fruits have been cut up, they can be marinated and cooked to order. The long skewers that the foods are threaded on are available at almost every good hardware shop and can be used over and over again. Lamb is usually used for kebabs (and how often I have stretched the 3 lamb chops to serve 4 in an emergency) but personally I think other meats, such as pork, liver (particularly chicken liver), sausages and kidneys, or a mixture, are just as good, if not better.

Once the meat is cut to about 1 inch (25 mm) cubes you will need small rings of onion, mushrooms, tomatoes, green peppers and bayleaves; or you can alternate the meat with bread cubes or different fruits as well as vegetables, such as cubes of pineapple for pork, while cubed peaches with liver is quite delicious. It really is up to you to try different combinations of taste, and to vary them as much as possible. Individual likes can be catered for with no trouble at all.

Once the skewers are threaded they can be grilled straight away, or try them smoked in a home smoker (page 11). There are several marinades, which again are a matter of taste and inclination. Usually I use a simple one, such as the following.

Marinade for kebabs (1)

Mix together about ½ cup of good oil, 3 tablespoons of wine vinegar and a squeeze of lemon. Add a couple of unpeeled garlic cloves (optional), some chopped herbs, particularly a small sprig of rosemary, salt and freshly-ground pepper. This should be enough for about 12 skewers. Pour it over them all, and turn at least once during the marinade time. This can be as long as 2 days, if they are left in a cool place. Sometimes I add a few whole allspice or fennel seeds to the marinade, but it is entirely how I feel at the moment, and each time I make it, I probably do so differently.

TO COOK THE KEBABS

Drain off the marinade but reserve it, paint the kebabs over with a little oil, and grill them under a moderately hot grill (to ensure that the food cooks through without burning) on both sides until done. This should take about 10 minutes in all.

If you only have a small grill and want to make a lot of kebabs, then put them all in a roasting tin in a hot oven (400°F/200°C/Gas Mark 6), turning them over at least once. Before serving, put them under a hot grill, to give them a touch of the fire. Put on to a warmed serving dish, either with or without plain boiled rice, then make the sauce as follows. Put the tin the kebabs were cooked in, with the pan juices, on top of the stove, then add the marinade, another squeeze of lemon juice and some more chopped herbs. Boil very rapidly, so that it reduces, and taste for seasoning. If you like you can add a teaspoon of tomato purée or even more mushrooms, just letting them soften, but not letting them brown. Pour this over the kebabs before serving. If you like a more spicy marinade then try this one, which is good with bacon, liver and sausage kebabs.

Marinade for kebabs (2)

½ cup wine vinegar
½ cup oil
1 teaspoon Worcestershire sauce
Few drops of Tabasco
1 crushed clove garlic
1 level tablespoon tomato chutney or purée

Pinch of dry mustard
Pinch of paprika
Squeeze of ½ lemon
Salt and freshly-ground pepper

Mix all ingredients well together and pour over the kebabs, then cook and use as above.

Shellfish such as scallops, prawns or lobster are excellent alternated on skewers with chunks of a thick white fish such as turbot, brill, angler fish and so on, also with a bayleaf or two and some tomatoes, while a little bacon is good as well, as are mushrooms. When the skewers are full marinate them in the following marinade.

Marinade for kebabs (3)

4 tablespoons olive oil
Juice of 1 large lemon
1 teaspoon chopped fennel or dill
Salt and freshly-ground pepper

½ glass dry white wine, cider or dry vermouth, or use equivalent amount lemon juice
Freshly-chopped parsley

Mix together the olive oil, lemon juice, fennel or dill and seasonings. Marinate the kebabs (of meat, poultry, liver, fish or shellfish) in this as above. When you have cooked the kebabs, add the marinade to the pan juices and add the wine. Reduce by rapid boiling to about half and serve over the kebabs with a lot of freshly-chopped parsley.

Beef kebabs

I have omitted beef from any of the previous ideas because unless you use top-quality meat, which is so expensive, it is liable to be tough. But you can make lovely kebabs with minced beef. Mix the mince with chopped herbs, a little grated onion or garlic, a pinch of curry powder or garam masala, or ground cinnamon or coriander, whichever you like. Then add 1 beaten egg to each 1 lb (450 g) of mince and mix very well. Dip your hands in flour and form the meat into little balls, adding more flour if it seems too sloppy. Then chill the small, walnut-sized meat balls, and when needed thread them on the skewers with the vegetables of your choice, and proceed as above. 1 lb (450 g) of mince will make ample kebabs for about six people with the added vegetables. *See also koftés* (page 119).

Vegetable and date kebabs go well with almost any meat kebab. Thread the skewers with stoned dates, small mushrooms, chunks of tomato, red and green sweet peppers. Then brush with oil and either grill or bake for about 10–15 minutes.

Fruit kebabs are also very good served as a sweet course. Almost any firm fruit can be used, cut into chunks, and alternated if liked with the firmer kinds of canned fruits, such as pineapple, pear or peaches. Apple, banana, grapes, cherries, plums, are all good done in this way, but stoned fruits should have the pits removed.

Alternate the fruits as much as possible, seeing that you get a variety of texture, colour and taste. Marinate the skewers in liquid honey, just enough to coat them slightly. Add some lemon juice, or orange juice if preferred, and turn them at least once before grilling. Sometimes I add a good pinch of ground coriander to the honey, or even a pinch of curry powder, and if the skewers have a lot of apple on them, then I might add a few whole cloves.

Put them as they are with the marinade under a hot grill and grill until they are just slightly crisp. It is not necessary to cook them through. They can be served plain, with creamy rice, or with yoghurt.

PORK

Pork can be expensive, but certain cuts and small amounts can make excellent meals for it has a pronounced flavour. The Chinese use it to great effect, and anyone who has eaten a Chinese meal will realize that very little need be used. The chicken Chow Mein on page 109 can be made with pork equally well.

Chinese pork with mushrooms was first made for me during the war by the painter Sir Francis Rose. He spent some time in China and is an excellent cook. A small piece of pork makes both a good soup and a main dish.

1 lb (450 g) lean pork	or use pak choy
Pinch of sugar	(Chinese cabbage)
2 tablespoons soy sauce	Small piece of green
4 oz (115 g) mushrooms	ginger (if available)
Salt	1 cup of water or stock
1 oz (25 g) noodles	
1 medium white cabbage	

First boil the pork and sugar in water barely to cover for 30 minutes, then take it out, but let the stock get cold and remove any fat from the top. Cut the pork into

2 inch (50 mm) squares or strips and cover them with the soy sauce.

To make the soup heat the stock and season with salt, then add the trimmed and sliced mushrooms and the noodles, broken into 1 inch (25 mm) pieces. Cook gently until the noodles are soft, and serve with a little soy sauce on the side. This soup is both delicate and good.

To prepare the pork dish, cut up the cabbage as for Chinese cabbage (page 79) and follow that recipe, tossing the cabbage in hot oil, until it is time to pour in the liquid. Put the chopped pork on top of the cabbage, first, then add the chopped ginger, and a cup of water or stock, cover and cook gently for 15–20 minutes. Serve with rice. Spinach can be used instead of cabbage, but double the quantity as it cooks down. Serves 4 with side dishes.

Sweet and sour pork is made by cubing lean pork, then dipping the cubes in batter, (*see pastella*, page 29), then deep frying them. Sweet and sour sauce is easily made as follows.

Sweet and sour sauce

½ cup white vinegar	½ cup water
1 tablespoon sugar or honey	½ teaspoon paprika
1 teaspoon soy sauce	1 tablespoon cornflour

Combine all ingredients except the cornflour in a saucepan and bring to the boil. Cream the cornflour in 2 tablespoons water and add to the mixture. Stir until it thickens; add a little more sugar or honey if liked and if the mixture seems too thick add a very little vinegar and water mixed. Or use the pineapple-flavoured sauce given on page 120.

Belly of pork is very good roasted, a most succulent little joint, and if it is salted and boiled, then served with pease pudding (page 91) it becomes a filling and tasty winter dish.

Pickled pork is an old-fashioned meal these days, but one which can be extremely good. Use either streaky or belly of pork, which can be roasted until crisp and is delicious, or simmered in one piece as a stew. It is particularly good cooked with rabbit, which I am glad to see again at a fairly reasonable price. Use plenty of onions, a bayleaf and parsley; cider is good mixed with half water as a stock. Season well, and cook gently for about 2 hours. If liked the rabbit can be taken from the bone when cool and layered with the pork in a deep dish. If the liquid is poured around it will jelly when cold and make a superb terrine.

Pork products, which include bacon and sausages, are indispensable to many households. They have always been eaten by Celtic peoples and by the poorer countries, for pigs require no grazing and can be kept on household scraps.

Dublin coddle was a great favourite of Dean Swift's and used to be a traditional Irish supper dish, after the pubs were closed on a Saturday night. I have found it popular with all ages, and a very good way with sausages.

8 large pork sausages or 16 of the smaller kind
8 slices bacon, cut in pieces
2 pints (1 l) boiling water

4 large onions, sliced
2 lb (1 kg) peeled and sliced potatoes
4 tablespoons chopped parsley
Salt and pepper

Boil the sausages and bacon in the boiling water for 10 minutes. Drain, but reserve the liquid. Put the meat into a large saucepan or casserole layered with the thinly sliced onions, potatoes and the chopped parsley. Season to taste, and add enough of the stock barely to cover. Lay foil or greaseproof paper over the top, then the lid, and simmer gently, or cook in a slow oven (250°F/120°C/Gas Mark 1) for about 2 hours or until the liquid is reduced by half and all the ingredients cooked, but not mushy. Serve hot with fresh slices of soda bread. Serves 6–8.

Savoury sausages with bananas and rice

1 chicken stock cube
1 medium onion, sliced
Pinch of fresh chopped herbs
Salt
1 lb (450 g) long-grain rice

8 rashers bacon
8–12 sausages
2 tablespoons oil
8 large bananas
Parsley

Boil up 2 pints (1 l) of water, and add the stock cube, the sliced onion, the chopped herbs and salt. When it is boiling add the rice. Let it come to the boil again, lower the heat until it is just simmering, cover, and let it cook for about 25 minutes or until all the liquid has been absorbed, then pile up on to a warmed dish. Meanwhile, while the rice is cooking, remove bacon rinds, cut the rashers in half and roll up. Grill or fry them with the sausages, heat up the oil and lightly fry the bananas

until they are soft and pale brown. Arrange them alternately on the rice and garnish with parsley. Mixed vegetables can be added to the rice when it is cooking if liked. Serves 8.

Sausages in beer

1 oz (25 g) butter or oil
1 medium to large onion, sliced
1 lb (450 g) skinless sausages

1 oz (25 g) flour
Salt and pepper
½ pint (300 ml) warmed beer, preferably draught

Heat up the butter or oil and lightly fry the onion until soft but not coloured. Then add the sausages, and let them just brown on all sides. Shake the flour over, and also season to taste, then add the beer and simmer gently with the lid on for about 10 minutes, turning them at least once. Serves 4.

Normandy sausages

I once had these in Normandy made with the rather coarsely-ground pork sausages available there and it was delicious.

1 lb (450 g) sausages, skinless or lightly grilled
2 tablespoons butter or oil
1 large onion, sliced
2 large apples, peeled, cored and sliced

2 cloves garlic
Sprinkle of flour
1 tablespoon tomato purée
½ pint (300 ml) dry cider
Salt and pepper

If not using skinless sausages grill them lightly first, so as to colour the outside; do not overcook them.

Heat up the butter or oil and lightly fry the onion,

apples and chopped garlic, so that they are softened but not brown. Add the sausages and cook for seven minutes, then shake the flour over, and mix the tomato purée into the cider. Pour this over, season to taste, and let it bubble up for a few minutes until it is thickened and the sausages cooked. Garnish with parsley if available and serve with mashed potatoes. Serves 4.

Bacon joints

Shoulder or collar of bacon is the best buy, for it is not too fatty and has a good flavour. It should be soaked first in cold water for at least 3 hours, unless it is a packaged variety which is pre-soaked.

Bacon or pork braised in cider with fruit and vegetables

This is a seventeenth-century recipe and very good.

2 tablespoons oil or fat	1 tablespoon flour
3 small onions	6 dates
3 medium apples	1 head celery
Salt and pepper	1 orange
1 boneless bacon joint (approx. 3 lb, 1½ kg), either collar or shoulder, soaked for at least 3 hours, or equivalent unsoaked joint of pork	4 oz (115 g) seeded grapes or sultanas ½ pint (300 ml) cider Sprig each of sage and parsley

Heat the oil or fat and fry, very lightly, the sliced onions and apples. When ready put them in the bottom of a casserole and season. Rub the bacon joint in flour, and place on top, then add the chopped dates, celery, herbs, finely chopped orange peel and the quarters of orange without pith or pips, the grapes and the cider, adding a little water if the liquid doesn't cover the meat.

Cover and cook in a slow oven for about 2 hours. For carving put the joint on separate dish, pouring some of the sauce and vegetables over it. Serves 8.

Bacon with barbecue relish

3 lb (1½ kg) joint of collar bacon	1 × 15 oz (425 g) tin tomatoes
1 onion, sliced	2 tablespoons cider vinegar
1 bayleaf	
Few peppercorns	2 tablespoons demerara sugar
Demerara sugar	
Cloves	2 tablespoons chutney
Barbecue relish:	½ teaspoon French mustard
1 onion, finely chopped	Dash of Worcestershire sauce
1 oz (25 g) butter	

First soak the joint for about 3 hours, then pat dry. *Either* boil the meat with the onion, bayleaf, peppercorns, starting with cold water, for 20 minutes to the pound (450 g) and 20 minutes over (but do not leave it on the boil: after reaching that point it should merely shudder in the water); *or* wrap the soaked bacon in foil with the onion, bayleaf and peppercorns and secure well, then roast at (425°F/210°C/Gas Mark 7) for 30 minutes to the pound (450 g). When cooked, strip off the rind, score the fat in criss-cross pattern, coat with the sugar and dot with cloves. Crisp off the joint in a moderate oven (350°F/180°C/Gas Mark 4) for 10–15 minutes. While the bacon is cooking make the sauce.

Cook the chopped onion in the butter without browning. Add remaining ingredients, bring to the boil, reduce heat and simmer for 10 minutes. Serves 8.

Boiled bacon is very good hot, with *avgolémono* sauce (page 119).

See also cassoulet (page 90) and pig's liver (page 139).

VEAL

The price of veal today puts it almost outside the scope of this book. However, breast of veal, trimmed and cubed, then simmered for 30 minutes to the pound (450 g) with a little bacon, onion, root vegetables, tomatoes and herbs makes a delicate dish, which can either be used for a pie or, with the stock thickened with eggyolks and a *beurre manié* of butter and flour, to make a delicious stew. When cold it will be a thick jelly.

Breast of veal can also be stuffed with a bread or oatmeal stuffing, or with chopped spinach and quartered hard-boiled eggs, then rolled, secured and simmered for at least 2 hours to make a fine roulade.

Osso bucco is braised shin of veal, which is still cheap in price and makes a really delicious meal.

3 oz (85 g) butter or margarine, or 3 tablespoons olive oil	2 cloves garlic
1 medium onion, sliced	1 lb (450 g) tomatoes, skinned and chopped, or equivalent tinned
4 lb (2 kg) shin of veal, sawn into pieces about 2 inches (50 mm) but check that it has a good coating of meat around it	$\frac{1}{2}$ pint (300 ml) stock ($\frac{1}{2}$ cube will do)
	Salt and pepper
	1 large lemon
	4 tablespoons chopped parsley
$\frac{1}{4}$ pint (150 ml) white wine	

Heat the butter or oil in a large pan and lightly fry the onion, then add the pieces of shin of veal (with the bone and the marrow inside) and brown them quickly on both sides. See that they are standing up, otherwise the marrow will spill out. Pour the white wine around and let it bubble up for about 5 minutes. Then transfer this to a casserole, add one of the garlic cloves, tomatoes, stock, salt and pepper, cover and cook in a slow oven for 2 hours, taking off the lid for the last $\frac{1}{2}$ hour. Meanwhile, grate the peel of the lemon very finely and add it to the chopped parsley and the other clove of garlic, very finely chopped. Put this mixture, known as *gremolata* in Italy, on top, 10 minutes before serving. Serves about 4.

Traditionally, this is served with *risotto Milanese* (page 68).

SOUP-STEWS AND HOT-POTS

Scotch broth has nurtured many a sturdy Scotsman, and is still a favourite winter dish which is difficult to stop eating. '... You never ate it before?' 'No, sir,' replied Johnson, 'but I don't care how soon I eat it again' (*Journal of a Tour to the Hebrides*, James Boswell, 1786).

2 lb (1 kg) neck of mutton, trimmed of fat, and a knuckle bone if possible	3 carrots, diced
	1 large onion, sliced
	White part of 1 large leek, sliced
5 pints (2.8 l) water	3 oz (85 g) pot barley
Salt and pepper	1 small cabbage, shredded
3 oz (85 g) shelled peas or $\frac{1}{2}$ cup soaked dried peas, according to season	2 tablespoons chopped parsley
2 medium white turnips, diced	

Put the meat into a large saucepan with the water, bring to the boil, and then skim the top. Season to taste, then simmer gently for about 1 hour. Add the peas (if dried, add them with the meat to begin with), diced turnip, carrot, onion, leek and the barley, cover and simmer for 20 minutes, then put in the shredded cabbage and test for seasoning. A few minutes before serving add the parsley. Serve hot with 1 cutlet per person. Some cooks prefer to serve the broth first and then the meat afterwards with a caper sauce. The vegetables can be varied according to whatever is in season, or to hand – kale instead of cabbage, celery, etc. Serves about 8.

Hotch-potch

Also called 'hairst bree', meaning harvest broth. 'A truly delicious soup, quite peculiar to Scotland...' (J. G. Lockhart, 1819).

The essence of this soup-stew is that it must be made with good, fresh meat, and at the time when all the vegetables are very young and crisp. In some parts of Scotland small cabbage is used instead of cauliflower, and in both Harris and Lewis young nettle tops, wild spinach, shemis (*Ligusticum scoticum*), a kind of wild lovage, nettles, wild carrot and garlic have also been used when fresh green vegetables were scarce.

2 lb (1 kg) neck of lamb chops	2 cups fresh shelled green peas
5 pints (2.8 l) water	1 medium cauliflower
1 teaspoon salt	1 small hearty lettuce
4 small yellow turnips	1 teaspoon sugar
4 medium carrots	2 teaspoons chopped mint
6 spring onions (with green)	Pepper
1 cup shelled young broad beans	1 tablespoon chopped parsley

Boil the lamb with the water and salt, very gently, and remove any scum from the top. Cover and simmer for 1 hour. (If liked, the meat can then be removed and taken from the bone before being replaced, but this is not traditional.) Add the chopped turnips, carrots, onions, beans and half the peas, cover again and simmer for 1½ hours. Then add the cauliflower, cut into flowerlets, the shredded lettuce, the rest of the peas, the sugar and the mint and season again to taste. Cover and simmer gently for about ½ hour, or until the vegetables and meat are tender, but not broken up. Add the parsley just before serving to give a nice fresh taste. The soup-stew should be very thick, and is a meal on its own. Serves 4–6.

Irish stew was originally made with kid, for no farmer would be so foolhardy as to kill off young stock. It should be creamy in consistency, not swimming in a lot of liquid.

3 lb (1½ kg) best end of neck of lamb chops, trimmed of fat, bone and gristle	1 tablespoon chopped parsley and thyme mixed
2 lb (1 kg) potatoes	Salt and pepper
1 lb (450 g) onions	¾ pint (450 ml) water

Cut the meat into fairly large pieces and see that the fat, bone, etc. are trimmed off. Peel and slice the potatoes and onions. Put a layer of potatoes in a pan, then herbs, then sliced meat and finally onion. Season each layer well and repeat this once more, finishing with a thick layer of potatoes. Pour the liquid over, cover with a sheet of foil, then the lid, and either bake in a slow oven (250°F/120°C/Gas Mark ½–1) or simmer very gently on top of the stove, shaking from time to time so that it does not stick, for about 2 hours. Add a very little more liquid if it seems to be getting very dry.

Another method is to place the trimmed neck chops around the inside edge of a saucepan, and put the sliced onions and small potatoes with herbs and seasonings in the middle. Add the water, put on the lid and then cook very slowly for about 2 hours until the meat is quite tender. If the meat is so placed, you will have no difficulty in serving.

Lancashire hot-pot

6 shoulder or neck of lamb chops, trimmed of bone
3 lamb's kidneys (optional but good)
5 medium to large potatoes
1 large onion

Salt and black pepper
1 tablespoon chopped parsley
Pinch of chopped thyme
½ pint (300 ml) meat stock

Trim the chops of fat and bone, then skin and cut the kidneys into quarters. Peel and slice the potatoes and onion, and take a deep dish and put a layer of potatoes in the bottom, then a layer of chops, followed by some kidney, seasonings, herbs and then a layer of onion. Repeat this until the dish is full, ending with a layer of potatoes. Add the stock (made from the bones), cover with a piece of buttered paper, then the lid. Bake in a moderate oven (325°F/160°C/Gas Mark 3–4) for about 2 hours, but for the last ½ hour remove the lid and the

paper so the potatoes will crisp up and become golden. This dish should be cooked and eaten straight away, as otherwise the potatoes might get soggy. It has a beautifully pure flavour of all the ingredients. Pickled red cabbage is traditionally served with it. Serves 6.

Pepperpot is a West Indian dish made from tripe and a knuckle bone of veal or a ham-bone.

1 knuckle bone of veal or ham-bone
4 pints (2.2 l) water
Salt
1 onion
Thyme
⅓ teaspoon peppercorns, finely pounded
1 lb (450 g) honeycomb tripe

1 tablespoon butter
3 tablespoons flour
3 tomatoes, peeled
2 sticks celery
1 red pepper or ½ teaspoon chilli powder
1½ cups potato cubes

Cook the knuckle bone in water with onion, salt, herbs, and peppercorns (tied in a piece of muslin) for 2 hours. Cut the tripe into thin strips and toss them lightly in melted butter. Add the flour and the stock (strained knuckle bone stock) and simmer until tripe is soft. Add the tomatoes, celery, red pepper, all chopped, and potato cubes and cook until they are done. Season well with salt and pepper. For pressure cooking of bones the time is 30 minutes; for tripe 20 minutes. Serves 3–4.

OFFAL

Brains, heart and tripe are all cheap compared to today's prices for other meats; all are nutritious, and if cooked well are extremely good.

BRAINS

To prepare them, first soak for about 1 hour in cold, salted water. Drain, and bring some more salted water to the boil to which you have added either 1 tablespoon of vinegar or the equivalent in lemon juice. Add the brains and simmer gently for about 20 minutes, then drain them. When cool, remove the skin and any membranes which are attached and leave them to get quite cold. When cold cut into cubes about the size of a walnut.

Fritôt of brains with beurre noir

4 sets brains
deep oil for frying

Batter:
Salt
4 oz (115 g) plain flour
1 tablespoon oil

½ pint (150 ml) tepid
    water
1 eggwhite

Sauce:
2 oz (60 g) butter
3 tablespoons vinegar
2 tablespoons capers

First make the batter by adding the salt to the flour, then pour in the oil, and then the warm water. Mix well so that it is a smooth, fairly thickish consistency. Set aside for ½ hour and meanwhile beat the eggwhite until stiff and get the deep oil hot enough for frying crisply. Add the eggwhite to the batter, stirring around with a fork and making sure that the white reaches down to the bottom. Dip each piece of brain (prepared as above) into the batter and fry until golden on both sides. This batter will puff up so don't put too many in together. Drain on kitchen paper.

To make the sauce, melt the butter in a saucepan and let it turn light brown, then add the vinegar and capers and keep hot. If the brains are fried only until pale gold they can be re-fried later in the day. If you are doing them to serve straight away, put the drained puffs on to a warm dish and serve with the hot sauce poured over. Serves 4.

Stuffed braised lamb's hearts

8 lamb's hearts
Salt and pepper
3 tablespoons oil
1 heaped tablespoon flour
2 cups meat stock (or a
    cube)
1 large onion, chopped
2 carrots, sliced
2 stalks celery, chopped
Pinch each of mace and
    powdered marjoram
2 bayleaves

Stuffing:
1 cup breadcrumbs
3 tablespoons milk
Grated peel of 1 lemon
1 small onion, grated
1 teaspoon each chopped
    thyme and parsley
Salt and pepper

Wash the hearts well and remove any fat, pipes or gristle. Make an incision from the top down one side of each to form pockets for the stuffing. Season the insides with salt and pepper, then make the stuffing. Pour about 3 tablespoons of milk over the breadcrumbs and let it soak in. Add the peel, onion, herbs, salt and pepper and mix well. Stuff the hearts with this mixture, pushing it down well, and if necessary secure with a skewer. Heat up the oil and brown the hearts on all sides; shake over the flour and let it brown for 1 minute, then add the stock, stirring well. Add the vegetables, spices and bayleaves and season to taste. Cover and cook in a slow oven for about 2 hours or until tender. Serve the hearts sliced with the vegetables and gravy. Tomatoes or any other vegetables can be added if liked, and the hearts can be stuffed with seasoned sausagemeat if preferred. A calf's heart can be treated in the same way, but will require 3 hours' cooking time. Serves 4–6.

KIDNEYS

'... Most of all he liked grilled mutton kidneys...' wrote James Joyce in *Ulysses* about his character

Leopold Bloom. There are, of course, many more ways of treating these delicious morsels, and the 4 distinct kinds of kidneys are all good if used for the right dishes. Beef or ox kidney should only be used in a casserole or for soup; veal kidneys (which, although not prominently displayed, are there for the asking) are extremely delicate in flavour and excellent when lightly braised or cooked in a chafing dish. Pig's kidneys make a good stew, and mutton kidneys are usually available and can be served in many ways.

Kidneys in their overcoats

These are simply mutton or veal kidneys baked in a pan in their fat casing for about 40 minutes in a moderate oven, or until the outside is quite crisp and brown. When broken open the juices are retained and the middle will be cooked, but juicy. Allow 2 to 3 kidneys per person, and serve either with toast, boiled potatoes or spinach, and salt and pepper.

Devilled kidneys are a good luncheon or supper dish. Mutton kidneys are the best for this method.

6 kidneys	Pinch each cayenne and
Little oil	salt
2 teaspoons mushroom	2 teaspoons
ketchup	Worcestershire sauce
2 teaspoons dry mustard	4 oz (115 g) butter or
and white pepper	margarine

Trim and skin the kidneys, brush them with oil and grill them on both sides until they are well-browned outside but still pink in the middle (about 7 minutes). Meanwhile, mix together all the other ingredients in a basin, spread over the kidneys just before serving, and heat for literally 1 minute under the grill. Allow 2–3 per person.

Pochki Smetanie is a Russian way with mutton kidneys which is excellent.

2 tablespoons oil	Salt and pepper
1 large onion	3 tablespoons red wine
12 mutton or 3 veal	$\frac{1}{2}$ pint (300 ml) plain
kidneys	yoghurt

Heat up the oil and fry the sliced onion until golden, then add the trimmed and skinned kidneys and also fry on both sides until brown, but do not overcook them. About 7 minutes is enough. Season to taste, pour over the wine and let it reduce, then just before serving add the yoghurt and mix well. Let it bubble up and serve at once. Serves 4–6.

Kidney casserole

1 large ox or 4 pig's	Salt and pepper
kidneys	Approx. $\frac{1}{2}$ pint (300 ml)
2 tablespoons flour	meat stock
1 large onion	or $\frac{1}{2}$ red wine and $\frac{1}{2}$
1 tablespoon mixed	water
chopped parsley and	
marjoram	

Ox kidneys make a very good casserole dish which can be cooked in advance and reheated to advantage. Pressure cooking time is 20–25 minutes.

Skin the kidney and cut out the central piece of fat, then cut into small pieces and coat with the flour. Put into a casserole with the sliced onion, herbs and seasonings and barely cover with the stock, or wine and water mixed. Cover and cook in a slow to moderate oven (225°–275°F/110°–140°C/Gas Mark $\frac{1}{2}$–1) for about 2 hours. Some people prefer to fry the kidney first, but doing it this way the juices come out and make a superb gravy. Serve with plain boiled rice, garnished with rings of crisp brown onions, and either a salad or a green vegetable such as peas or beans. Serves 4.

LIVER is quite expensive, but there is no wastage and it is important as food value. If you have your liver in one piece you might try stuffing and baking it: calf's, lamb's or pig's liver can be used.

Stuffed liver

2 lb (1 kg) liver in one piece	*Stuffing:*
Oil	3 slices crustless bread soaked in milk
Sprinkling of flour	1 small onion, grated
½ pint (300 ml) stock (dissolved cube will do)	1 teaspoon finely chopped lovage or parsley
Salt and pepper	Salt and pepper
6 rashers streaky bacon	Pinch of mace or nutmeg
1 tablespoon redcurrant jelly	Finely grated peel of ½ lemon

Mix all the stuffing ingredients together, then make a deep cut or pocket in the liver, but don't cut the whole way through. Put the stuffing in, and secure with a small skewer. Melt the oil in a casserole, and then quickly seal the liver all over in it, sprinkle with flour, and add the seasoned stock. Lay the rashers criss-cross fashion over the top, cover and cook in a slow oven for about 1¼ hours. Half an hour before it is ready add the redcurrant jelly (any sharp jelly will do, such as apple, if you don't have the redcurrant) and a little more stock (or a little red wine) if it seems to be running dry. Cover and continue cooking.

It can, of course, be made without the stuffing, but this lightens the meaty taste of the liver. If the liver has already been sliced, it can still be baked, layered with sliced onion, and bacon rashers, ending with a layer of rashers to keep the top basted. Barely cover with stock,

put the lid on, and bake in a moderate oven for not longer than 1 hour. Pig's liver cooked this way has a most excellent taste, almost like the famous goose liver of Germany or Austria.

Faggots

Faggots are exactly the same as the French *crépines* or *crépinettes* and yet another link with Brittany for they are a speciality of Wales, although a similar dish called 'savoury ducks' is found in the North of England and I suspect that these were a Welsh inheritance. As in France, they were always made around pig-killing time, usually from not only the liver but also other intestines, and traditionally they were wrapped in the pig's flead – that is, the thin lacy membrane, marbled with fat, from the pig's inside. They are still made daily in Wales, and can be found in many butchers.

Both faggots and various pasties were eaten a lot in Wales, especially by miners, quarry and furnace workers, for they were easy to transport, could be made at least the day before and provided the valuable protein needed for such strenuous work. They are extremely good, and much enjoyed by all ages.

2 lb (1 kg) pig's liver, minced (if this is difficult to get calf's or lamb's liver can be used) or ½ liver and ½ sausagemeat	butter or margarine Approx. ½ teaspoon mace or nutmeg 2 teaspoons chopped sage (bog myrtle was originally used)
2 large onions, minced	1 teaspoon chopped thyme
4 oz (115 g) breadcrumbs or oatmeal	2 teaspoons salt
4 oz (115 g) grated suet,	½ teaspoon black pepper

Put the finely minced liver and onions into a large bowl, then add the breadcrumbs or oatmeal and all the other ingredients and mix very thoroughly. Grease a large meat tin and put the mixture in, and if possible cover with a sheet of pork flead, but if this is not available use greased foil. Cook in a slow to moderate oven (250°F/ 130°C/Gas Mark ½–1) for 40–60 minutes, but after 20 minutes take from the oven and mark into squares with a knife. 15 minutes before it is ready remove the foil (not the flead if using it) to let the tops get brown. Leave in the tin to get cold and when serving break them apart. They can be eaten cold with salad and apple sauce or, if wanted hot, pour over about ½ pint (300 ml) of good stock to make a gravy, and reheat. Serves 4–6.

TONGUE

I can never make out why canned tongue is so expensive, for uncooked tongue can be bought from any butcher at a very reasonable price, compared to lean cuts of meat. Most butchers will keep a tongue for you if it is ordered about midweek. It usually comes elaborately tied up with string, and the first thing to do is untie it and see that it is properly trimmed of all horny parts or bone, and leave it untied.

To boil an ox or calf tongue

If it has been in pickle, it is advisable to soak it overnight in cold water, so that it isn't too salty. Put it in a large saucepan with an onion stuck with 2 cloves, a sliced carrot or two, turnip, celery or whatever is to hand in the root vegetable line. Add a bayleaf, some thyme or parsley, and a good sprinkling of black pepper. Cover with cold water, put the lid on and simmer very gently for about 2½–3 hours, but test with a fork to see it is tender after that time, if the tongue is a very large one. If you have a pressure cooker, a tongue weighing about 3 lb (1½ kg) will take 45–60 minutes.

When cooked, plunge it into cold water and the skin will come off easily; also see that it is well trimmed of any gristle.

To serve tongue cold

Put the tongue in a suitable basin, curled round so that it is a tight roll. Taste the stock to see if it is salty, in which case it is better to throw it away, for nothing is more difficult than trying to eradicate salt from stock. If the stock is no use, then dissolve about 2 tablespoons of aspic powder in water and pour this around and over the tongue. Cover, and put in a cold place to set. There is no need to press it; I find that it sets very well, and the interspersed jelly has a good flavour. Once cooked, the tongue can be served in any number of ways, and I usually serve it hot at least once, and then put what remains in aspic if there is enough left over.

Polish sauce for tongue

Cook the tongue as above, and taste stock for saltiness: if too salty, use a dissolved stock cube as in sweet and sour tongue.

1 tablespoon margarine or butter	1 tablespoon tarragon vinegar
1 heaped tablespoon flour	2 oz (60 g) sultanas
½ pint (300 ml) stock	2 oz (60 g) almonds, blanched and chopped
½ pint (300 ml) sweet white wine or cider	Pinch of cinnamon
Juice and finely grated peel of 1 lemon	1 tablespoon brown sugar

Melt the butter and stir in the flour, then add the warm stock, stirring well to avoid lumps. Add the wine and all other ingredients, stirring well after each addition. Serve hot, over the tongue as above.

Tongue with sweet and sour sauce

1 ox or calf tongue
    (approx. 3 lb, 1½ kg)
Root vegetables and
    herbs as above

Sauce:
1 pint (600 ml) tongue
    stock (if this is too
    salty use a dissolved
    chicken stock or
    bouillon cube)
1 tablespoon brown
    sugar
1 tablespoon honey

Grated peel of ½ orange
    and ½ lemon, and a
    good squeeze of juice
    from each
3 tablespoons white
    wine vinegar
1 tablespoon chopped
    fresh parsley
Pinch of paprika and
    black pepper
1 heaped tablespoon
    cornflour

Take out 1 pint of stock for sauce then warm up the tongue in the remaining stock. Put all sauce ingredients together in a separate saucepan, except the cornflour. Cream the cornflour with a little cold water, then add to the sauce ingredients when they are boiling. Stir well to avoid lumps, and keep warm. Slice the drained tongue into thick slices on a warmed dish, and pour the sauce over. Serves about 6.

Trippa alla Romana (Tripe Roman style)

3¼ lb (1½ kg) tripe,
    preferably honeycomb
    veal tripe
6 tablespoons olive oil
1 large onion, sliced
1 large clove garlic,
    chopped
2 carrots, sliced
4 stalks celery, chopped
Salt and freshly-ground
    pepper

¼ pint (150 ml) white
    wine
1 tablespoon chopped
    mint
1 × 16 oz (450 g) tin
    tomatoes
6 tablespoons grated
    hard cheese, e.g.
    Pecorino or Parmesan

This tripe is very delicious, the fresh mint giving it an unexpectedly good flavour.

First trim the tripe of any fat, then wash it well in tepid water. Put into a large saucepan, cover with cold water and bring to the boil. Throw off the first water and repeat this operation, then simmer slowly in fresh water for about 3 hours or until the tripe is quite tender. (Sometimes tripe is sold half-cooked, in which case simmer for only 2 hours.) Leave it to get cold, then cut into strips of about 3 inches (75 mm).

Fry the onion in the heated oil with the garlic, carrots and celery, until they are soft but not coloured, then season. Add the tripe strips and mix well, letting it heat gently. Pour in the wine and the mint, then let it bubble up and reduce slightly. When it has reduced add the tomatoes and their juice, mixing well. Cook again, gently, for ¾ hour and, when serving, sprinkle the tripe with the grated cheese, allowing 1 tablespoon per person and letting it melt a little before serving. Serves 6–8.

11. Miscellaneous

PASTRY

Many of the dishes in this book require pastry of one kind or another. Pastry is one of the oldest forms of cookery, flour and water being mixed together then used as a wrapping around various foods to enclose the juices. It is a good way to cook, and also supplies extra nourishment with small amounts of meat, etc. such as in a Cornish pasty. Pasties, and turnovers have been the staple food for centuries in Cornwall and Lancashire. Originally they were used as food for the miners to take to work with them, for almost any food can be put in the pastry crust, such as meat, fish, bacon, vegetables (especially leeks), herbs, eggs and even fruit pasties and turnovers are made. Nowadays they are enjoyed by all and are excellent picnic food.

A joint of bacon or a stuffed shoulder of lamb wrapped in a pastry crust and then roasted is an old-fashioned but excellent way of cooking. In France many dishes are cooked in this way, *pâté en croûte* being perhaps the best known. Baked apple dumplings are seldom seen today, but how well I remember the ones my grandmother made for me when I was a child. The cored apple was filled with a little cinnamon or clove butter and either brown sugar or golden syrup, then wrapped in its pastry crust, and served hot from the oven, the spicy, butter, syrupy juices running out as I broke into it. Sometimes they would be made with the potato and flour mixture given for potato cakes (2) (page 85), and then I would be given extra butter and brown sugar to sprinkle over the top. Apple dumplings, boiled, were another favourite of mine, made with a suet crust, or better still a boiled apple pudding, for then one got more apple than pastry, and sometimes a second helping. These old-fashioned 'granny' puddings are both cheap and nutritious, and never refused when made. I have an American friend who spent two terms at an English public school, and whenever I stay with him the first thing I am asked to do is to 'make some of those gorgeous English puddings'. You really need very little for a first course if one of those puddings is to follow.

VARIOUS KINDS OF PASTRY

Shortcrust pastry

4 oz (115 g) margarine, or margarine and lard mixed	Pinch of salt 8 oz (225 g) SR flour 2–3 tablespoons water

Mix the fat and a pinch of salt into the flour and make into a stiff dough with the water. See that all ingredients are kept cold. Turn out on to a floured board and roll into a sheet.

Rich shortcrust pastry

4 oz (115 g) butter	2 teaspoons castor sugar
8 oz (225 g) plain flour	3 tablespoons iced water
Pinch of salt	1 eggyolk

Mix the butter into the flour, salt and castor sugar. Add a tablespoon of iced water to the eggyolk. Mix this into the flour mixture and finally add the remaining iced water, mixing it all to a stiff paste. Put on to a floured board, and roll to required size.

Suet-crust pastry

8 oz SR flour or 8 heaped tablespoons	Pinch of salt Water
4 heaped tablespoons grated suet	

Mix the flour, suet and salt together, and then add just enough water to make a stiff dough (about ½ cup should be enough). Turn on to a floured board and roll into a sheet about ¼ inch (6 mm) thick.

Puff pastry

6 oz (170 g) plain flour	1 tablespoon sugar (for sweet dishes)
Pinch of salt	
6 oz (170 g) butter	3–4 tablespoons iced water

Stir flour in a basin with the salt (and sugar, if making sweet pastry); cut half the butter into pieces and mix well into the flour in lumps, then add enough water to make a firm dough. Roll out on a floured board to a rectangle about ½ inch (12 mm) thick. Add the remaining butter in little pieces on to half the dough, then fold over, pressing the edges well together. Let it stand for 10 minutes. With the sealed end towards you, roll away from you; then fold the dough into three, and turn round again so that the open edge faces you, then roll again. Repeat this twice more so that in all the pastry has six turns of rolling and resting. Keep everything as cold as possible, and store in a cool place until you need it.

RAISED MEAT PIES

The raised pie is made of hot pastry and moulded, or raised around wooden moulds. This is the oldest form of pastry case, and was known as a 'coffyn' or 'coffer', that is, a little box, hence the following lines from a fourteenth-century document. 'PYG PYE: Flea Pyg and cut him in pieces, season with pepper and salt, and nutmeg, and large mace, and lay in your coffyn good store of raisins and currants, and fill with sweet butter and close it, and serve hot or cold.'

Any meat can be made into a raised pie, but the two most popular pies are pork, and veal and ham mixed. All these pies can of course be made in a pie-dish and covered with ordinary shortcrust. The great advantage of raised pies is that they do not need a dish, and were always taken by shooting parties, men working a distance from home like shepherds, or people picnicking.

The method of preparing and cooking is the same for all meats, so I will give the essentials here.

The meat must be chopped, not minced, quite small, and not too much fat left on it. In some cases it can be cooked a little beforehand; this is advisable if making the pies small, as the pastry would be cooked before the meat. The stock should be rendered down until it is certain to jelly. This is not difficult, as pork and veal are known for their gelatinous quality. However, for a mutton or beef pie it might be advisable to add a little gelatine or aspic to the stock. A few chopped herbs, such as sage and marjoram, should be added to the pie as well as a bunch put into the stock, and plenty of good black pepper and salt. In the case of veal and ham pie, hard-boiled eggs are sliced and scattered throughout the pie. In country districts home-made mutton and pork pies are sometimes interspersed with tart windfall apples. Whatever is used, there must be a good, tasty, jellied stock to pour in afterwards.

Hot-water crust for raised meat pie

To make 1 large pie 6 inches (15 cm) across and about 6 inches (15 cm) high, or several small ones.

Pinch of salt	4 tablespoons lard
1 lb (450 g) flour	½ pint (190 ml) water

Unlike any other kind of pastry, hot-water crust must be kept warm.

Mix the salt into the flour in a mixing basin. Bring the lard and water to boiling point and pour immediately into a well made in the flour. Mix thoroughly and quickly with a wooden spoon and the hands. This has to be all done quickly, for the paste must be moulded into shape before the lard has time to set and the paste becomes brittle. Set aside about a third of the pastry for the top lid and then roll out the remainder. In the middle of it set a wide-bottomed, straight jar which has been warmed – earthenware is best, about 4–5 inches (10–13 cm) diameter. Shape the paste around this and up the sides, patting with the hand and working as quickly as possible. When the mould is made, carefully lift out the jar and tightly pack in the chopped meat, either raw or partly cooked, and herbs.

Roll out the top to fit, dampen the edges and put on the lid, pressing gently to make sure it is closed. Cut a neat hole in the lid and make a little leaf or rosette to cover this, but do not press it on. If a glazed outside crust is desired, brush with beaten egg in milk. Then bake in a slow to moderate oven for 1–1½ hours. Have a well-flavoured stock hot, and immediately the pie is cooked pour it through a funnel into the pie until it is quite full. Put the rosette back and leave the pie to stand overnight. Do not refrigerate as this will make the pastry hard. Raised meat pies are not as difficult to make as they might sound, and they are excellent. At least 2 lb (1 kg) meat would be needed to fill the above case.

Mutton pies have a little minced onion in them, and they used to be decorated on the market stands with a sprig of mint to distinguish them from pork pies.

In the country around Nottingham they used to make a raised fruit pie, often from gooseberries, and to fill it afterwards with hot apple jelly.

I have seen meat pies made in a long bread tin: this is quite a good idea if you are timid about making the raised crust, but then only the top can be glazed and the tin must be greased to avoid sticking. Leave in the tin until cold, otherwise you may break the pie getting it out. Or use a spring-sided tin, which are available at many good shops stocking kitchenware.

A FEW PUDDINGS

There are many sweet pudings given throughout the book (*see* Index) and many more fruit tarts or flans can be made with the above pastries. Excellent fillings for a 9 inch (23 cm) flan are gooseberries, plums or peeled and cored pears (sprinkle with lemon juice to avoid discoloration), covered with ½ pint (300 ml) yoghurt, or

K

a 5 oz (150 ml) carton of yoghurt topped up with the cream from the milk, 3–4 tablespoons sugar, according to taste, and 1 eggyolk all beaten together. Pour this over the fruit in the unbaked pastry case and cook for about ½ hour in a (375°F/190°C/Gas Mark 5) oven.

Cobblers are easier to make than steamed puddings or pies. They stem from the days when the oven range was on day and night and fruits of the fields like blackberries, or plums from the kitchen garden, were plentiful. Sometimes they are made with the fruit at the bottom only, but gradually they evolved into almost oven-baked moist dumplings with the fruit in the middle. This plum cobbler is really delicious and can be made with almost any fruit.

1 lb (450 g) ripe plums, stoned
4 oz (115 g) light brown sugar
1 tablespoon lemon juice
6 oz (170 g) plain flour
2 teaspoons baking powder
2½ oz (70 g) margarine or butter, cut into pieces
Approx. ½ pint (300 ml) creamy milk
2 tablespoons white sugar

Put the plums, brown sugar and lemon juice into a saucepan and cook for 3 minutes. Then combine the flour and baking powder together, and mix in the fat until it resembles fine breadcrumbs. Add the milk, just enough so that it will form soft mounds when dropped from a spoon in a stream. Butter a 9 inch (23 cm) deep dish well, then pour in half the batter, put the plum mixture on top and the rest of the batter over.

Sprinkle the white sugar over the top and bake in a preheated hot oven (425°F/210°C/Gas Mark 7) for about 25 minutes or until the top is golden and the batter is cooked when tested with a skewer in the middle. Serves at least 4.

Lemon pudding is a similar idea which produces a sort of lemon sauce under a spongy top. It is excellent served after a cold meal.

2 eggs	1 lemon
1½ heaped tablespoons butter	3 tablespoons sifted flour
4 oz (115 g) sugar	1 pint (600 ml) milk
Grated rind and juice of	Sugar for garnish

Separate the yolks from the whites of the eggs, then cream the butter and sugar, and mix in the yolks, the grated rind and juice of the lemon and the flour. Beat well and gradually add the milk. Finally fold in the beaten eggwhites. Grease a deep dish and pour the mixture in, then stand in a larger dish with 1 inch (25 mm) of water in it. Bake at (350°F/180°C/Gas Mark 4) for about 35 minutes, or until it is puffed up and golden brown. Dust with sugar before serving, and eat hot. Enough for 4.

Canary pudding

Also for date, fig or marmalade pudding.

This is one of the basic English light steamed puddings. It can have many other flavourings added, such as preserved ginger, chopped dates, figs, marmalade, sultanas, currants, candied peel or orange. If it is made without flavouring or fruit added, then the bottom of the basin is lined with jam or golden syrup. It has a spongy texture, and can be very good. If made in individual small moulds they are called 'castle puddings'.

2 eggs, and their weight in butter, castor sugar and SR flour (the average egg weighs 2 oz, 60 g)	Grated rind of 1 lemon Jam
	For a steamed fruit pudding:
	3 oz (85 g) fruit, chopped

Cream the butter and add sugar gradually, beating very well. Beat a spoonful of the flour into the eggs, then fold in the remainder with the lemon rind, and mix all together very thoroughly (if using fruit stir it in now, but omit the jam in bottom of basin). Put a tablespoon or so of jam in the bottom of a greased pudding basin and pour the mixture in, seeing that it does not come to more than three-quarters of the way up, to allow for rising. Cover and steam for 1½–2 hours. Turn out carefully on to a warm plate and serve with extra warmed jam if liked. Serves 4.

Hasty pudding

One of the oldest English puddings, and very simple to make. It stems from the days when, with milk, flour, butter and spices always in the house, the pudding could be made reasonably quickly to put before unexpected callers. Well-made it can be very good, and much better than it sounds. Before 1800 it always had an egg in it, but since then it is made without, and I think it is better.

Almost any sweet spice can be used, and if you are out of those a bayleaf is a very good substitute.

2 oz (60 g) butter	Pinch of mace or
1 heaped tablespoon	nutmeg, or 1 bayleaf
flour (or use cornflour)	2 tablespoons castor
¾ pint (425 ml) warm	sugar
milk	1 teaspoon cinnamon or
	nutmeg

Melt half the butter in a saucepan and stir in the flour until it is well mixed. Gradually add the warm milk, stirring all the time, so that the mixture is smooth and thick. Add the pinch of mace, nutmeg or bayleaf and let it just simmer a while, but do not stop stirring. Have a grill hot and a well buttered dish ready. Then pour it boiling into the dish, and at once put the rest of the butter on top in small lumps; then cover thickly with the sugar and finally the powdered cinnamon or nutmeg. Put under the grill for just a few minutes until the top is well heated and the butter, sugar and spice topping is just browned. It is best eaten hot, but is also good cold. Serves 4.

Malvern pudding

This traditional English pudding originates from Malvern, Worcestershire. It is made as above, but put into a pie-dish with alternate layers of cooked sweetened apple pulp which has had a little grated lemon rind added. The top layer is hasty pudding, which is strewn with sugar and spices as above, and it is then put into a moderate oven for 20 minutes and served either hot or cold.

Lemon cream is a Victorian refinement on the country-type hasty pudding.

2 large lemons	2 large eggs
1 pint (600 ml) water	¼ pint (150 ml) double
4–6 oz (115–170 g)	cream, or ½ cottage
sugar (according to	cheese and ½ yoghurt
taste)	beaten together
2 oz (60 g) cornflour	

Grate lemon rind finely, add water and boil for 5 minutes, then strain. Put the sugar and cornflour into a bowl with the lemon juice, beat well, then add to the strained warm lemon water and mix thoroughly and bring to the boil, stirring well. Separate the yolks from the whites of the eggs, and add the yolks to the mixture, whisking as you pour. Cool, then add the stiffly beaten eggwhites. Whip the cream or cheese and yoghurt mixture until thick, and fold in. Chill before serving, either in one large bowl or individual dishes. Serves 4–6.

Bananas, either baked or fried, make an economical pudding. A good way is to peel them, then slice lengthways in half if large and put them into an ovenproof dish. Grate over the rind of an orange, then squeeze the juice and pour over. Use 2 oranges if they are small, and see that the juice comes to halfway up the bananas. Sprinkle over about 2 tablespoons brown sugar, then add 1 teaspoon rum essence mixed with 2 tablespoons water. Bake in a hot oven (400°F/200°C/Gas Mark 6) for about 40 minutes. When cold the juice will be jellied.

Or, if you don't want to use the oven then heat about 1 tablespoon butter in a frying pan and sauté the bananas in it. Pour over the orange juice, and some sugar, also a squeeze of lemon as the butter makes this dish much richer. Serve hot, as the butter becomes solid when cold.

Egg fluff is a very light sweet dish which can be made in seconds. It is useful for invalids or when you haven't much time, and is very good served over cooked or soft fruit in place of cream. It can also be cooked in a low oven like a meringue.

For two people separate the yolk from the white of 1 egg. Beat up the white stiffly with sugar to taste, and then beat the yolk and fold it in gently.

Yiaourtopeta is a Greek cake made with yoghurt, which is very light, and can be used for a dessert.

4 oz (115 g) butter	½ pint (300 ml) plain
12 oz (340 g) sugar	yoghurt (or use fruit-
2 eggs	flavoured)
10 oz (280 g) plain	
flour	*Syrup:*
½ teaspoon baking	1½ pints (900 ml) water
powder	10 oz (280 g) sugar
Pinch of salt	

Cream the butter and sugar together, then beat in the eggs. Mix the flour, baking powder and salt together, and add to the butter mixture alternately with the yoghurt. Grease a pan about 10 × 14 inches (25 × 40 cm) and pour in the mixture. Bake in a moderate oven (375°F/190°C/Gas Mark 5) for 30–40 minutes, or until the cake is cooked through (you can check this by putting a thin skewer into the centre). Let it cool for a minute before taking from the pan and cooling on a rack. Then put it on to a deep plate, and pour over the syrup, made by boiling the water with the sugar for 10 minutes and then allowing it to cool.

Variation: Add the grated rind of 1 lemon to the mix, and separate the whites from the yolks of the eggs, adding the stiffly beaten eggwhites last, then bake as above.

Yoghurt and cottage cheese combined make an excellent filling for a baked pastry crust with fruit such as strawberries.

Put a layer of fresh fruit on the bottom of the cooked pastry case and sprinkle with sugar to taste. Beat together 1 cup yoghurt and 1 cup cottage cheese, 3 tablespoons honey and a pinch of cinnamon or a few drops of rum or vanilla essence. Sieve it, then pour into the pie shell and cover the top with more fruit. Chill for 24 hours before serving. This is also called *yiaourtopeta* in Greece, and it can be made without the fruit.

CHUTNEYS

These are expensive to buy, but easy and quite cheap to make. They also use up windfall apples. The basic recipe is the same whether you use apples as the main ingredient or rhubarb, gooseberries, or vegetable marrow, but with the latter it is advisable to peel and chop the marrow and salt it overnight, then to drain it before making the chutney. Raisins are used according to taste: they can be omitted, but slightly increase the sugar content.

Indian chutney

3 lb (1½ g) apples	8 oz (225 g) chopped
2 large onions	crystallized ginger
1½ pints (900 ml) malt	½ teaspoon cayenne
vinegar	pepper
2 lb (1 kg) brown sugar	2 teaspoons dry mustard
1 teaspoon salt	Approx. 1 tablespoon
1 lb (450 g) stoned and	turmeric (to taste)
chopped raisins	

Peel, core and chop the apples and onions. Add the vinegar and boil to a pulp. Add the other ingredients and mix well. Boil again for ½ hour, stirring often. Put into jars and cover when cool. This amount makes approximately 3–4 lb (1.3–1.8 kg) chutney.

A spoonful added to stews just before dishing up gives an added piquancy. Either without the turmeric and ginger, it is a very good apple chutney.

Sweet lemon pickle goes well with curries and is easy to make.

Slice up about 6 lemons finely and mix with 2 tablespoons salt, ½ teaspoon turmeric, a pinch of cumin, 4 oz (115 g) soft brown sugar, and a pinch of cayenne pepper. Put into jars, then heat up and cool ½ pint (300 ml) oil, and cover the lemon with it. Keep in a warm place for 3 days, stirring from time to time, and when the skins are tender it is ready.

12. Free foods from Nature

There are so many wild plants, fungi and shellfish that this chapter will serve only to remind you not to overlook them. There are several good books on the subject (*Food for Free*, Richard Mabey, Fontana/Collins, 1972 is one that comes to mind) and I am concerned purely with plants I regularly use and have done for some years. There is something thrilling in finding unexpected food in fields, woods or on the seashore, but do take care to avoid verges which might have been sprayed with insecticide or be otherwise polluted. Similarly, do not take mussels or cockles from a polluted harbour or near a sewage outlet, and always scrub and wash them well in at least two changes of water.

Blackberries are the beautiful bonus of autumn and lend themselves to many dishes. They also make a very good, pale lavender dye, if boiled in water, drained, and the water used for the dyeing. Articles for dyeing can be boiled in it. I have often dipped yellowing white articles with great success, and it is fairly permanent. Blackberries can be used, and indeed were in the past, in place of currants in cakes or puddings and they make very good jelly and blackberry curd. I don't like jam made with them on account of the pips.

Bramble jelly

One of the simplest preserves to make, and one which can be used for many sweet dishes throughout the winter. It is excellent spread on top of sliced apples which have been cooked gently in butter and sprinkled with sugar.

Barely cover the blackberries with water. (They require no picking over, just a light wash in a colander.) Boil them until the fruit is quite soft, but before it loses colour. Drain them well, until all the juice is out, then add 1 lb (450 g) of sugar for every 1 pint (600 ml) of juice. Boil up until a little set on a saucer jellies. About 20–30 minutes' fierce boiling should be enough. If the taste of scented geranium leaves is liked, add 1 or 2 to the final boiling. Pour into warmed jars and tie down when cool.

A little more trouble than bramble jelly but well worth the effort, is blackberry curd or bramble curd. It is like lemon curd.

Blackberry curd

4 lb (2 kg) blackberries	Few rose geranium
1½ lb (675 g) apples	leaves (optional)
½ pint (300 ml) water	8 oz (225 g) butter
Juice of 3 lemons	4 lb (2 kg) lump sugar
	6 eggs

Simmer together the blackberries, the peeled and cored apples, the scented geranium leaves, and water until the fruit is soft. Pour through a sieve, pressing down to extract all the juice, and transfer to a double boiler. Add the lemon juice, the butter and the lump sugar. When it has all melted, very gradually add the well-beaten eggs, stirring all the time, until the mixture thickens. The water under the curd should be just gently simmering, not boiling furiously.

Bottle into warmed jars, and seal down when cool. The curd makes the basis for a good blackberry meringue pie, which is made like a lemon meringue pie in a pastry shell which has been baked blind.

Blackberry cheese

'Cheese' is the old-fashioned term for a very firm conserve which can be used, cut into cubes, as a sweetmeat.

4 lb (2 kg) ripe blackberries	Water (see recipe)
2 level teaspoons citric or tartaric acid	Sugar (see recipe)

Put the picked fruit into a pan and barely cover it with water, then bring to the boil. Simmer gently until the fruit is soft and mushy. Put through a sieve or a mouli-mill, weigh the pulp and add 1 lb (450 g) sugar to each 1lb (450 g) of pump. Put into a preserving pan with citric or tartaric acid, dissolve well, then bring to the boil and boil until a semi-solid consistency is reached. Pour into a lined and greased tin to set and cut into slices when cold. Gooseberries, damsons, plums, apples, etc. can also be used. If using as sweets, roll cubes in sugar.

Blackberry wine

An excellent wine can also be easily made from blackberries.

Place alternate layers of blackberries and sugar in wide-mouthed jars; allow to stand for 3 weeks. Cover with a piece of sterilized muslin to keep out insects. Then strain off the liquid and bottle, adding a small handful of raisins to each bottle. Cork lightly at first, and later more tightly.

This is very simple to make, and will keep in good condition for a year. It tastes not unlike a good port.

Black cumin (not to be confused with cumin, which it does not resemble) comes from the seeds of Love-in-the-Mist (*Nigella sativa*). It is also known as fennel flower, and the seeds have a good peppery taste and can be used instead of pepper. In Turkey they are sprinkled on top of bread before cooking.

Dandelion is full of vitamins A, B and C and is very good if a stripped leaf or two is put into salads. If blanched under an upturned bucket, or lifted before the frosts and put into a pot, the leaves are far less bitter and make a pleasant winter salad herb. In France they are often served with a sauce made from chopped fried bacon with the fat poured over, with a spoonful of wine vinegar and some chopped parsley then added and all mixed well.

Elderflowers make a quite delicious wine, called 'champagne' in the West Country. Simply macerate about 6 heads of the white flowers with the juice and rind of 1 lemon, then add 1½ lb (675 g) sugar, 2 tablespoons white wine vinegar and 1 gallon (approx. 4 l) cold water. Mix well then leave in a cool place, covered, for 24 hours. Strain off into screw-topped bottles and leave for at least a week. I recently opened a bottle from last year which had been overlooked and it was truly like champagne.

A head of elderflower plunged into gooseberries just as they come to the boil makes them taste like muscatel grapes.

Elderberries also make a wine; it is not as delicate as the flower one, but the berries make a good relish to accompany grilled or roast meats, called Pontack sauce. Pontack's was a well known restaurant in Lombard Street in the last century.

For Pontack sauce put 1 lb (450 g) elderberries into a large container, then pour over 1 pint (600 ml) boiling wine vinegar, or red wine which has gone vinegary. Cover and put the container overnight in the lowest possible oven. The next day, strain and add 1 medium finely chopped shallot or onion, 12 cloves, a 1 inch (25 mm) blade of mace, 1 dessertspoon peppercorns, ½ teaspoon ground ginger, 2 mashed anchovies, and a teaspoon salt. Boil up for 10 minutes, then bottle with the spices and leave for at least 1 month and preferably 6 months.

Fennel, with its feathery leaves which smell strongly of aniseed, can often be found growing wild in sandy soils. In fact I found my plant, now seven years old, on the strand of Killiney Bay. A pinch of the leaves will tell you what it is. Both the leaves and the seeds are excellent with fish dishes, or used for a tea.

> The Fennel with its yellow flowers,
> In an earlier age than ours,
> Was gifted with the wondrous powers,
> Lost vision to restore . . . [Longfellow]

Fungi

I'm very wary about mushrooms and advise my readers to get a good book with coloured photographs before being too adventurous. However the field and horse mushrooms are fairly easy to identify for they resemble the cultivated pink-gilled mushrooms but are larger, and the pink gill darkens to brown. The stem is short with a ring, but there is no sheath at the base of the stem and no unpleasant smell. Beware of any white-gilled mushroom and also any that stain pink or yellow almost immediately on cutting.

Chanterelle is really my favourite, and as I write these words a large basketful are reposing in my kitchen. They cannot be mistaken for any other fungi, for they are a vivid apricot colour, have a vaguely apricot smell, and are funnel-shaped, the gills continuous with the stem, with no ring. At their largest they are about 2–3 inches (50–75 mm) across. They are common in woodlands and also in or near bracken, which is where my store is. In the autumn they look like a cluster of bright orange leaves swept into a huddle by a capricious wind, but look again and you will find they are chanterelles. Some writers think them tough and stew them in milk, but my hoard, freshly picked, are exquisitely tender quickly turned in butter. Served over the top of a herb omelette, the taste and appearance (the butter having turned a dark apricot colour), are truly memorable. They are also good with scrambled or cocotte eggs, and they make a wonderful dish with pasta and a little grated cheese. They can be found between July and December.

Hedgerow jelly

This, in jam form, was the first thing I ever cooked, aged about eight years old, and I still think it's delicious.

8 oz (225 g) wild rosehips	1 lb (450 g) elderberries
8 oz (225 g) hawthorn berries	1 lb (450 g) crab apples or cooking apples
8 oz (225 g) rowanberries	Water to cover
8 oz (225 g) sloes	Lemons (*see* recipe)
1 lb (450 g) blackberries	Sugar (*see* recipe)

Put all the fruit into a large saucepan, barely cover with water and boil rapidly until the fruit is soft, about ½ hour. Pour it all into a muslin bag or a jelly-bag over a large deep bowl, then hang up the pulp to drain overnight. Measure the juice next day and for every 1 pint (600 ml) of juice allow the juice of 1 lemon and 1 lb (450 g) of sugar. Put it all into a saucepan and slowly bring to the boil, allowing the sugar to dissolve, then boil rapidly until setting point is reached which should be about 20 minutes. Pour into warm sterilized jars and tie down. Makes about 6 lb (2.7 kg).

Marigold petals are good in a potato salad and also in a baked custard.

Nasturtiums

The peppery leaves are good in sandwiches or a salad, and the flowers (which can also be eaten) look very attractive on a cold rice dish. The seeds make a pickle which resembles capers, which are now extremely expensive.

Nasturtium seed pickle

1 lb (450 g) nasturtium seeds	1 tablespoon sugar
Salt	1¼ pints (750 ml) white wine vinegar
Pinch each of ground cloves, mace and nutmeg	1 shallot or small onion
Pepper	1 tablespoon grated horseradish

First put the seeds in cold water and some salt for 3 days. Then drain. Add the spices, a pinch more salt, pepper and the sugar to the vinegar and bring to the boil, and keep boiling for 5 minutes. Then let it get cold. Put the seeds into jars with a little piece of shallot and horseradish in each, and then pour over the spiced vinegar. Seal, and keep for at least 2 weeks before using, although the pickled seeds will keep well for many months. This amount makes approximately 2–3 lb (1–1½ kg).

Nettles are one of my spring standbys when greenstuff is scarce and expensive. Pick only the tops (with gloves on and a pair of scissors) and use them as you would spinach, stripping the leaves from the stalk. A pinch of nutmeg and a knob of butter are good when the nettles are cooked. Sometimes I liquidize them and make a purée which I mix with mashed potato, a little minced, cooked meat, an egg and seasonings. Then I shape them into little cakes, fry them and serve with tomato sauce (page 27). They make delicious little spring rissoles.

Nettle soup is well known in Ireland (*see brotchán roy*, page 14), and also in Sweden, where it is called *nässelkål*. It is made from a purée of 1 lb (450 g) nettles, prepared and cooked as above, mixed with a sauce made from a roux of 1 tablespoon each of butter and flour. Then 2 cups of nettle broth (the water from drained, cooked nettles) added and it is stirred until it boils and is smooth. The soup is garnished with sliced hard-boiled eggs.

Nuts such as hazel, chestnut (with the pink blossom), beech and walnuts should be looked for and gathered.

Rowanberries from the rowan or mountain ash tree tempt me every autumn when their vivid clusters of red berries nod to me with every breeze, and I think of the slightly smoky distinctive taste which marries well with game and meat.

Rowanberry jelly and other berry jellies, such as red-currant, blackberry, etc. are made in the same way. Cook the fruit in water barely to cover and strain (as for bramble jelly, page 151), then add 1 lb (450 g) sugar and the juice of 1 lemon for every 1 pint (600 ml) of juice, and boil. Rowanberry jelly is so good with ham, lamb or chicken. A little apple can be added if liked, in the proportions of 1 lb (450 g) apples to 3 lb (1½ kg) rowanberries.

Samphire, the rock variety, grows on the cliff adjoining my garden. In late summer and autumn it is the source of one of our choicest vegetables. Usually we eat it as a first course, the way one would seakale or asparagus.

Pick the fleshy, solid, branchy leaves from the stems and steam or boil them with salt for no longer than 15 minutes. Strain and serve with melted butter with a squeeze of lemon in it. It has a flavour all its own, slightly reminiscent of a coriander leaf. Samphire was the diarist John Evelyn's favourite vegetable and he gives a receipt for it used as a pickle in wine vinegar and salt. It can also be used as a sauce with cucumber, capers, lemon peel, nutmeg and pepper simmered in a little wine vinegar, then thickened with butter and an egg yolk. This was popular with meat in the seventeenth century.

Seaweeds of many kinds abound on our coasts and have been used for centuries by the Irish, Welsh and Scots. Even if you don't cook it, use it for poaching or baking fish for it gives a delicious flavour. It is also a good garden fertilizer.

Sloes

The sloe is the ancestor of the cultivated plum and makes a good jelly, but it is perhaps best known for sloe gin. This is easy to make and is an excellent liqueur for Christmas, when it will just be at its best if made in late autumn.

Sloe gin

This can also be made with damsons, or small unripe plums.

Sloes　　　　　　　　　　　Gin or vodka
White sugar

Wash and prick the sloes (a small knitting needle is a good implement for this). Mix them with an equal weight of white sugar. Half-fill the bottles with this, then fill up with gin. Cork tightly. It is ready to drink in about 3 months.

It is a very strong drink, and the sloes are also very potent. At the age of eight I extracted the sloes from an empty bottle of sloe gin and ate them. To this moment I have vivid memories of that day!

Snails

The ordinary garden kind, are traditional to the West Country of England and are a regular feature on the menu of the Miner's Arms, Priddy, near Wells, Somerset.

They must be immersed (with a covering lid) in salted water (1 tablespoon per gallon, $4\frac{1}{2}$ l) for 6 hours, then 2 more tablespoons of salt are added, and after another 6 hours or overnight a further 2 more tablespoonsful are added and it is left for 24–36 hours. By this time the snails will be dead, and they should be drained and then boiled up twice, then finally rinsed under the tap. They are then simmered for 4 hours in a *court bouillon* of cider, water, herbs and vegetables.

The snails are now ready for use, either by filling the shells up with garlic butter as in France, or by using a mixture of butter, grated Cheddar cheese, cream, fresh herbs, salt and pepper (which is the West Country method), and heated in a hot oven or under the grill.

Sorrel is good used in omelettes or scrambled eggs, in sauces (*see* page 105) or soup (page 20). It also makes a good salad herb mixed with lettuce, or vegetable cooked with spinach.

HERBS

Wild herbs such as mint, thyme, marjoram, yarrow and garlic can all be traced by their smell and can be used as the cultivated varieties. Some of them, such as mint and yarrow, make good 'tea' or tisane. Put a handful into a jug and pour over boiling water, then let it stand to infuse, as you would ordinary tea.

Fresh coriander is very easy to grow. Crush the seeds slightly and plant in a well-drained soil and in about 2 weeks you will have plenty of the parsley-like leaves, called Chinese parsley in Mexico and South America, although the flavour is not like parsley at all. It is very good used with potatoes, fish, or in curries.

Parsley, even if it has gone to seed, makes a delicious honey-like preserve, but you need quite a lot of it.

Parsley honey

Pack a large saucepan with clean, wet parsley and just cover with water, then bring to the boil and simmer for ½ hour. Strain through muslin, and let it hang for a few hours. For every 1 pint (600 ml) juice add 1 lb (450 g) sugar and boil rapidly for about 45 minutes or until a little wrinkles up if put on a cold saucer. Add the juice of a small lemon with the sugar if you like, but the pure parsley honey is very delicate on its own. It looks and tastes like a thinnish honey.

Rose geranium leaves are good for cooking with rhubarb or blackberries, and can also be used for flavouring cottage cheese.

Herbs can be preserved in several ways: for using freshly, they can be washed and picked over, small quantities put into plastic bags and frozen. To use, simply bring them out and crush them in their frozen state, then add to whatever you need them for. A sprig or two of herbs such as rosemary, tarragon, basil or fennel can be put into vinegar bottles, then filled up with vinegar. I have also done this with oil, and it gives the oil a pleasant flavour.

They can be dried, but I think this is the least successful method. I prefer to chop an assortment of herbs, mix them up, making certain that the very strong-flavoured do not predominate, then cover them entirely with lemon juice, and keep very cold in a screw-top jar. These herbs acquire a wonderful flavour and the juice as well, and if kept in the fridge the mixture will keep a year. Sometimes a little mould grows in the centre, but this can be removed without spoiling the taste.

Finally, I would say, do try and grow your own herbs, for nothing can take their place and they enliven even the most pedestrian of dishes. Their sweet fragrance in the corner of a flower bed, or even on a windowsill will give so much pleasure, and the evergreen ones such as rosemary always bring a taste of summertime into the winter.

How could such sweet and wholesome hours
Be reckoned but with herbs and flowers!

[Andrew Marvell] (1621–78), 'The Garden'

Index